...e, suddenly
.., people quietly start to cry
.d to cry. You do not know if you
: – all your blood is in your body! You'r.
ou are having them anyway. They are jangled
:d shapes and do not feel in any way good). He
ling he's bleeding. He's actually— he's sort of stopp
use there's not much else left to bleed. You look at th
: of him on the pavement and know that he is goin,
watching the final moments of a life. It's not a life yc
rich full life and you only get to watch the end of it
nd he has family and he has friends. He has hobbi'
hts and he loves things (what? Nike or Adidas
? What's his McDonald's order? What's his c'
slightly, on the pavement; he's holding h
' as if that will help him. He'll die ir
out here in 90 seconds, m~
~onsciousness

FOUR STARS

A LIFE. REVIEWED.

JOEL GOLBY

MUDLARK

Mudlark
HarperCollins*Publishers*
1 London Bridge Street
London SE1 9GF

www.harpercollins.co.uk

HarperCollins*Publishers*
Macken House, 39/40 Mayor Street Upper
Dublin 1, D01 C9W8, Ireland

First published by Mudlark 2024

1 3 5 7 9 10 8 6 4 2

© Joel Golby 2024

Joel Golby asserts the moral right to
be identified as the author of this work

A catalogue record of this book is
available from the British Library

ISBN 978-0-00-828409-1
Printed and bound in the UK using 100%
renewable electricity at CPI Group (UK) Ltd

All rights reserved. No part of this publication may be
reproduced, stored in a retrieval system, or transmitted,
in any form or by any means, electronic, mechanical,
photocopying, recording or otherwise, without the prior
written permission of the publishers.

This book contains FSC™ certified paper and other controlled
sources to ensure responsible forest management.

For more information visit: www.harpercollins.co.uk/green

SUNDAY BRUNCH

However much you think you hate Tim Lovejoy, I promise you I hate him more. He's staring at me from the TV now, look, because *Sunday Brunch* is back on our screens, although it never really goes away: it slank into the swamp during the COVID-19 pandemic, and then it crept back, the guests all spaced out at a long curved table, the laughter even more staccato now, the jokes bouncing through yet more air to die on the floor. *Sunday Brunch* (2012–present), of course, is just *Something for the Weekend* (2006–2012) but rebadged with a slightly different name and studio, and in that way the Sunday morning cooking-and-banter format is a sort of unkillable monster: you can cut its head off and think you'll never see Tim Lovejoy squint at an autocue again, and then he springs up on Channel 4, as bored as a teenage girl in the back of a maths class, arms folded across his chest, asking Emeli Sandé what her new album's about, making it exceptionally clear he hasn't listened to a second of it. I want to jump through the screen and attack him. I hate him with my life.

What is *Sunday Brunch*, and who is it for? These are both good questions, one more answerable than the other. At its core, *Sunday Brunch* is a three-hour (it is insane that it is three hours long! That is such a long time for a TV show to be on for!) magazine format where two hosts and five guests compete to see who can be the most visibly bored and confused over the course of a morning. You experience palpable shifts in mood while *Sunday Brunch* is playing – first you slip into an uneasy watching stupor, and then, as you see Tim Lovejoy fail and fail again to make any sort of connection with even one of the guests, you start to relive every dreadful social interaction of your life (I am in a neighbour's kitchen politely drinking wine and trying to care what their job is about; I am on a first date and they have just lied to me about why they have to go outside for a bit and look at their phone; I am at a party and said "nice to meet you" and someone's coldly said "we've actually met, before, many many times"). Simon Rimmer, the show's co-host and the resident chef, keeps trying to gee the mood up a bit by cooking some food – I baked an onion, look! I breadcrumbed some hake! – but his too-cheerful attempts to make tarts and stews are always timed calamitously and incongruously, almost always at the exact moment a frosty guest finally finds their rhythm and starts to talk. The show starts at 9.30 a.m., and everyone involved is often visibly tired and disorientated when it starts – tufts of hair sticking up, skin wan under too-bright studio lights, outfits chosen in the grey half-light of a messy hotel room – and the sort-of format of the show (sometimes there are quizzes and activities, sometimes there's just nothing, just seven people in a room with bad acoustics saying

FOUR STARS

"yeah, well— sorry, no, you go") starts to slip into chaos around the 90-minute mark. And reigning over his pasture is Tim Lovejoy, my nemesis, my foe.

It is very strange that Tim Lovejoy has chosen a front-facing career in TV, because he doesn't seem to like doing it and nobody seems to like watching it. He leans on countertops and sort of looks at his notes and audibly thinks – one second, two seconds, three – about what to ask someone. He listens to a one-minute story a guest has rehearsed and rehearsed again – "Yeah, well I obviously welcomed my new baby daughter—" – while looking down and scratching his cheek with one finger then asking a question absolutely not related to anything at all. He half-hears jokes people say, ignores prompts for conversation, is constantly looking at the wrong person. Sometimes he'll stop a sentence halfway through because someone else has tried to interject – "What's that?" – then a glower at a guest, an awkward continuation. Often, the queasy unstructure of *Sunday Brunch* evokes the feeling of a fever dream: Simon Rimmer is grinning and whizzing up a fresh salsa, Tim Lovejoy is asking you about your favourite biscuit, music you've never heard is playing quietly in the background, forced laughs bounce hard off walls. Three hours have gone by. What did you actually just watch? Recall a single detail from an episode of *Sunday Brunch*. You can't. Your brain wipes it out the same way hormone flushes delete the horror of childbirth.

It is easy to hate Tim Lovejoy: obvious, even. People have been hating him for years, from *Soccer AM* through until now. He is a certain type of turn-of-the-millennium man – you don't get Lovejoys anymore, do you? Bottled lager, balsamic vinegar, supporting Chelsea, those strange black trainers that don't have any details on them – and, as a totem of that, he's been a punchline object of hatred for a number of years. But I want to reiterate that he deserves all of it and more. The government should be making plans to terminate the Tim Lovejoy experiment and build a monument to say sorry about ever engaging in it. As a nation we should apologise for him as much as we would a war crime.

—though maybe of course the problem with Lovejoy is not with him but with me; that I see a smeared reflection of myself in his anti-banter, his chilling awkwardness, his magnetic repulsion from charm. When I had finished the wine with my neighbour – they invited us over because apparently there had been some problem with the bins and I had been responsible for the long slow descent of the bins and they informed me they had been dipping into my bins and sorting out all the rubbish I had just been throwing in the bins – because that is how I thought bins worked, by throwing things into them, but apparently there is a system, instead – and there was a lot of bin-related chat and bin-related questions, and I was nudged to apologise regarding bin misuse by my girlfriend, but I really didn't want to, so I didn't, and it turned into this great long ice-out game of chicken, where they very much wanted me to apologise about using bins wrong for many many months on end and I very much did not want to use

FOUR STARS

the hard-S "sorry" about a very minor bin infraction, and the mood in the room started to swell like a bubble – and when we finally got through that frost I made small talk in their living room about a painting, and I said isn't it weird the paintings you get in these rented flats – soulless little pastorals made by someone with no talent and no joy and they said we don't rent our place we bought it, and I said oh, and then they said of course my mother painted that, and I said oh again, and they informed me then that their mother had recently died, and I said, yeah, a–huh. But fair dues must be given to me because it really was a tawdry little excuse for a watercolour—

I have been told in the past by long-term editors of this fun weekly column that I am not allowed to be overly negative or make bodily threats against the people I am reviewing the TV shows of – ever since that thing with Robbie Savage – so I must fold away my hatred for Tim Lovejoy, stuff it into a tiny dark box within me, metabolise it like a pellet of poison. The man has no business being on television but then neither has Eamonn Holmes, and look how long we've had to put up with him. Britain, it seems, is a country that deserves joyless TV presenters to ruin the landscape of their mornings. This country is addicted to bad things – we love the taste of the boot, we hate the vibrancy of youth, and we actively revel in how grey and mediocre our weather is – and *Sunday Brunch* is just another three-hour punishment we feel we must endure. I welcome the day I won't have to know who Tim Lovejoy is anymore, but I fear it will not come soon. Until then I must watch him, but at least I am allowed to loathe him. **ZERO STARS**

THIS PHONE CALL FROM MY EDITOR

I was at Stratford Westfield to escape the outer reaches of my insanity when my phone rang in my hand. The Instagram video I was watching was: a man building a tent out of a cardboard box then watching morosely from underneath it as it melted down to pulp. He kept saying, *it's not working, it's not working.* Weeks previously he had made a video announcing his divorce. Close viewers of his videos (me, the guys on the forums) sort of saw this one coming. Something within him had changed, lately. Broken and dropped. Plus he was eating way more strange grey meat from tinned cans, which is never a good sign.

"Joel? It's Gruff," the voice said.

"OK."

"From the *Guardian*."

"Yeah, I know."

"Oh. Then why would you not say, 'hello'?"

I thought about it. "Don't know. What's up, Gruff?"

What I love most about Stratford Westfield – although it does apply to most mega-malls, it just so happens that this one is the closest to my house – is that once you enter it via the DLR, train or Tube, you

FOUR STARS

cease to become a person anymore. You become, completely, an *unperson*, a sort of roving customer, constantly pressed with samples of oud and beard oil, a grey pixel on a CCTV camera pointed at the double-shutter doors of JD Sports. I come to Stratford Westfield when it feels like the chainsaw inside my head is revving, because I find peace there, giving up my soul to the mighty ancient gods of consumerism. I am no longer 'Joel Golby'. I am 'man who bought face soap in Kiehl's, man who walked the wrong way around Flying Tiger, man who walked past three donut stands and bought a donut from two of them'. You are never less of a person than when a 22-year-old in a tight suit is telling you H. Samuel don't stock the watch you want, and have you maybe tried looking online?

"Yeah: did you get my e-mail earlier?"

There was an e-mail but I forgot to reply to it and came here instead. I bought three sticks of butter from Waitrose that are currently growing dewy in my backpack. I bought some saucisson and some chocolate-coated Brazil nuts, too. I spent fucking £39, somehow.

"E-mail ... e-mail ..."

"The one about changes to the latest TV column."

"The one about Tim Lovejoy?"

"Yeah."

"What was wrong with it?"

"Joel, you can't say, 'I hate Tim Lovejoy, I loathe Tim Lovejoy'. You can't say, and I'm quoting, 'I want to attack Tim Lovejoy like he's an animal; I want to watch what little life there is behind Tim Lovejoy's Chelsea-supporting eyes flicker out.'"

"Right."

"A lot of people don't really know who Tim Lovejoy is enough for that bit to work—"

"Sorry, am I on speakerphone?"

"Yes."

"Is that Louisa?"

"Yes."

"Louisa, do you know who Tim Lovejoy is?"

"I do, but—"

"Do you like him?"

"..."

"Do you both like Tim Lovejoy?"

"This isn't about whether we like Tim Lovejoy or not, Joel—"

"*I do*, actually."

"—This is about you saying you want to beat him limp with a spade."

There was a pause. The endless queue for Pink-Berry shuffled forward a little. I peered over the balcony to the escalators slowly rolling below. If I jumped from here I'd just crumple my legs, I wouldn't die. Everyone would look at me as my shin bones splintered out through the flesh of my thighs. A guy in a hi-vis jacket would have to walk over, sighing because I pulled him away from a puddle of sick he was trying to cordon off with WET FLOOR signs. A walkie-talkie bleeps on his shoulder. No one knows what to say. I'm just feeling embarrassed. I think in this scenario, realistically, I would be too afraid to

FOUR STARS

scream in case someone started videoing me and put it on the internet. Accepting a massive injury with a small stoic groan is somehow more respectable than accepting your shins are poking out of the raw red meat of your legs, to me anyway. Of course everyone around me is staring in shocked silence. No one really knows what to say to help.

I really should stop reacting to even the most mild inconveniences by thinking about jumping off something, but that's not a problem for now, it's a problem for later.

"Um, OK. I'm just queueing up for PinkBerry now, but when I get home I can change it."

"Well, the print deadline's gone."

"Gone?"

"Yeah, we had to send it to the printers."

"So what's gone in?"

"Ed Warburton has covered the column with a bit about *Saturday Night Takeaway*. It took him less than 20 minutes."

"Well that won't be any good, then."

"It's actually really funny."

"And also very crucially *on wordcount*."

"Can I be taken off speakerphone please? It feels like there's too many of you."

"No."

It's nearly 4 p.m., now, which I can tell from the slow steady influx of uniform-wearing school children. I should get out of here before a gang of them decide to run really fast around me and say something mean. Last time this happened they called me 'big mong' while I was eating a burrito bowl and tried to grab at my hat. They didn't leave me alone until a guy with a litter-picking claw and a long orange beard came along and mutely snapped at them. I didn't even know you could say 'mong' anymore. Let alone: 'big mong'.

"Yeah, can I get Original please?"

"Sorry: are you still queuing for PinkBerry?"

"Well I mean you should see this queue, Gruff. It's hard to describe."

"Try."

"... long."

"Can you get out of the queue for PinkBerry please, Joel? This is quite serious."

"Uhh ...?"

"It's really quite serious."

"*Fine.*"

It turns out everyone has been mad at me for months. You sort of always think people are mad at you, don't you? And then you dismiss that idea as being the idle wanderings of an unstable mind. But then they call you up in the middle of the PinkBerry queue (I watched the 30-or-so strong queue of frozen yoghurt eaters stomp past it behind me. The person after me chose *jelly gums* to go on theirs. An in-real-life psychopath.) and confirm that every fear you've had was actually true and also there were a couple of other fears you hadn't previously considered that were also true and now they've said them out loud, yes, you are quite scared of them.

"So from three weeks ago: 'Victoria Pedretti's lips and face crumple in a way that make me soften inside.

FOUR STARS

It used to be very cool to fancy actors and actresses, didn't it – my father always went very quiet for instance when Demi Moore was on screen – but now you're not allowed to do that, to sexualise them. You are not allowed to look at them like they are meat. Which personally made me watching Victoria Pedretti in *The Haunting of Hill House* very difficult.' I mean what is that about, Joel?"

"OK, well— I mean, culturally. Like. You're not allowed to fancy actors anymore."

"And what's that got to do with *The Haunting of Hill House*?"

"Well I found myself very distracted by Victoria Pedretti's lips and face. And eyebrows, I have a bit of an eyebrow thing."

"And what has that got to do with *anything*?"

"Ah. Ahm. I mean yeah, when you put it like that—"

There was a section that didn't make the edit where I'd fantasised about taking Victoria Pedretti on a road-trip. In this fantasy we had both been in that first frenzied flush of love. I'd noticed her at a party and plucked up the courage to say hello. I'd complimented her eyebrows, her lips, things like that. Her performances as an actress. She'd gone: *Great, amazing, no one ever notices the eyebrows. And also thanks for complimenting my work.* Things had escalated from there: a drink, a hand-brush in a high-tension elevator journey, a lazy summer Sunday spent entwined in a linen-made bed. She'd rocked up outside my house in a gleaming '50s-style convertible with a scarf wrapped around her head and she was laughing so hard she was showing teeth, those perfect teeth that always just rest on the cushion of her bottom lip. I threw a holdall in the back and hopped over the passenger-side door instead of opening it and going through it. She turned to me and said: *It's completely OK you can't drive, I don't mind doing all the driving.* I lit a cigarette, I fiddled with the radio. She said: *I'd really prefer you don't smoke in the car.*

I said: *I mean I'm not smoking* in *the car, am I, Victoria Pedretti? The roof is not on the car. I am basically smoking, like: out in the world.*

She said: *You know how I feel about the smoking stuff anyway. It's not that it's unhealthy, it's that, when you do it, it's affected.*

I said: *How can it be affected? How can it possibly be affected? I'm just smoking a cigarette.*

She said: *I know but I've never really seen you smoke a cigarette before. Because like, you don't smoke. So now I'm asking why now, why today? It just sort of seems like you're putting it on.*

I threw the cigarette out of the car and said *Fine.* in a really firm voice.

Anyway all of this got edited out so I don't know why I'm bringing it up again.

"I just don't really understand why in the fantasy version of your road-trip with Victoria Pedretti – a fantasy *you made up* – she gets mad at you for smoking?"

"Yeah I don't know why I've done that either."

"So, for future reference, a review is ... well, do you know what a review is?"

"Yes."

"Can you describe it to me?"

"I ... I know a lot of words I cannot fully describe the meaning of, Gruff."

"OK so what we look for in a review is: well firstly, 575 words. And then after that, the point is you experience something – in your particular case, a TV show, but sometimes it can be music, or theatre, or art – and you distil that experience into a neat and on-wordcount column describing what it is and whether it is worth our readers' time."

"Right. So I live life so they can decide whether they have to or not?"

"That is absolutely *not* what I am saying, no."

"Who sighed just then? Was that Louisa?"

If I lose this job then that's the last job I've lost, now. If I lose this job I no longer have a job. If I lose this writing job, I suppose, I immediately cease to become a writer, because I'm not writing anyway. Which obviously would be disastrous for my internal self-belief systems, all of which are predicated upon me being a writer. I really, really like telling people I'm 'a writer' in a cool offhand way at parties. They always think that's so so interesting and good. If I don't have that then what do I have to say. Also realistically I have absolutely no transferable skills, so if I can't write I am doomed to poverty. There is no Plan B. If I turn up on a building site and offer to carry things around they will simply laugh at me. Builders have a very specific, evil laugh on hand for this exact scenario.

"Erm. Right then. Well, ah, I guess I'll try harder with ... more. Next week I'll do—"

"No."
"OK."
"We're going to take a little break from the column. With you. Specifically with you."
"OK."
"So, yeah. Take a beat. Figure out what a review is. Figure out whatever . . . is going on. Then, you know."
"E-mail you?"
". . ."
"Which one of you sighed then?"
"Sure. You can e-mail me."
"OK."
Click.
ZERO STARS

THE RESULTING PINKBERRY

I had to re-queue up again and got the same guy who got mad at me for side-stepping out of the queue last time and he had saved my medium-sized original scoop — felt like a bit of a passive-aggressive move from a man who wears translucent oversized gloves all day and slings frozen yoghurt for a dispassionate franchise, but not my place to say — so it had mostly melted already, a firm enough island of froyo poking up through the centre but the rest just gloop, and in my dizzy overwhelmedness I did get some jelly gums sprinkled over it as well as my usual topping (cookie bites, M&Ms, white chocolate curls), and the resulting combination was disastrous, frankly, repulsive. I ate a few bites but the whole thing tasted like failure and fruit so I tried to throw it away but the flap on the bin was wired quite tight so when I pushed the half-full tub of Pinkberry against it it tried to push it back out at me again quite hard, and while most of the tub fell with a clunk into the bin a fair arc of spray did make its way onto my trousers and up to my t-shirt and onto my hand, which was sticky all the way home, so I had to hold it in that way where it didn't get on anything in case it made that thing sticky, too. The few scoops I had with just cookie dough were nice though, obviously. **ONE STAR**

HAVING TO TELL MEGAN ABOUT ALL OF THE ABOVE AND HER BEING, WELL, NOT MAD ABOUT IT EXACTLY BUT DISAPPOINTED IN A VERY DISHEARTENING WAY

I waited until she'd made dinner (paneer curry – you simply cannot go wrong with a paneer curry on a midweek night!) and let her choose what show we watched this time (some sort of show where Khloé Kardashian undergoes hours of full glam to go to lunch with a woman who tells her gravely that she's been cheated on) and then said the thing about the phone

call and the work and how they're not doing the column anymore. She pulled a clove out of her mouth and chewed the flavour away for a second then said:
"OK."
Which wasn't helpful.
"They sacked you by *phone*?" – and I can hear her wondering why she trapped her youth and vitality and happiness to this sinking rock – "Wow. Does anyone even get fired by the *Guardian*?"
"Not really. You can say some really TERF-y stuff on Twitter and they don't even fire you."
"So to get fired for some reviews is—"
"Bad."
"Bad, yeah."
Which is the worse conversation I've had today? Hard to tell, hard to rank them. Maybe someone will ring me at one minute to midnight and pip them to the post, somehow: tell me I'm the prime suspect in an assassination that just happened, something like that. A lieutenant calls to tell me I've been drafted into the army. One of the concierge workers in our building says they've had a number of complaints about how often I walk around the house naked – and that despite me calculating all the angles of our windows, figuring out who can see in and who cannot, and being really really careful about closing the curtains, actually everyone can see me naked, all the time, and the guy in 310 specifically e-mailed in to note that my dick looks weird.
"Yeah so um. Yeah so I don't know."
"Yeah. Hmm. Well that's no good."

"Yeah."

"How, um— hmm. But you're OK to pay rent?"

"Yeah I can cover rent for a little bit. Like a little bit. Like I still have some money left over from the first book—"

"— the one no one bought?"

"— the one no one bought, yeah."

"And how long will that last?"

"Ahh, erm. You know, a month or two, something like that."

"Hrm."

"... yeah"

"Um, OK. Unideal. Ah. Well, I'm not going to say it, because I know how you get, but—"

She means it is perhaps time for me to get a real job. Like with a salary and a tie and an ugly e-mail address. That maybe this experiment – relying financially on my creativity – has not worked. That I have painted myself into a corner and the simple way out of it is to submit to the agony of a normal life. And you know maybe just ... maybe I should just get a job. Like an actual *job*. Which for a hundred different obvious and unobvious reasons, I do not want to do.

"Yeah, no, yeah, no. But ah ... you know things always work out in the end."

"Do they?"

"Yeah."

"Well what about with that housing column?"

"That went in a different direction. That became a different thing."

"OK. And the TV thing—?"

"TV thing didn't work out. The production company e-mailed me about it."

"When? You didn't say."

"Yeah I didn't want to say."

"Huh."

Khloé Kardashian was still going for lunch through all of this. The volume was down but she was still moving.

"Huh."

I made a big show of really doing the washing-up and making sure the bed was nice before we got in it but she was very quiet for most of the rest of the night and her phone was buzzing a lot and whenever I glanced over to look at it she was talking on WhatsApp with the girls, which has never been good news, for me. Things will work out, things will work out. Things always tend to ... to work out. Well, hmm. Yeah. A few things haven't worked out. But this will surely just sort of work itself out. It would be great to stop feeling like this for literally one second of my life, wouldn't it. One day, one day, one day. **ZERO STARS**

A MONDAY MORNING WITH NOTHING TO DO

So far today I have: woken up, beheld a perfect honey-coloured patch of sunlight the size of a newspaper as it fell across my bedspread, watched three YouTube videos featuring creators I actively hate, sucked at a watermelon ice-flavoured CBD vape pen until I got lightheaded, watched 1 hour and five minutes of Instagram videos on my phone until my phone got all hot and I realised the phone (which I charged overnight) was already at 42% battery so I had to plug it in to charge again, got annoyed at the neighbour who runs down the corridor in flip-flops (flip-flops should fit! The name is a misnomer! They should not audibly 'flop'!), had a piss the colour of European Fanta and then two extremely large glasses of tap water and then a 45-minute Google about the dangers of tap water vs bottled leading to the purchase of a fridge-door water filter that cost, for some reason, sixty-six pounds and ninety-nine pence plus shipping, watched the patch of sunlight grow slender and yolk-like, watched it fizzle out to nothing via grey. It is almost 1 p.m.

    I kind of figured going to a coffee shop would be a good idea – if nothing else, if no work is happening, (and it isn't: once I got there I checked my e-mail compulsively then read Reddit then flipped back to my e-mail tab then checked Reddit, again and again on a loop, occasionally maybe checking the BBC Gossip page to see if there was any movement on any

Arsenal signings but obviously because the transfer window isn't even remotely near to being open yet there isn't, so I don't know why I looked, then e-mail again, and—), then at least I would be somewhere else, and at least I would be in a place *where work was happening* – albeit, by other people – and somewhere that *feasibly* I could do work *if I were commissioned to do any* or *if I somehow was struck with an original idea, which I haven't had for eight months now*. But by the time I got my shit together – a too-long shower and a too-long look at my urine colour and a too-long toothbrush and a too-long getting dressed routine and too-long to find my laptop charger and pack a backpack and also the walk to the coffee shop took too-long, also, because I kept trying to walk while looking at my phone – once I actually got to the coffee shop they were no longer serving lunch, according to the gorgeous-faced coffee girl who explained that to me, with soft eyebrows but not really any form of, like, empathy. I made a very small joke about how that's fine, I am used to the city stiffing me on lunchtimes (I am a 2 p.m. to 3 p.m. lunch kind of person, in a city that is very hostile to anyone who wants to have lunch anytime beyond exactly one minute past 1 p.m., and it's embarrassing a capital city can't do sub-£10 lunch plates beyond very, very early afternoon) and she did a genuine-seeming laugh at that and I was like, *oh great, now I'm in love with her.*

You wonder, as a straight adult man, when you will outgrow the curse of falling in love with coffee girls when they are even slightly polite or beautiful to

FOUR STARS

you – I fell in love with my first one at a Caffè Nero aged 19, and another one a year later at a sandwich shop near my university house, and variously over my career I have probably fallen in love with, what, four or five more of them? – because the whole routine is so pathetic and obvious and embarrassing, but *oh great, here we go again.* Another fraught six months of misinterpreting every shy smile, every small laugh, every "Do you want this oat latte? We accidentally made two oat lattes", a tap on the forearm when a sandwich is bought to my table, noticing she had a haircut, the day she wears new jeans. And then, of course, one day something cold will run through me and I will suddenly look at her as if I would a lamp, or a recycling bin, or a leaf on the floor. And then I'll have to find a whole new coffee place to go to all over again. And so the dance begins. Anyway I wrote zero words and received zero e-mails apart from that one from Uber Eats saying they "missed me". Don't lie, you *machine.* **ONE STAR**

I MEAN–

—why do I even try and make jokes with the coffee girl, anyway? I have a girlfriend. I have all the attention I could need (do I? I do. I both desire attention and loathe it. I love to be known, I hate to be perceived), and yet every interaction I have with someone serving me something – a coffee, a beer, a meal, a ticket – has to for some reason end with me getting a laugh out of them. Why? Why? Why am I so in need of the approval of others? Why do I constantly need to be thought of as charming? "That guy over there, the one on the table on his own but with three books for some reason, as if he's ever going to read three books in one go, like bring one book to the café, sure, but three? Come on," I imagine the wait staff whisper to each other, after a glancing little interaction with me results in yet another firm-but-polite titter, "he's not like the other customers: he's *funny*," I imagine them saying, "he sees us as human beings, toiling endlessly at our jobs, and he and he alone has come to brighten our day." The other wait staff gaze at the hallowed waiter who bought me a bircher muesli bowl, the closest thing they have to touching the face of God. "Should we show our appreciation for this man?" they whisper, "should we bring him his second coffee for free, maybe, or comp him a *pain aux raisins*?" but the other waiter shushes them. *He does not do it for the plaudits*, he says. *He does not do it for the adoration, or recognition. He does it for us. Charge him full price, especially for that smoothie. He had a scoop of Super Greens in it as well as an extra banana. Fucking four thousand calorie-ass smoothie—* **ZERO STARS**

KILLING A PLANT

Doesn't feel good, killing a plant. Feels like a basic biological failure. When you consider that we are all just animals – I know we have evolved beyond that slightly, and that there are a few things that separate us now from the beasts (language; an up-to-date iPhone), but fundamentally we are just naked, hairy creatures made of flesh, and no amount of 'paying council tax' will ever really change that – we should be good at looking after plants. Plants were here before us. Plants *do not need to be cared for*. The entire planet is geared up to make a plant flourish and grow. We are a planet sloshing with water. We are a planet lit by the warm hazy fire of the sun. There is basically no circumstance on earth where a plant should be choosing to die. And yet this monstera has somehow gone yellow because I left it on a windowsill in the afternoon when it should've been the morning, or some bullshit.

I have never had to care about anything in my life, before, apart from myself, and I didn't even realise I was in charge of that ship until I was about 28, 29: fundamentally, unless you are a parent or a dog-owner or whatever, it is quite easy to forget that you are in charge of life and keeping life alive, which I suppose is my excuse for every day I got distracted and forgot to eat until 6 p.m. and, even then, when I did eat, all I had was a share-sized bag of Nik Naks and some flat Diet Coke. Plants pull all of this into sharp focus: *we need tending, and small attention*, plants sing, *we need fresh clean water and good access to light. We need the tendrils snipping off of us, and the right soil to sit in. With three or four very simple environmental changes, we – like you have the capability to! – can thrive.* Then somehow the cactus on my desk dies – a cactus! Dying! Come on! How dramatic can you get! – and I start to wonder what the throughline is between all these failing plants. The snake plant, which apparently I was meant to dust, before it choked. That sort of bruise-purple bulbous sub-cactus thing that barely did six weeks. That fern I bought from Walthamstow – why was I in Walthamstow? Why did I buy a fern? Why did I bring it back, for 45 minutes, on the bus? What ever compels me to do these things? – that went brown and crackled when tended to on a bedroom shelf. The aubergine in the fridge that I bought from the good grocer near me but then I forgot about, until I found it, shrivelled but filled with its own soggy juice, prostrate on the bottom of the salad crisper. I feel like some deep inky poison lives within me and bleeds out. This cannot be a good sign, any of this. Crop failure is always the omen of an apocalypse, a drought, a plague. Why does my body feel like it is curdling? Why do my teeth singe inside my skull? Why did I ever think I was ready for a fiddle-leaf fig? **ONE STAR**

ALMOND CROISSANT

The French really know what's up. Every time I go to France it is the same: good bread, good wine, good butter, good cheese, good pastries, cobbled streets, classically beautiful brunettes and being rude to people. This is my exact wheelhouse. There is nothing else, particularly, that I need to be able to live. I would thrive in France, if I could speak French and had the constitution to smoke the amount of thin dirty cigarettes required, and if I had some very rum opinions about the northern African nations. I'm one good sex scandal away from being the president there.

My world was rocked, obviously, when I learned the truth about the almond croissant. The almond croissant, for me, has always been the pinnacle of lamination: though *le connoisseur* might argue that the perfect croissant is one that is puffed up like a dome – and shatters into a thousand brown splinters the second you bite into the shell of it, and so then once it's got down your jeans you realise it has to actually be torn apart into thumb-printed little chunks, and dipped in to coffee, and it's 20 minutes later and somehow you're still eating the same croissant – to them I say, *non*. The almond croissant softens the traditional inelegant croissant down into a squidgy little sea creature, covered in coarse marzipan and almond splinters and an entirely artless dusting of icing sugar, creating something sweet and softly chewy and dense. Something magical happens to the constitution of the almond croissant, in the almonding of it: it glues the component parts together, softens them down like an overripe fruit, creating a single heavy handful of pastry: more like the crescent of a Cornish pasty than the cathedralesque croissant from whence it came. And that's why when I was 32 and I learned that almond croissants were just yesterday's stale croissants, spatchcocked and refilled and sold to me, not at the same price but *at a profit*, I had to have a sit-down. I had been eating garbage. I had been going to France and cheerfully eating French *garbage*.

After a period of reflection, in which I tried half-heartedly to defect over to eating actual croissant (a six-week dalliance that didn't sit right with me: eating a plain croissant and getting it all down myself felt, no matter how hard I tried, like I was a child trying to eat adult food in order to look sophisticated in front of people I wanted to impress: once, as an 11-year-old out to dinner in the big city with my sister and her cool older friends, I pretended I liked olives, and eating a plain croissant felt much the same – false, and embarrassing, like I was trying to be somebody I wasn't because I was ashamed of who I am) (this is similar to when, a few years later, I went to a more middle-class friend's house and pretended the moussaka his dad had made us was 'actually nice' and not 'just a horrible sloppy oily mess that for some reason has purple in it', which in itself led to a good 18 months of class-panic: was I born too poor to ever really like quinoa? Would I ever earn enough to like muesli?), I realised this didn't matter.

FOUR STARS

The almond croissant never lied to me: society did. So I wasn't the first person to be offered this pastry: *so what*? So yesterday the almond croissant sat behind the sneeze guard of this shop and was ignored by tens, dozens, maybe hundreds of customers: *irrelevant*. So a baker took my little croissant in the middle of the night, sliced it open down the middle, and filled it with a rough paste made of frangipane: *eh*. Society is obsessed with regeneration, the new, knocking down the old castles and building new grey apartment blocks in their place. We are constantly replacing perfectly usable smartphones and buying new cars and replacing TVs with slightly bigger ones. People with real taste – people who care about the future of this doomed planet! – prefer vintage. I buy and consume almond croissants not for me, but for the children of tomorrow.

(There is a side-theory that being bothered that your almond croissant was just yesterday's croissant is akin to getting mad that your partner has previously had sex with someone other than yourself, which is also a waste of time: *Oh, they had sex? They practised having sex? And now they are really good at sex? Oh, no!* In the same way, the almond croissant has spent a full day practising being a croissant in front of a succession of other men, and now, finally, it is ready to be something magical for you. Do not slut-shame the almond croissant for the crime of living in a world that is fleeting and cruel.)

That said, there is a limit. Once I had an almond croissant which had a stiff little bloc of *pain au chocolat* chocolate in it – I assume this is what they do with an almond croissant on Day 3 of trying to sell the thing? What the fuck do they do on Day 4, bake it in custard? – and, no. At some point, decadence can become too much. There is a lot the almond croissant can teach us about life – how to age gracefully, how subtle tweaks can add to a greater bigger picture, recycling, how to unlearn classism – but putting a stick of chocolate down the middle is not one of them. *Know when to stop*, the almond croissant whispers to us, from the little crinkled brown paper bag you've kept it in in your pocket. *Learn some restraint.* **ONE HUNDRED STARS**

HOWARD LEIGHT LASER LITE 35dB EAR PLUGS

A list of sounds I hate: trains going overhead, children squealing in the hard bouncing walls of a pub, builders (why do builders have to start work at 7 a.m.? Why is that? This has never been explained to me.) doing their early morning clanking, shouting, coughing up from smoking. Other sounds: someone who is getting a lot of text messages having their phone on buzz, most amateur singing, people with loud voices in quiet rooms, people having conversations on wireless headsets (the wireless headset has a microphone directly next to your mouth, so it is not necessary to shout,

FOUR STARS

but the wireless headset people do not, for whatever reason, understand this). I do not like ambulance sirens but I will concede there are functional and necessary. I do not understand why every TikTok my girlfriend watches needs to be so loud (but also, with their little TikTok voices, so affected: I know with gun-to-my-head graveness that one day I will have a mortgage application turned down by someone who was raised on TikTok voices, just a gestative teenager now but doomed to be a bank employee by 25, and they will fix me with a perfunctory administrative glare and say: "OK guys so— OK. Storytime. Erm? Kind of crazy noise I just made with my throat, there! OK so your combined salary does not even get *close* to qualifying for a 4.5x loan—") but I cannot do anything about it. A trainer squeaking on a tiled floor: no. The noises other people make in the gym, and all the music they play there. Self-service checkouts. Coffee machines that use a lot of steam (if I screamed every 90 seconds in a coffee shop, I would be asked to leave. Not the coffee machine, though! That is *allowed* to scream!). Football chants. The high metallic squeal of the Tube. Dogs that yap instead of bark. Anyone who talks – out loud, in public – about how much their houses cost.

    I keep trying to work in coffee shops or quiet murmuring pubs during the day – I cannot work at home, for various normal and non-insane reasons – but I can't focus because of the sheer *noises* people are making, all of the time, every single second of the day. The world is full of sound I do not want to hear.

At a gig a couple of years ago, I discovered the Howard Leight Laser Lite 35dB ear plug, and that has changed everything. Firstly, gigs, which everyone thinks are good for some reason but are actually cacophonously bad: all those angular, bad-shaped noises; sticky floors, the close damp smell of people; a man carries five pints of lager through a crowd and is annoyed when he inevitably spills them. I hate gigs because I am always in the way and other people are always in the way and I'm standing up and it sucks but also, crucially, because they *sound* bad, no gig venue on earth able to make a single noise that sounds even halfway as nice as 'a CD'. Gigs, as I keep telling my girlfriend who nevertheless 'likes them', are the great swindle of modern society – to truly love and appreciate music, you must hear it performed live, then buy a t-shirt afterwards! – and ear plugs help with all of this. I am still bristling and annoyed and bombarded with bad sounds but at least only the good notes are getting in.

I have taken, then, to wearing ear plugs everywhere, which friends tell me is strange. The Howard Leight Laser Lite 35dB is a lurid yellow and pink, so it looks like I have wadded children's chewing gum into my ears to avoid conversation. Consistency-wise, the Laser Lite suggests this, too: satisfyingly squidgy and bouncy to play with, they roll up tight into a little tube (I am convinced I have unexpectedly elegant and petite earholes for a man of my size) and expand out gooily to mute my own personal ear canal. Put in a pair of Laser Lites and the pub, or the library, or the

FOUR STARS

coffee shop, or the train I have to take to another doomed meeting with a new media company who don't want to hire me but do want to 'pick my brains' – all of that recedes and washes down to a more muted tone. The muffled, scratchy thump of other people talking, the shoreline hum of blood in your ears: a serenity that only comes with dull silence. I bought a sack of them on eBay (these are meant to be taped up outside building sites, I believe, but—) and will be working through them until I die.

When I first moved to London we had a downstairs neighbour who was always yelling at her children, which I didn't love: I'm no great fan of kids but I do think they should be able to live in homes where they don't recoil in horror every time they are a bit slow to put their shoes on, or when they stay up a minute past bedtime, or whatever non-transgressions they commit over the course of growing up become too much. Occasionally I would *womp* a heavy shoe on the floor of my bedroom – "STOP YELLING!", I would sometimes say, and she would yell back a tirade of sentences I couldn't really hear because it was coming through a ceiling – and I grew irritatingly accustomed to coming home after a long day and having to spend an evening listening to a woman yell constantly at her two kids. My hungover mornings were affected and my relaxing night-times were, too. If I'd had access to the cosy squidge of some Howard Leights then I wouldn't have had to be troubled by that in any way. Anyway she died. I didn't do it, but she did die. There is no moral to this story. **FIVE STARS**

MY FAVOURITE INSTAGRAM SOAP SHAVER ANNOUNCING THEIR RETIREMENT

My favourite Instagram soap shaver announced her retirement from the soap-shaving game recently, and though I am not 'bereft' or 'grieving' exactly, I do feel the pulsing soreness of their absence. But then part of me is like: *what sequence of dramatically bad decisions have led you to here, to this, to soap-shaving ASMR Instagram and the tang of grief that comes with a particularly good soap shaver leaving the scene? How would you explain what you have become to your father, your father's father, or the series of men who struggled hard through thousands of years of cruel tundra and arid farmland to breed and care for the man who became the man who became the man who came before you?* Sometimes I just think: if confronted with my most ancient, neanderthal forebears, how would I communicate to them that sometimes looking at my phone too much makes me sad? But then I also think: frankly, I could just try explaining this to my cousin, who is also physically hairy and likes tools and speaks in simple sentences. And he would simply call me 'a nutty fuck'.

I discovered soap shaving while profoundly stoned, which I suppose goes some way to explaining it. The Instagram Explore page algorithm knows me better than I know myself, so it shows me a sequence of things I didn't even know I wanted to see – footballers

FOUR STARS

scoring goals in the year 2006, extremely expensive Japanese cotton trousers that the shop selling them insists on calling 'fatigues', girls from anonymous American states showing off their thrifting haul by pouting by a good natural-light window, extreme Turkish butchers, beautiful watches I will never afford held artlessly by unmanicured fingers, and every outfit Justin Bieber has worn and every haircut Justin Bieber has had since the high peak of dirtbag Bieber-ism, the 2019 video to 'No Brainer'. Sometimes it shows me how to properly wash a kombucha scoby, or shows me how to delicately plate food using precise tongs, or how gymnastically drunk Australians can backflip into a paddling pool, but I skip past those rapidly and further shape the mass of plasticine and nerve-endings that make up my personality according to the Instagram AI. And then: soap shaving.

Soap shaving is simple: you freeze a bar of soap and then you shave it, and then you take that mass of frozen shavings and you crunch them with your hands (this produces a noise I call a 'good noise'). You can also carve the outer edge of a soap bar into tiny cubes by criss-crossing it with a razor blade, then freeze, then carve, so these perfect little pixels of soap tinkle to the aesthetic background (a piece of greaseproof paper, maybe, or some assembled flowers) beneath. You are asking why they freeze the soap: the heat of your puckered little hands would make the outer layer of a particularly aesthetic soap bar soft and grimy to the touch within seconds, and dipping the soap to low temperatures makes for a better carve. You are asking how many videos of this I can watch, soundlessly, in a row: it is in the many hundreds. You are wondering what I am getting out of this, what anyone is getting out of this: it is hard, really, to know. I just like looking at soap being carved up and crunched. It doesn't make my brain tingle, or send electric shudders through my nervous system. It's just soothing. Watching a pair of hands maniacally slice into a soap bar with an unguarded razor blade as part of a worldwide community of soap carving, as part of a long line of soap carves: it makes me feel whole, it makes me feel peaceful, it makes me feel well.

> NEANDERTHAL GOLBY: Ooh, ooh! Ooh ooh, ooh! Ooh ooh, ooh ooh, OOH!
> ME: No it's like— God how to describe soap? It's like ... have you seen *Fight Club*?
> NEANDERTHAL GOLBY: Ooh! Ooh ohh OOH!
> ME: Right, right right. Well uh ... you know what let me Google it— yeah it's like. It's fat. But it's not? God what the fuck is soa—
> NEANDERTHAL GOLBY: Ooh ooh AH ooh ooh ooh
> ME: Yeah, sort of like ... sort of like that. I think it's like ... ash mixed with animal grease? Would that count?
> NEANDERTHAL GOLBY: OOH ooh
> ME: Yeah now you're saying it I'm realising that if I were zapped back into pre-history – or any history, really, I mean take me back to the 1920s and this still applies – I have literally zero

real-world knowledge that would make me in any way useful or important or, in fact, able to survive. And I haven't memorised any important sports scores so I couldn't even get rich doing a 5,000-1 bet. Basically: send me back in time any further than like, today, and I will just instantly die.
NEANDERTHAL GOLBY: Ooh ooh ih ooh ooh?
ME: This also applies to prison, yes. Though I always assumed I'd be alright in prison because I can read and write
NEANDERTHAL GOLBY: [*A rudimentary form of laughter.*]
ME: No they wouldn't beat me up, yeah? Because then who would write to their lawyers and mistresses? Think about it!
NEANDERTHAL GOLBY: Oooh ooh ah ooh!
ME: We don't make jokes like that anymore.

Anyway my favourite soap carver announced their retirement from the soap-carving game. I have tried following other carvers but they just don't match up: they are too ungainly with their hands, they focus too much on the soap being pretty instead of the carving, the background music they use is too jaunty, there are too many pleas to like and subscribe. What I want from a soap carver is a good, solid bar of soap, a strong and sturdy carve, and to be kissed and be on my way. Everyone else focuses on the showmanship. What I need is core game.

Everything we do now, of course, is content. You cannot just like something: you have to film it, you have to develop a special little language of filming it, and then you have to strap yourself to the stone plinth and allow the rough hands of The Algorithm to whip against you until you are made anew. The Victorians had workhouses, and we have a little unseen computer filled with lines of code that punish us for not uploading enough or uploading in the wrong way or swearing or showing tit or not showing enough tit or not being energetic enough, and it seems weird we have made society in this way, where we are beholden to a robot (I don't remember the full moral of *Terminator 2* – because I watched it at a sleepover and fell asleep 40 minutes in then woke up because a kid with a big plaster over one eye had wet himself and everyone was screaming, and kid piss really does smell so much worse than adult piss, doesn't it, it smells all *sweet* – but it feels like giving social power over to robots is bad, or something.), and being beholden to that machine made my favourite soap shaver go away and so now I don't have anything to lose a half-hour a day to staring at on Instagram. What else will the overlords take from us? What else will I love that shall be destroyed? **ONE STAR**

COMPULSIVELY BUYING BOOKS AT A RATE THAT OUT-EXCEEDS HOW MANY I AM READING BY AROUND 12 TO 1

I had a dazed little walk around that good bookshop in Fulham after a production meeting that went nowhere (one guy younger than me and visibly richer than me but bald, so I still win, one woman called 'Aggie': they made me come all the way out to their offices just to ask if I had any ideas and when I told them that one about cowboys they both wrinkled their noses in a very private school way and went, "We more do British crime series where a woman stands next to a window and stares at the sea, do you have any of those?" and I said, "No", and they really brightly said, "OK!" and on the way down in the lift I realised I hadn't actually tapped out of the Tube gate so today was going to cost me about £16, maybe more with a fine.). Anyway I bought a good little stack of books: six paperbacks, one really cool vintage sci-fi cover I'll never read but I will display, and two Henry Miller *Tropic* hardbacks from the '80s that have cool matching asymmetrical covers, so obviously now I will have to get the paperback versions of those to actually read because I don't like reading hardbacks, especially not ones as nice as this. I stopped off for a very middling coffee and croissant and realised I had nothing else to do today so I got the train back home and it took 75 minutes.

I started reading more voraciously a couple of years ago, which I enjoyed: it made me actually feel as smart as I always told people I was for a couple of decades beforehand. Whenever someone is trying to out-boy you at a party – show that they earn more than you, or actually understand politics more than you, or are married to someone and you are not, or they've been on nicer holidays than you, or that they went to a school that has a really long Wikipedia page *and* a separate Wikipedia page for alumni – a really good way of outmanoeuvring them is just by having read a book they haven't, and I have enjoyed having that new special power. *Yeah nice wife mate: tell me, what did you make of Michael Chabon's* A Model World? They never, ever know what to say to that. And I am the winner.

I realised I was compulsively buying books maybe two years too late. I just like old bookshops: the sandy-dusty smell, the strange men who work in them (I once went to a bookshop for a short-stack – four paperbacks, barely worth the backpack space – and the guy serving me slickly opened the first leaves of the book with a stiff fake hand. And then he closed the book back up again and pushed it towards me with *another fake wooden hand*! What happened there! How have you lost both of them! You simply do not get this in a Waterstones!), the gloopy way time pools around you there, the calming atmosphere, the fact that I am one of the few people who can see the high shelves so I often find really good stuff up there that everyone else has missed. The books are £1, or

FOUR STARS

£2, or sometimes £4, but if you buy enough in one stack the bookseller will often just sigh and round it down to the nearest solid number because they don't want to think about numbers. The quiet washing calm of a bookshop isn't the only angle of the problem, obviously: I can never resist a single book recommendation anyone ever makes me and as aforementioned I keep trying to impress people at parties with the fact that I am literate, and so quite often in the morning I will wake from a drunken daze to discover I have bought four or five more books online last night while I was trying to look cool in front of someone with a PPE degree from a top-five university. They keep flopping towards my house in the post, an onwards march of grey plastic-wrapped paperbacks, and into the to-read system they go.

A word on the to-read system, which is just piles: a pile of fiction written by men, a pile of fiction written by women. A teetering non-fiction pile. A short story pile. A graphic novel pile. A pile of hardbacks that look nice and whose spines I am never going to crack. A very, very small (but I am trying) poetry pile. Whenever I am in need of a book, I can turn to the system and pluck something perfectly selected for my mood, and that feels satisfying, like I am an at-home librarian. Of course these piles are scattered insanely around the room, many of them precariously, and should I die the system will make no visible sense to anyone but me. But if you need a copy of *The Bonfire of the Vanities* I have both a hardback and a paperback I can find you within six or seven minutes of rummaging.

When I got back I realised I had bought what now constitutes my third copy of *Travels in the Scriptorium*, two paperback one hardback, and also I had already read it and also I didn't really get it. The non-fiction pile wobbled, paused, then slid over in a pile. I sat cross-legged on the floor of my office and counted: in the past 30 months I have bought just north of 600 books and read approximately sixty of those. What is the goal of this? To own every piece of post-modern literature written since the late '60s? And what will I feel, then, if I do? And if I figure how much I'd spent I— no. Let's not do that. Let's not do that at all. This isn't problem behaviour because it isn't a problem – I'm just buying books, aren't I! They're neat little objects to have! – but. Mm no maybe it is. **TWO STARS**

SLEEPING

I love sleeping and wish I could do a lot more of it. You think I mean like: stay in bed another half-hour, something cute like that. No. I wish I could sleep for maybe 18, 19 hours in a row. I would like to see if I could lose an entire day. This is how I wish I could sleep: deeply, infinitely. Sadly something happened to me that I never consented to (I turned 30.) and now I can never do that again. Something in the core of my sleep function has irreparably cracked and drifted. We

FOUR STARS

cannot push Pangea back together with sheer force of will. We cannot make me sleep like a 22-year-old version of myself on a Saturday hangover with nothing to wake up for. Sure, we've all evolved. But we don't have to be happy with what we've lost.

The day after I turned 30, I woke up at 8 a.m. and did not get back to sleep again. This happened the day after that, too. Sometimes it's earlier: there have been 7 a.m. wake-ups, deranged pre-6 a.m. ones. But the form is always the same: once my stupid brain wakes up inside its stupid skull, that is it, I am awake now. I am tortured by the reality of the morning. It does not matter if I screw my eyes up and chant in my head: *don't think don't think don't think.* I am doomed to do it. I am doomed to have a thought. And then I may as well put Birkenstocks on and go and make the coffee. There is no drifting away again until I go back to bed 14 hours later.

I read about 'sleep hygiene' sometimes and I laugh (not a fun laugh – the kind of laugh an anime villain does from his spire when he sees the hero has defeated one of his lackeys. The kind of gruesome low laugh goths teach themselves to do as teenagers instead of getting laid). I go to bed at 10 p.m. most nights, frankly. I have close to impeccable sleep hygiene. The whole toothbrushing routine. Big thing with washing my face. Pillow mist, clean sheets. Read a book instead of looking at my iPad (I am at the age where I think looking at an iPad is a more fun way of looking at a phone than just looking at a phone – this, truly, marks the slippery descent into middle-age. After this it's just chain-playing *Candy Crush* and having long conversations every January about changing insurance providers). Then I watch the inside of my eyelids go orange then purple then black and then a soft, cosy grey, and ... I am pinned in a dreamless sleep. Until—

No the new thing is I just wake up in the middle of the night for an hour. Like fully awake. No mechanical need within my body to pee, or anything like that (though I deeply, deeply fear that reality: the movie *The Green Mile* taught me that inter-nocturnal pissing may occur as early as 43, the age Tom Hanks is in that film, which gives me eight good years of sleeping through the night without pissing, minimum, but I just do not want to be up and down those stairs all night: I see badly in the dark, I don't keep a particularly neat and tidy hallway, I am doomed to slip over and die doing that). I am just awake. Not awake enough to open my eyes, just awake enough to be awake. Maybe I'll think things but I won't write them down, so I'll just be haunted by a half-idea or a reminder that I need to do something that I will chant over and over again, eyes screwed closed, hoping to remember it the next day (I have lost about ten great novel ideas to this). Maybe my mouth is dry and I can just about feel around for a tumbler of water to take a tiny little prone sip. But other than that, no. Every night, in the middle of the night, for no reason at all, I have to spend an hour in the company of myself. This is a punishment no one deserves.

What even can I do about this? Every morning I swallow a puck of magnesium complex, which is meant to make me 'good at sleeping' and 'nice at having knee cartilage', but so far I see no benefit. Sometimes, after trips from America, I smuggle back melatonin gummies that always promise to deeply knock me out, but the sleep it gives me is fluttery and ineffective: unnaturally heavy, feverish, too forced to count as rest. I could smoke a joint every night but that's like saying 'I could have an arm-full of cool tattoos!': sure, I could, but history has proven repeatedly that I am not the kind of man who can get away with behaviour that is so effortless and cool. So I guess every night we will play this game, dancing just out of time with that impish mistress *Madame Sleep*, waking up rested but not, never at my liveliest, never at my worst. We think of the worst curses we can throw at someone as being poverty, destitution, madness, death. But I would say if you really want your enemies to suffer, get a witch to make it so they wake up exactly one hour a night to contend with themselves. **THREE STARS**

THIS LUNCH I JUST HAD WITH MICHAEL

Michael just moved in around the corner which I couldn't remember was awkward or not after we had that year-long beef about the coat (did we quash that? I don't remember. We went for that drink, didn't we? But it wasn't a very good drink. So is it resolved, or ... no?) (really must keep on top of my various beefs) but I guess he got over it because he text me in that deeply frustrating way he does, like, "when are you taking me for lunch", which I hate – I feel the blood turning red in my body! I feel the old creak of beef rise up again! – but the words weren't really coming out today so I said, "now", more of a power play than anything, and he said, "OK", so I said, "OK", so now we're at lunch.

Lunch started fine I suppose – I opened with my bit about how there's no good coffee near our houses except for this place, which is a "hard thirteen minutes away", and really city living isn't about being a hard thirteen minutes away from a good coffee, a good coffee in a city should be at maximum a soft seven away, but then this is an 'up-and-coming area' I suppose which is why he could afford to buy here and why I can't get a coffee without switching postcodes. He smiled without laughing and then said, "How are you?", which I also hate, and then when I went to answer he said, "You're yelling" and it turns out I'd left my ear plugs in and been shouting the whole time. Things loosened up slightly after that. I got the chicken sandwich, obviously, while Michael got soup. A younger version of me would've really got into the weeds about ordering soup in restaurants – what a waste! What a waste of an opportunity of a treat! *Broth*! – but actually I have really come around to restaurant soup in recent years. Fundamentally, fresh soup made well is better than 90% of the meals you have at home. I'm really entering my soup era, I think.

FOUR STARS

But this one was beetroot and I really need that craze to pass because I've already ruined enough white t-shirts trying to eat it.

Michael is gay and I think that's fine, I'm really fine with that, but he's the kind of gay that I can't suss out and that always wrongfoots me. I get on pretty well with most gay men, I think. I figured out fairly early on that to win a gay man onside you just have to say something really catty about a mutual friend you both have (using ten words or fewer, ideally – gay men *j'adore* succinction), and also still have a favourite Spice Girl. Mine is Posh and I never say anything nice about anyone so as long as I am not trampling into safe spaces I think most gay men accept or at least tolerate me. Michael's gay in a different kind of way, though: careful with his buttons, unknowingly elegant hand gestures, Moroccan cookbooks. He listens to music that doesn't sound like a panic alarm. He doesn't really watch television. I'll never really get him.

"So how are you?" he says again, which I am begrudgingly used to. If there is a lull in conversation Michael will always ask, "So how are you?" It has a certain lilt to it, a rhythm: soft on the *so*, higher on the *how*, unpressing on the *are* (too many people ask "how are you" with emphasis on the *are*. Tiresome! We get it!), a gymnast's landing on the *you*. Go for a meal with Michael and you might get How Are You'd six, maybe seven times. He just loves it. Anyway I say my usual response, which is: "Yeah, good."

"Are you?"

"Yeah."

"*Are* you?"

"Yeah."

"Good," he says, then he does a soft smile to himself and eats soup (so careful – like an exotic tall bird dipping its head into soft mud!).

There is a pause, which I never like.

"And how's writing?"

"Writing's fine. Writing's always fine. I'm writing things."

"What things?"

"Reviews."

"TV reviews?"

"No not TV reviews. Things … reviews. Thing reviews."

"Thing reviews?"

"Yes!"

This is what it's like talking to Michael, sometimes. Agonising.

"It's just," he says, "well." He folds his hands on his lap. It takes him, I am not kidding, like 35 minutes to eat a bowl of soup. "I've heard things."

"What things? Heard things?"

"Lloyd said you hadn't been texting him."

"That's literally a lie? I sent him—" it took far too long to get my phone out of my jeans pocket, I'll admit that, and it wasn't elegant at all "— look at that. I sent him a sunglasses emoji two days ago."

"His mum died."

"I'm not very good when parents die. You have to do the whole 'parents die' thing."

FOUR STARS

"You don't have to do the whole 'parents die' thing. You literally have to just text and say you're thinking of them."

"I hated when people texted me 'I'm thinking of you' when my parents died. Like oh, great, another chore I got, responding to this text."

"And you think that's the normal response? Your response?"

"Michael, I'm begging you to eat your soup."

There was a mood after that. Apparently Lloyd had been having a really hard time and Michael had held a big dinner with everyone to help lift him, and he had text me about it (he remembered that old aversion I used to have towards WhatsApp, so he texted – "I literally don't text anyone else. You're the last person I text." "I did wonder why you text so much." "Because you made me!") but actually I use WhatsApp now and I guess I hadn't seen it and so obviously didn't come, and Lloyd was quietly quite upset because he'd brought me a book he thought I might like from his mum's house which, admittedly, is very thoughtful.

"What book?"

"Doesn't matter, now."

"Hardback or paperback?"

"It really doesn't matter."

"I think it matters—"

"It was a Graham Greene."

"Hardback?"

"Yes."

"Bodley Head or Heinemann?"

"I have no way of knowing. I have no way of knowing that."

"I should text him."

"*Yes.*"

Anyway the rest of lunch went fine. Michael is making a documentary, or something. He doesn't seem very into it so I didn't really need to pretend to be too into it either, which is a nice break for me. It's about ... it's on the tip of my tongue. Michael's documentary is about: no, it's gone. *Vegan incels?* Is that a thing? No. The chicken sandwich as ever was astounding and the coffee is from that nice roasters I like in Cardiff. The coffee girl wasn't there that particular morning which I think was probably for the best. The bit about interrogating whether I'd been a good friend for the last five months was less good but overall I give the lunch a hard— **FOUR STARS**

TEXTING A FRIEND SOMETHING EARNEST

I think it always sucks to send a friend an earnest text (or WhatsApp) (or 'Instagram DM') (e-mail, I suppose, but that feels psychotic) because sincerity just doesn't come naturally to me in any way. I mean what do you say? What *do* you say? When someone is stinging, what do you say? The rationale here is like: you do not need to say the magical combination of words that

FOUR STARS

will instantly make them feel better, to reverse all wrongs. You do not need to solve unsolvable problems. You just need to be like: "Hey." But not: "Hey, I'm here." He knows you're *here*. And you can't offer to like, "Let me know if I can do anything to help". Because then the onus is on them: they have to type back, "Thanks" (imagine if they actually took you up on that offer! Calamity!). So all you need to do is reach softly across the void and make them aware that you know that they are hurting. But you can't be like: "Hey, I know you're in a degree of mental agony right now. Yikes!" They hate when you say, "Yikes". You can never say, "Yikes". It's been— it can't be. It's been twenty minutes I've spent on this. It's a *text*. "Hey Lloyd—" No, no. Using their entire full name feels like you're calling them up to the headmaster's office to be expelled. "Hey dude—" Dude? Can I say *dude*? If your mum's just died, can you still be a dude? I feel like there is a statute of limitations on dudeism. He is not, currently, in the dude-zone. Delete that. Twenty-two minutes. The nightmare here of course is you accidentally press SEND when you're halfway through the empathy text, so you accidentally send Lloyd (grieving, sad, motherless) a text that just says: "Hey dude, Yikes!", which is what it currently looks like while I'm deleting it. It is best to draft these things in Notes. I have a lot of these things in Notes, in among my Notes. It is a litter of like shopping lists, ideas for film scripts ('*Joker* road trip movie') and earnest, overwritten texts to my friends. Sometimes I scroll through them – who was I apologising to in 2018? Do I even know anyone called 'James'? – and they catch me off-guard. It's like a language not of my own, an alien writing through my fingers. What would you want to receive, as a text, five weeks after your mum died? I should lead with like, a shared interest we have. Find some Instagram photos and say I think they might be 'on your vibe'. Then subtly, like a rabbit punch, hit him with some empathy. "Hey so long time no speak" kind of thing. "Hope things r cool. Let me know if you want to grab a sandwich or something." That, to me, feels like a soft little hittable underhand shot over the net. He can smash that back at me if he wants to, or he can let it bounce into touch. I have put no expectations on him, and I have rid myself of the profound and rotten guilt of inaction. This is perfect. This is the perfect text. I fo— fuck me. I forgot to delete the "Yikes". **ONE STAR**

THE DOG

So we got a dog. He flew from Cyprus to Belgium then got in a truck for five hours to a motorway services on the edge of the city, and when he came out he was all greasy and small and crap. When we are home alone together he looks at me and starts shivering, as if he is freezing, because he knows (from his time on the streets) this makes him look more pathetic and thus more likely to get a small snack or a bite of whatever I

FOUR STARS

am eating. He has very soft ears and an even softer head. He wears little jumpers when it's cold. His name is Bam.

I don't know how I feel about Bam, because he's less my dog and more just a simp we got for Megan, who occasionally allows me to pet him or lift him up really high in the air and go, "Yah!" He has a completely perfect face and weighs eight kilos and is really short (I like to joke to him that he is "no foot eleven inches tall", to really make the point that he is little, but he doesn't really get it) and is slightly scared of men, because he grew up on the streets of Cyprus and must have got shooed and kicked or something, because he sometimes gets really afraid of men wearing boots. When I think too much of that I get so enraged I want to fly out to South Cyprus and just tear every man I see apart with my bare hands. *Who of you was mean once to my dog? Show yourselves! He is a soft little prince! He just wanted some food because he was hungry! He wears little tiny jumpers!* Then I realise: Bam is a simp for my girlfriend, and I am a simp for him. There is a natural pecking order, and I have inverted it to my own detriment, because the little boy who lives in my house looks really cute in the Carhartt jacket we bought especially for him.

He doesn't like walking to the pub with me so I have to carry him all the way there. This makes both of us look pathetic. What you don't realise about dog ownership is a major component part of it is talking to other dog owners or people who are interested in petting your dog, about the dog, and because the dog can't talk you really are holding up exactly one side of the conversation, just saying facts about your dog to a stranger. Bam will go and get tangled in another animal's lead and start sniffing them directly on the dick and I just have to mildly say like, "Oh, yes, well we think he's three." He will try and keep pace with two whippets and absolutely blow himself out in less than a minute while I am telling some guy in a Barbour, "We don't really know what he is, he's a mix." This is all people ask about your dog: What Kind Of Dog Is He, What's His Name, How Old Is He? I have never asked these questions back. Don't you want to see deeper than his age, his name, his breed? Bam is an enigma. He is a complete one-off. His ears are so attuned to the sound of a Babybel that he knows just from the crinkle of the plastic around the wax that I am trying to eat one without him. Don't you see that? I haven't eaten a Babybel alone for 14 straight months because every time I get one out of the fridge I hear that little midget clunk down the stairs – *ker–clunk ker–clunk ker–clunk* – to come and shiver and stare at me. Ask about that! Ask about who he is! He is more than a name and an age and a dog breed! He is a person!

Today we have been left alone together and he just keeps looking at me. Occasionally he slumps over to me on the sofa and really inelegantly flops sideways onto me – onto my leg, or an errant arm. He makes little sighing noises as if he's got a job and it's not going very well. I went to the kitchen to eat a single plain cracker and he just watched me, huge wet brown eyes, pleading and yearning, so I gave him a special

FOUR STARS

dog chew that supposedly cleans his teeth, which he held delicately between his two front paws and gnawed at without thanks. It's not helping that I haven't had an idea today and the dog is just looking at me, occasionally shivering, occasionally gently raising his head from a light sleep, always judging. I, obviously, cannot go anywhere in the house to brain-clearingly masturbate, because he'll either try to watch or I'll hear a little *snrrk!* dog-noise at a crucial moment in the procedure and that will put me off. It is impossible to do anything in this house without him trying to nudge against my legs. I love him, but creatively he is sapping a lot of my energy. It's 3 p.m. and the alarm just went off telling me I have to carry him outside for a shit.

Anyway, as I say, he's not really my dog. I technically own him and I look after him and I've picked his mess up with two plastic bags over my hands and I pay for half of his food and I bought him six entire presents for Christmas, but he is not really mine. He is my girlfriend's dog and he stares at her constantly, adoringly. When she goes out and we are left alone he sits on the sofa with me long enough to get a bite of Babybel and technically be polite and then he takes himself off to bed. Do you not understand how devastating a review of my company that is? I cannot even captivate a *dog*. One of his favourite toys is that little coil of cardboard you get from unwrapping an Amazon parcel, and he can barely spend five minutes in my company. "You talk to him in a normal voice," Megan says, "do you know how psychotic that is?", and I say, "No." Also every night he jumps into bed between the two of us, contorts his body sideways, then spends the next four hours until the dim grey light of the morning slowly pushing me out of the bed. Every day I wake up pressed thin on the side of the mattress on the bed I paid for with two tiny paws pressed into my side and his eyes open, looking at me, as if daring me to do something. I paid for a bit of deer antler for you for Christmas, you little fuck! I pick your shit up with my hands! I haven't had a full snack-cheese since 2020! So yes, the dog is adorable, and I love him so hard it makes me feel like my heart is larger than it was before I met him. But he disrespects me at every turn. As a result of this, the dog only gets— **THREE STARS**

BEING TRAPPED IN A TOILET IN SPITALFIELDS MARKET AND LIKE 16 PEOPLE WATCHING ME COME OUT ONCE THEY FINALLY GOT THE DOOR DOWN

I don't want to talk about how exactly (backpack strap got caught on the handle and somehow sheared the entire piece of metal off, while also *yurk!*-ing me backwards in a way that quite hurt my neck and throat) but I got imprisoned in the disabled bathroom underneath Spitalfields Market. This was a shame, because up until that incident Spitalfields Market was in my top

FOUR STARS

three pisses in London – London is a particularly hostile city to people who need to have a piss, or a shit, or to sit down, and so you need to learn the various publicly accessible bathrooms and keep them close to your heart like secrets, and Spitalfields Market serves my bathroom needs whenever I am in Spitalfields, Shoreditch, Brick Lane and even sometimes Liverpool St. Station (they moved the toilet facilities there a couple of years ago and I don't like the long walk to and from them, through all the slow-moving station crowd. It is far easier to go to Spitalfields Market and dip). It's right up there with the McDonald's on Tottenham Court Road, the door-less clean facilities in the middle of St Pancras station, or the really nice second-floor toilets in Liberty. There are of course pubs, but some pubs have stringent rules about whether customers can use their bathrooms or not – normally "no" – so you have to know the pubs, and also know how busy they are (you cannot walk into a quiet pub and use the toilet: they are watching your every move) and, I find, it helps to go into pubs where you know where the bathrooms are, and march into them with purpose, which I do at the Wetherspoons in Angel whenever I need to piss around there. It goes without saying that I mainly use public facilities for urination only: I have taken shits in public bathrooms on only three occasions in my life (June '18, August '20, then August '20, again), and all three were extremely dire emergencies, the details of which are unnecessary.

Anyway here are some observations from the as-it-turns-out 46 *minutes* I spent locked in the disabled bathroom beneath one of London's premiere food-and-trinket markets, while someone knocked on the door and said, "Is anybody in there?" and I said, "Yes" and they said, "What?" and I said, "YES", again but louder, and they said, "Are you OK?" and I said, "I'm locked in, the handle sheared off" and I could sort of tell from the tone of voice they were using that they were talking in very simple tones to me because they thought, from the disabled sign on the toilet, that perhaps there was a chance I was pissing in there because I had impaired faculties, whereas actually I did it because there was a huge sloshing puddle of sewage on the floor of the Gents' toilet and I didn't want to tiptoe around that (or sort of piss while straddling over it) in my new Reeboks. But that was hard to communicate through a door. I simply said, "Can you get someone, please?" and it took a really really long time to get someone. I mean, who is there? It's not like Spitalfields Market has any roving staff, or any disabled toilet specialists. There is maybe a guy in hi-vis, *maybe*. Anyway:

- This is a paper towel bathroom, which I always respect (apart from the industry-standard Dyson Airblade™, no electric hand dryer in Britain really gets close to drying a hand, it just sort of blows on them, maybe warmly maybe not, so to get a truly dry hand you need a paper towel, although also it helps to have a paper towel to put over the handle of the door when you open it, because a lot of people do not wash their hands at all after the bathroom, or if they do they don't dry them properly, so the bathroom

FOUR STARS

handle is, germ-wise, a nightmare. Often I will try and open a bathroom door with my foot – I am surprisingly agile with my legs for a man of my size – but obviously you cannot do that with other people in the bathroom, for instance in a urinal set-up in a pub, because anyone watching you stretch your leg to door handle height to open the door handle will go back to their group at the table and go: "You see that big bloke over there? I just saw him do something *mental*", and they will all turn to look at you, which obviously is unideal. I do not know why pubs don't just, by default, fix their bathroom doors so you push them to open with a flat hand, rather than having to pull them open with your fingers scooped round a filthy handle. That is baffling, to me), but it means that this bathroom is now a tip: piles of towels fallen on the floor, sodden towels in thick pats sort of near but not in the bin, a big paper towel adhered with dampness to the wall. It is strange what we become in the private cubicles of a bathroom: we throw things around, we spill things, we leave smears and odours, we make an outsized amount of mess compared to the default messiness of our personalities. We become *chimps*. Normal people walk among you every day who make obscene and dreadful scenes inside public bathrooms. They say "Hello" to you, they nod and smile. Who are you when no one else is watching? Lock the door to a toilet cubicle and find out;

- It is insane to me that the multiple people knocking on the door – there was the initial knock-and-check, and then a subsequent one a few minutes later, and now they keep knocking at semi-urgent intervals – are getting mad at me, the victim, here. I am the one locked in a bathroom filled with the steam of other people's pisses and shits. Normally I try and hold my breath for as long as possible in a public bathroom – I always imagine a fine particle mist of other people's piss and shit in the air, and I don't want to inhale that – but that has obviously gone by the wayside over the course of 46 minutes. But it's the tone that's rubbing me up the wrong way here, as if *I* am inconveniencing *them* and not the other way around. "Hello?!", this new voice is saying, "you've been in there quite a while now!" I have stopped communicating with them because they are morons, but, like, obviously (I have to assume help is coming: the only other option now is to use the sheared half-handle as a sort of digging device to try and gut out the lock, but I feel that will take hours of hacking, and then what if – once I get out, panting, sweating, covered in a miasma of piss and shit – I incur some sort of fee for damaging the toilet door? I am not paying to be locked in a disabled toilet, I promise you that. That is not the way round I would like this to be!). I should walk out of there and point to every person there and say: "You are cretins. You are CRETINOUS!";

- The sink here is a robot sink, which I hate. They took the concept of the sink and made it worse with technology. You put your hands under a sensor that I assume was devised with hardware developed before the moon landing and, minutes later, it dribbles out a

FOUR STARS

wad of pink soap. Then you have to put your hand under a tap, which runs thin and unwarm water over you for like nine seconds. You cannot get a lather going in nine seconds and you certainly cannot get a rinse. They didn't test this? They didn't get a single human being to wash their hands with these, before putting them in the disabled facilities beneath Spitalfields Market? And then when I put my hand under the sensor for another squirt of water, the sensor now pretends it's never seen a hand before, that it doesn't understand what a hand is? It took me longer to wash my hands in here than it took me to take a piss. In a way it's good I have 46 minutes locked in here with the sink, because after a few minutes I did notice a greasy film (cheap soap) on my hands, still, so had to re-rinse and re-dry them again (there was a robotic hand dryer, too, but as aforementioned that simply does not work, which, whoever is in charge of the facilities here – and who cannot be found in the labyrinth of Spitalfields Market, apparently! – does acknowledge, hence the raw wad of paper towels on the side for drying);

- That maybe being locked in a disabled bathroom for 46 minutes, even though it's an accident, even though it's not my or anyone else's fault, feels like a low-point and should be treated like a low-point and maybe this should be a low-point and I should learn from my low-point. I mean all my friends are at *work* right now;

- How come one in maybe every three times I am confronted with a toilet seat, the seat is twisted off at a mad angle from the ceramic bowl itself, and I have to edge it back towards parity with the edge of my leg? There is a gap between the design of the human *hole* and the toilet seat that does not allow for a natural twist when standing from a seated position, meaning the seat pops and pings with the motion from it and does not return. It's not a big problem but it is a problem, and it's strange that none of the mega-billion industries – I assume being in toilet seat manufacture is lucrative, as every toilet needs a seat and every building has dozens of toilets in it – in charge of this have done anything at all to fix it. We've been shitting and pissing for millions of years. We should have got it down by now;

- Anyway turns out I could have unlocked the door myself with a lower lock that perhaps could have been just about screwed open with a couple of credit cards held close together and my being in the disabled toilet for 46 minutes was a complete waste of time, and also if I pulled the emergency cord someone would have been here faster, and by the time I did walk out a small group of gawkers had assembled presumably to see if there was visible damage to the person trapped in the bathroom or just unseen mental stuff, and once the door did open I did the only reasonable thing which was to march through the crowd of people wordlessly with my head held high, bashing through a couple of elderly gentlemen as I did so, which on the way home I did feel a bit bad about, actually. I do not rate this activity very highly at all. **ZERO STARS**

AGARIC FLY – UHURU

I came back from a long weekend a few weeks ago and smelled what my house smells like. *Oh*, I said. *So it smells like that.* I always thought it was strange when I was a kid that all of my friends' houses had a particular smell – Paddy H., a sort of soupy, lentilly scent; Charlie C. had a bright, lemony flavour; Steven H., whose house was kept beyond immaculate by his mother, had that hotel-room, new-laundry air to it throughout – but my house had no discernible odour at all. Then I came home from university for the first time and it hit me: stewed tea, dusty carpeting, the light but looming smell of a basement a cat had diarrhoea in. This is what my friends smelled when they smelled my house. And now, on a hangover after four days of drinking every single pint the city of Leeds had in its taps, it struck me again: damp towels, old curtains, the smell of the fridge that always has one wet shelf in it.

My aim is to make my house smell like a 'fancy shop', so I turned to incense. This is because incense is potent, and immediate, and because there is some form of ritual to the lighting and enjoyment of it; and also because those mist diffusers are a fucking faff and nobody seems to sell tasteful blends of essential oils to put in them so it's just me, fingers greasy, a mug of cold water sloshing in my hand after being carried upstairs from the kitchen, trying to get three precious little drops of 'lavender' into a rapidly yellowing tank.

Incense you light with a lighter and then it smells nice. If you don't like one smell you just light another. This is the exact level of aggravation I need.

I first picked up a packet of Uhuru at 194Local in Shoreditch, which I should never have been in in the first place because I was born in the '80s. The point of 194Local is to give you an unerring experience that is nothing like shopping: it's more like walking into a conversation at a party where everyone is talking about you, and then they abruptly turn, and stop, and look you in the eyes, as if this was all your fault in the first place. I always know I'm in a tastemaker shop because the guy behind the counter is having a full conversation with someone who isn't looking at him, and none of the prices are on anything. I walked past a rack of £160 vintage t-shirts and bought my pathetic little packet of Uhuru to the counter. "Yeah," the kid said (was he talking to me? He was on AirPods). "This is my second-favourite incense you know."

My second-favourite incense, you know.

This remains the most intriguing sentence anyone has ever said to me, ever. I cycled home with my Uhuru. I carefully cut open the top of my Uhuru (no incense on earth is packaged in a useful and usable way, and Uhuru is no different: it's in a sealed-shut silver pouch with no reseal to it at all, so once it's open, it's on you). I pulled one stick of Uhuru out of the container and smelled it like a fine cigar. *My second-favourite,* the voice echoed, *you know.* The phrase "second-favourite" alone contains a world: the idea of a man constantly ranking and re-ranking various incenses, a 24/7 internal stock ticker, and Uhuru was good enough to place second but crucially *not* first. There was no attempt by the 20-year-old boy in AirPods to tell me what his actual #1 ranked incense was. That was not what his comment was about. If you want to know his favourite, you will have to buy it, completely by accident, and have him tell you. And then, ringing like a bell, the "you know". *No, I do not know.* But something within the way he said "you know" suggested he did slightly expect me to know.

Uhuru smells of cassia (fancy cinnamon), grapefruit (you know what grapefruit is) and oud (dark, resinous wood), and those notes tangle together beautifully across the stale air of my flat: the cassia is bitter, the grapefruit lifts with a sultry zing, the oud adds a barky crunch, like stepping through a wood-chip path through the back of a late summer festival. Together, they smell dry and sandy: it smells like being near the sea, but not being near the beach. Long, dry wan strands of grass stretch out of clumps of green weeds. A single wire fence taps you away from the edge of the cliff. The waves, deep beneath, rise against the shore and sound like a deep inward breath. The moon and the sun hang together in the sky.

When I was a kid I asked my parents why we never went on holiday and they both realised with a jolt that they'd never thought to take me anywhere. The first place we went was Filey, a grey and brown and just-about cheerful north-eastern seaside town. There I first saw the sea, and scrunched my feet onto the

JOEL GOLBY

beach, and spent a day digging breathlessly into the sand. I ate milk-white ice cream and scored a deliriously improbable hole-in-one at crazy golf. A year later we went again, but something was off: the sea was mean against the shore, the beachside arcade was roped off menacingly, the bed-and-breakfast we'd had such a jolly time in the year before had been sold to a young husband and wife. The first night we all woke to the clonking sounds of them rowing, feet scuffling against the polished floor above us, and at breakfast the next day the wife slinked downstairs with a newly purple eye. My parents packed their bags in silence and told me the holiday was off. We drove home mostly in silence. I wasn't happy about it but I got it. And all I remember was: the strange sideways smile of the B&B manager when he asked us why we were leaving. It was like he knew why, he knew exactly why, and he was proud of it. Uhuru smells like the long, quiet drive back from that holiday: stuffed in the back of a juddering Volvo on its last summer on earth, packed in with every bag and toy and outfit I was supposed to be enjoying on holiday, instead crawling back home, again, not even long enough to smell what the house was like when we first got in. I *must* go back and ask that AirPod boy what his #1 incense is. I! Have! To! Know! **TWO STARS**

TWO SLICES OF PIZZA AT VOODOO RAY'S

I was walking through Shoreditch when I got my '3 p.m. hunger', which is a special hunger only I get at around 3 p.m., when somehow the constant on-ness of adult life has crept up on me and I have forgotten somehow to feed myself over lunch. This happens a lot. This happens more than you'd think. This happens a lot more than I would like to admit. This happens in a way that you really should think I'd learn from because it happens so often – me, rushing into a restaurant at one minute to 3 p.m., time and time again, watching a flushed group of kitchen workers exhaustedly wipe all their surfaces down, shaking their head and their hands "no, no, no!" – and yet I keep doing it, I keep letting 1 p.m. turn into 3 p.m. because I'm too stupid to just eat lunch. Sometimes I really do wonder how I make it day-to-day without another more grown-up person giving me constant supervision.

It did not help that I was wandering aimlessly around Shoreditch, which never helps, because Shoreditch is a cursed place that defies human habitation. You should only ever go to Shoreditch at 10 a.m. on your bike to have exactly one coffee with a girl in a beret who works in PR in a way she can't really ever explain but will e-mail you about, or at 10 p.m. in an Uber to have an overpriced cocktail in a member's only club you keep saying "doesn't have a vibe" but you are still pathetically excited to go there because you once saw a famous person (who lawyers have urgently suggested you redact the name of!) walking out of the toilets while sniffing very deeply. The hours in between, there is no reason for anyone to wander around Shoreditch, seeing what new shop they have that does £6 cupcakes, being handed small whatever promotional freebie they are passing out outside the station, thinking 'that vintage shop looks nice' but once you go in you see the first jumper you touch costs £400 despite having a hole in the collar and now you have to stay in the shop for like five more minutes pretending you're actually interested in the clothes and the boots and things so the French fashion student working the till solo doesn't know that you're poor. Maybe in the afternoon you can go to a hotel you can't ever really quite find the door for first time and sit in a co-working space and fail to get a waiter's attention to order a beer for no-joking 45 minutes. That's Shoreditch.

So I ended up at Voodoo Ray's for a slice (two slices.). Voodoo Ray's is good because it's there, and it tastes good enough, though obviously it has its faults (the staff are all cool but in a very intimidating way, so rather than going there and thinking, 'I am among cool people! That must mean I am cool!' it actually ends up feeling a lot more like 'it is your first day of art college and you are the only person wearing chinos'; also the paper plate system is still fairly inept). I got a margherita slice (I think whenever you order pizza from a good place you need at least one slice which is

FOUR STARS

exceptionally plain – life is not designed to be an unending party) (in fact, this goes for all restaurants: the plainest item on the menu should also be the best. Every curry house should have an outstanding korma, for instance) and also something with like nduja and fior di latte on it, and then a good big cold Diet Coke. This was all fine until I remembered I always used to go to Voodoo Ray's with that guy, and then I got doleful.

Ah it's not much it's just I always used to go to Voodoo Ray's with the same guy. Good guy! Couple of slices, some Diet Cokes, a little conversation. You walk back and you cut in and out of Shoreditch like it isn't there. But like the main reason I'm here and he's not is on me: I didn't text enough, didn't do enough reach-outs, you let a friendship fizzle and without enough light and enough action, it withers. I mean yes I could text him and see if he "wants a pint" now, but I know it'll feel too forced. He'll say, "So what've you been up to?" and I won't have any information to fill the void with and I'll say, "So what've *you* been up to" and it'll be something so startlingly and life-changingly significant that I'll feel bad for not already knowing it (a kid, or something. People always have kids.). So I just won't, so that friendship is over. That sucks! I could've kept that guy around – a couple slices every now and again! Some D.C.s! Maybe on a Friday, a cheeky frozen margarita! – but instead I fucked up. Now I'll probably just see him awkwardly in the street some time and have to do that whole thing. *Fuck.* Anyway the slices were good and the Coke was big and cold, but when I got to the train station they were handing out free SIM cards and I didn't know until I'd accidentally taken one and it's like, oh great, what am I going to do with that? **THREE STARS**

GETTING WAY TOO INTO VITAMINS

I try and take the Cod Liver Oil tablet first because it tastes the worst (obviously, a good vitamin swallow doesn't involve tasting the pellet at all, but the Cod Liver Oil caplet is a slippery, writhing little thing, and can sometimes squirm onto your tongue, and it tastes exactly what something called 'Cod Liver Oil' sounds like it tastes like, which is: fish and grease) and the Vitamin D tablet towards the end of the vitamin-taking session, which I always finish with a large ovoid of Bee Pollen (this is good for seasonal allergies and local immunity, I think, but also tastes like dessert). In between there are a few moving parts, but briefly: turmeric is in there, for blood health; Ginkgo Biloba, which I am convinced is good for my brain; a puck of Magnesium, good for joints and also supposedly healthy sleep, though I have seen none of that, lately, none of that at all. Then, the sprays – a daily mist of cherry-flavoured Air Defence, because I am afraid of the toxic smog in London (they will write history books about this toxic smog. They will say things like: "It is insane nine million people swanned around in this smog, all day every day, and didn't all die instantly when exposed to it. Anyway now we know—"), and an additional dose of Vitamin D, because I really cannot articulate how convincing the YouTube video about a guy who takes 118 vitamins a day and 'wants to live long enough to upload his brain to a computer' was about it (in the minutes after watching this video, I decided to get Way Too Into Vitamins, then ignored a deadline to fuck around and spend over £100 on the Holland & Barrett website). I take 5-HTP because it's supposed to be good for mood, also, though why I always pause on the middle of bridges and think what shape my body would explode into if I hit the ground below like a watermelon, I do not know. I take Zinc because it's good for my immune system and also, privately, because it makes me cum in a far more massive volume than usual. I take two caplets of Ultra Greens because they are very green, and it feels like I just *should* be consuming something that green every day, as if I am somewhere between Gwyneth Paltrow and an Olympic powerlifter, who for some reason are the only north stars of internal health I can think of right now.

    I take Collagen because I'm worried I'm at the age where my hair might, at any moment, start thinning and falling out, and I need my hair (and nails, and skin) to look as glossy and healthy as possible if that is ever going to happen, because aesthetically I really am nothing without my hair, nothing at all. I take Saw Palmetto because I am at that age where prostate health is, just distantly, starting to rear its looming head, and based on anecdotal data (men I piss next to at public urinals always seem to shoot their urine out with such venom that it seems they are actively mad at the porcelain, whereas I have always had a much more casual, louche flow) I feel like maybe it will be good for me to get some decent blood supply in that department to ward off a senile final few decades marked by constantly going to the bathroom for an underwhelming, dribbling little piss. It takes about a litre of water to get all these things down. I need to take a caffeine-free herbal tea afterwards – a Rooibos, maybe, with a touch of honey – to calm down all the anxiety I feel about my hair, blood, brain, bones, sleep, hair again, and piss.

Why am I doing this? I think it is because I spent my twenties treating my body like a toilet and I have spent my thirties gripped with an unquenchable fear of death, and taking 15 white label tablets every morning feels like some sort of uneasy parlay between the two. I think about that party I spent slurping from a communal punch bowl before finding a 16-pack of reconstituted crabsticks in the fridge, eating them in silence, then walking home via a McDonald's breakfast (I fell asleep on the 5 a.m. night bus back and spilled scalding black coffee on myself. I still had the wherewithal to save an anaemic-looking pancake from the takeout box by my feet, which I chewed at miserably like an apple). The famous '19 pints of beer, four shots of tequila' Saturday that I still wish – even now, years later – that I'd been smart enough to puke up. I think about that time at an afterparty where I was

FOUR STARS

offered a fairly chunky line of what I assumed was cocaine – lovely, dark, delicious cocaine; yum *yum* – but actually turned out to be a fairly hefty dose of ketamine, which almost immediately put me into a K-hole (me, prostrate on a sofa for two hours, incapable of thought or movement or blinking, really, gazing through time and space), and the only person who checked I was, say, alive, was the one Christian girl at the party, who sat next to me and said, "Are you OK, Joel?" in a soothing saviour's voice and I, about twenty minutes later, vaguely pulled one arm up and made an assertive moaning sound like a monster then stumbled into an Uber outside. What, of course, was a Christian girl doing at a party where someone could accidentally do ketamine off a photo-book and spend the next two hours staring into the abyss? It makes you wonder, does it not. I think, of course, that God sees the world not from above, but through the eyes of His believers, and so thinks everything down here is more-or-less fine, because all He really sees are little slices of wholesomeness – a bric-a-brac sale in a church hall, a weekend visit to a lake with bracing views, watching *Antiques Roadshow* with the sound turned down so you can hear the neighbours arguing, having clean squirtless sex once a month on starched linen sheets – and so does not see the horror true that makes up His world. Apart from that night, when I K-holed into infinity because I don't ask what goes in my body. Don't worry about me, God. I'm on the Bee Pollen now. I cum in half-litre loads. You won't be seeing me for a long, long time. **FOUR STARS**

WASTING A SINGLE DAY OF YOUR FINITE LIFE AT AN OFFICE JOB WHERE ALL YOU HAVE TO DO IS A SIMPLE EXCEL MAIL MERGE BECAUSE YOU'RE THE ONLY PERSON IN THE OFFICE WHO CONSISTENTLY KNOWS HOW TO DO THAT AND SO YOU DISGUISE HOW DIFFICULT IT IS (SIMPLE.) SO NO ONE EXPECTS YOU TO DO ANY FURTHER WORK FOR THE REST OF THE DAY

Microsoft Excel (1987) is a spreadsheet software that everyone on earth pretends to know how to use, for some reason, and that includes me. Microsoft Excel is exactly as old as I am, and towards the end of our dual gawky teens, our lives became entwined – me, a large boy in an ill-fitting wide-collared shirt doing an IT A-Level; Microsoft Excel, the thuddingly unglamorous software I was supposed to learn the deep formulaic intricacies of via a grey-and-brown textbook – and we got to know each other, a little, a little bit. Every day I would come to school, put a floppy disk into one of the lab PCs, and incredibly slowly build a multicoloured spreadsheet that added up items purchased at a shop (the shop did not exist – I invented it. I was given a rare opportunity to use the absolute outer reaches of my imagination to add any stock I wanted to this shop – Unicorn tails! Diamond condoms! – and I came up instead with 'three different kinds of egg').

FOUR STARS

Why would someone install Excel on a till machine, at an *egg shop*, when, for at least a hundred years beforehand, more elegant and simple analogue tills had existed? This question was not in any way answered by my coursework. I was graded a very low 'C'.

At university, like any weak adolescent friendship, Excel and I drifted apart. I got into light beer, and extended *Lord of the Rings* DVDs, and standing at parties in a very strange and unapproachable silence. They got into, I dunno, 'VLOOKUP'.

My first job took two and a half years of my life away from me and did not give it back. The problem, of course, was the job was too easy – the hum of day-to-day low-pressure administrative work in the back office of a university drama department, where the most pressing thing I had to do every week was print out three or four official-looking letters so that students in leotards could send to the council to exempt them from paying tax. Occasionally I had to fill out (by hand, in triplicate, like it was the *nineteen hundreds*) some contract forms for freelance tutors, and send them via internal mail to a very ill-tempered Ukrainian woman a couple of departments over, who apparently received them and did absolutely nothing with them then got mad at me when I called her a month later to ask why nobody had been paid. There was some soothing melody to filling those out: going down each row with a ruler, ticking off afternoons and mornings on a great huge year-long calendar, scrawling a changeable hourly rate at the top. But mostly I e-mailed my friend Sacha about Chinese food, monsters, Casio watches and women. Mostly I angled my computer screen away from the rest of the office and played *Minesweeper* at a low-to-medium level of expertise. Mostly I went on *Football365* and sent strange e-mails to the editors at the start of each season, ranking the various new kits. Mostly, whenever someone else in the office had a mild computer problem, I went over and stood behind them, looming over and taking control of their mouse, then hitting Ctrl+Alt+Del because a program had crashed and somehow looking like an expert in doing so. "You hit F5 so now Internet Explorer is full screen," I would say. "Try hitting F5 again to undo it." And they would reply: you are the all-knowing master of the universe. You are the Golden God.

Sometimes I would think distantly about how my mother had worked office jobs on-and-off unheralded for 40 straight years and now, early in her sixties, she was still working them now; that big sparking brain and full capacity of intellectual potential had been blocked at every turn by circumstance and unambition and the drudgery of comfort, reduced only to "Hazel is good at typing" and a series of unimportant cog-like roles of administration; and how, flashing forward slightly, I could see myself at her age, still here, still in this office, only slightly better at *Minesweeper*, still not the boss, because I didn't do anything and nobody could ever take me seriously in an authoritative manner, still not really heralded or recognised in any way, still hitting F5, still e-mailing just way too long missives about Liverpool's home kit this year (another classic). Then I would just ignore that thought forever until the dread did rise again.

Sometimes I would get so bored by doing nothing at work that I would spend my lunch hour going down a street I had never been down before, or an alleyway, or up the ramps of a car park. I think there is something interesting about unfamiliar streets (and something incredibly tedious about familiar streets), something strange: when I would walk up my childhood street on the 'wrong' side of the road (i.e. the one we didn't live on) I would feel off, alien, inverted, wrong. When I would walk back from the Londis down the road the 'weird way' – up and round and down, rather than along and across – I would feel like I was experiencing the street for the very first time all over again. This is fine in a small town where there are only a finite number of streets and re-discovering the ones you already know can be interesting, slightly. In London there are one billion streets and they are repurposing them or rebuilding them all of the time. There is no way to know this city and it is foolish to try. Still, at lunch, I would walk a bit of a wrong way back to the office and discover a grey-looking café or some bookshop that seemed to only serve a religion I'd never heard of. A magician supply shop I didn't ever go in because it looked like I might have to answer riddles before I could buy anything. A park that was only open to lawyers. A falafel shop where the only guy in there stared out of the window like he was plotting to avenge his brother's murder. A coffee shop with a penny-farthing parked outside.

I was thinking about all of this as I walked home (a slightly new and different way!) from a failed outing to a temp agency where they turned down my application form for a number of reasons but mainly because I was too '35 years old' for them to take me on. Part of me feels very bad about this, because of money, and part of me feels very very good indeed, because I am no longer on an infinite slide downwards into gloom, but mostly it just makes me feel like the systems we have built are not fit for purpose. The longer you work a job you feel nothing for and pays you nothing for it, the more you realise we made society backwards. There was some story once, right, about a great bountiful garden, lush and dense with plants and flowers and naked long-haired chicks gallivanting in clean cool water, and how insane a fantasy that seems in a world where we have sentences like, "no, you filled out the wrong form" and "I noticed you were a little bit late back from lunch". So maybe it's actually good that I failed to qualify for a grey office job that would piecemeal destroy every single molecule of my soul in a way that it would never ever grow back. That said paying rent this month is going to be very difficult, very difficult indeed. **THREE STARS**

RANK THESE IN ORDER

- I don't know if Megan is mad at me or disappointed with me but I know right now she isn't *happy* with me and I cannot solve that illness until I diagnose it
- But right now we are in an argument and as ever I am defaulting to my 100% ineffective tactic of: not talking to her, not texting her back, actively avoiding her, and I will have to slink home and apologise later but it will *not* be convincing
- Is it worth interrogating the fact that I'm really into 4K glossily staged casting couch pornography almost exclusively now? It's like I have a job interview kink
- Cannot keep trying to search for a job by just writing 'writer' into a job website, you have been a writer for a number of years and this has never worked
- Perhaps this is the age you sit down and consider whether it was worth burning all those bridges
- Pound-for-pound a Gü pudding is one of the most delicious items consistently available in supermarkets and cornershops, however I will acknowledge they have dropped off recently with the new range and the Tiramisu is a 'certified flop'
- I don't think I should have spent so much of my teenage years listening to Jamiroquai. I think I should have been trying to have sex.
- Megan said, "Let's go to brunch!" and I said yes and then she suggested a place and then I must have pulled one of those faces I don't know I'm doing because she went "What? What's the problem now?"

and I couldn't explain that the place just had 'bad brunch vibes' so we went and like, yeah, yet another £4.50 smoothie and £11 avocado-sourdough place in London, then. Really loud coffee machine and an iPad they turn around for a tip. Not even run by Australians so what's the point?. "But it's 4.4-star rated on TripAdvisor!" These places juice their reviews by getting their friends to submit five-star approvals of them! Wake up! Grow up!
- The only opinion I can trust is my own!
- It's 2023 you should be able to make a decent flat white by now! They are not a new concept!
- There are so many bones in your body you do not know about, so many muscles that work for you whose names you don't know. It feels churlish to pick things up without thanking all the component parts that made you. I mean what the fuck's an 'ulna'?
- Maybe she is mad because when she came home today she cheerily said, "How was your day!" and instead of answering her I immediately got quite boorishly defensive and basically started an argument in an empty room and all because I couldn't admit what I'd actually done all day which was: watch old *Takeshi's Castle* videos on YouTube.
- I think about what Mark Wahlberg's quote about 9/11 – "If I was on that plane with my kids, it wouldn't have went down like it did" – only it's about me and the Killdozer
- If I was piloting that bulldozer they would have had to change a lot of laws.

FOUR STARS

- "The ulna is one of the two long forearm bones." Oh. OK. I'm not really missing that much with that information then.
- I mean she only asks me because she loves me and she's worried about me but I can never actually see that *in the moment* because physically I feel like I'm up to my nostrils in mud. Maybe not physically, actually. "Metaphorically." Although, hmm, no. Actually physically
- There is a year between childhood and full horny adolescence when teenage boys are just fucking obsessed with empty quarries. Why is that.
- *Stupid, stupid, stupid, stupid*: I shouldn't have asked that cool Instagram menswear influencer who was at the pub last week, "How many dead bodies have you seen?" For God's sake. The man runs a hat company!
- I need to stop taking cocaine
- I need to stop taking *bad* cocaine
- (If I got a good cocaine dealer, I would be dead within one year, so it is probably best that I don't do that, actually)
- Alright, I've got it: I need to stop getting high on cocaine and going round the room making all my friends admit to me in turn that they think I am a good writer
- Actually I prefer the term 'gifted'
- We got there in the end.
- All non-murder mob crimes should be legal. They contribute so much to culture.
- More rich people should buy hospitals. It's an incredible flex. If you have the money to afford

a hospital – and still have the money left over to be rich! – it's insane you wouldn't just buy a hospital. I don't know how much hospitals cost but like if you can afford to buy a hospital, you should definitely buy a hospital. A lot of people are walking around with hospital-buying money who are not buying hospitals.
- If you can afford to buy a hospital and you've never bought a hospital then that's really embarrassing, actually
- I'm convinced that, under the right circumstances, tzatziki is a tastier and better dip than hummus, but no one ever wants to sit down and have the hard conversations
- I wonder if I will ever let a single mention of the Beastie Boys go by without saying "they made a really good ambient album, actually" or if that's just a locked-in part of my personality forever
- You have to rank these, in order, remember.
- Spiritually I would find it very refreshing to kill one person per year
- Maybe one a year is too many, actually. The World Cup is special because it's once every four years.
- It has been 77 days since I last got an invoice paid. Sometimes I wonder how close I came to becoming 'one of those teenagers who teaches themselves to laugh like the Joker' and then I realise that era of risk is not technically over
- I want to write the first movie The Rock stars in when he's old. Action stars get old and then start making very interesting, or very fucking weird, films. I cannot wait for that era of The Rock.

FOUR STARS

- (It would be called *Mahalo* and it's about a retired CIA operative taking one more job, defending his fortress-like compound on the beautiful island of Hawaii, something like that) (the thing is, like every action film, it doesn't really need to be interesting it just has to have at least one really cool driving scene.)
- The transformation from 'person who spends all their spare money on beer' to 'person who always buys really expensive butter when they see it on the shelves' happens so subtly you don't see it happen, but you can't cross back from one to the other. Once you've spent £8 on one stick of cultured butter ... a new phase of your life has started.
- That said nothing has really come close to Beillevaire Demi-Sel Croquant which is like less than £3 a stick
- I think I think about being hit by a bus way too much for it to be healthy. I think it would just be such a solid *thonk!* I wouldn't die but I would be life-changingly hurt.
- Am I even a real writer? Google that later maybe
- I hate meeting someone when their primary personality trait is they don't like coriander. I have nothing to say to you.
- I really should try and learn the Heimlich Manoeuvre. I mean what am I really doing out here if I don't know that?
- How is one supposed to rank these (*This one still needs to be ranked!*)
- I'm really coming round on nepotism babies, actually. Of course a kid is going to grow up charming if their dad was a producer and, like, Hugh Grant used to

come round their house for dinner sometimes. If the working class wants to defeat nepotism then it needs to start having more charismatic babies!
- A lot of my friends have started having children and it has made me realise that they became adults in private without me and didn't mention it, which of course is rude. I was still out here being a child!
- What I think about parenthood re: myself is: if I had a child in my house, I would find so many new and interesting and previously unexplored ways to get mad at something that science would have to study me in a laboratory.
- I just really miss Geocities websites. Maybe that's when it all started to go wrong
- I shouldn't let it get to me but I find nothing more depressing than being stuck at a checkout when the customer and the server are having too-long and too-friendly an interaction. Come on. Surely you both have better things to be doing than this
- Would I die in LA or thrive in LA? It cannot be both
- God, I just had a thought: I would be a far more annoying person if I was good at picking up other languages
- I think I've figured it out: there are exactly, *exactly*, two types of men. There are men who watched pornography with their friends as teenagers, and men who didn't. And that's men.
- You cannot smoke a cigar in a movie without doing the 'cigar movie laugh' (*Weh-heh-heh-heh!*). It is illegal, for some reason

FOUR STARS

- Why have I never had an adult hobby
- Who am I?
- Have I ever felt love with the right intensity that music and films and culture tells me I should
- Carly Rae Jepsen's 'Take Me to the Feeling' is undoubtedly one of the top 50 songs ever recorded but you never see it on the lists, do you
- (In a very normal way) I don't want to die but if there were a big buzzer-beater button in my house that would kill me if I touched it then I would definitely underhand-toss a tennis ball at it once or twice a day, just to see
- Nobody in London knows what to do with their elbows apart from me.
- I really need to stop begrudging people things
- I really need to stop begrudging *people who are not Ed Warburton* things
- Just really really convinced vinegar is going to have a big year, but no one seems to want to listen when I say it.
- It's been a while since someone made something unexpectedly electric. The 'electric kettle', that sort of thing. Just feels like it's been a while since I've been excited by electricity
- Was writing all this down a better use of my time and energy than just getting up and saying sorry and getting a job, or was it actually an extremely toxic use of my time that has made me, perversely, a more mentally unwell person than I was before? One to ponder, one to ponder, one to mull.

MAKING HERBAL TEA WITH A TEASPOON THAT HAS A LITTLE BIT OF VEGAN MAYONNAISE STILL ON IT FROM YESTERDAY

This morning I made herbal tea with a teaspoon that had a residual little bit of vegan mayonnaise on it from yesterday. I am trying to make it a morning routine where I wake up with a herbal tea instead of just straight and raw on the strong caffeine – I love coffee, and as a personality I am right on the cusp of being one of those people who becomes 'too into coffee', that I start caring about how my bean has been washed and roasted and ground, the source of my water, the slow perfect press of an inverted coffee-maker, I am *this* close to being so boring about coffee that it erases a vital piece of light from my personality forever – but right now I am trying to start with a calm soothing mint-and-liquorice cup and a 20-minute read of a book. Reading for 20 minutes in the morning is a magic trick: for some reason, the time just doesn't count at all, and then you get up and do your routines and ablutions – long shower, extra-long tooth brush, dress and scent up and tousle hair, and then that 15-minute faff before you leave the house – that is all the same, and the time on the clock is the same, but you've done about 17 pages of *The Interestings* (which is definitely not going anywhere: I know already that *The Interestings* is not going anywhere) and drank a

FOUR STARS

herbal tea and felt, for a moment at least, still and silent and calm.

But today I used a teaspoon on the side that looked like it was clean and unused but actually, when I dunked it into the mug and bought it out again, it had a lurid greasy half-moon of vegan mayonnaise on the edge of it, probably from spreading on some sort of sandwich (Megan has taken to eating great inelegant sandwiches, filled with a huge fistful of alfalfa and smeared with mayo, stacked on stale old tiger bread, which is entirely the wrong bread for a sandwich. I've tried critiquing the entire set-up but she does not want to hear it and it isn't worth the row.). We used vegan mayonnaise because there is still not a good shelf-stable garlic mayonnaise worth a damn that you can buy in the UK, apart from the pink-lidded Follow Your Heart veganaise that costs £3.49 a jar (a *jar*!) and, whenever I see in the high teetering fridges of whole food stores, I buy as many as will fit in my backpack. It's a good mayonnaise – fantastic with chicken nuggets – but I do have to admit that, today at least, its presence did shatter my peace. *This herbal tea tastes garlic-y*, I thought, then went back to the page (Jules was once again thinking too much about Spirit-in-the-Woods – Jules, you are deep into your forties, I am begging you to get over summer camp!) but the feeling wouldn't shift. *If I were a good person, a complete person, a person who made correct decisions and didn't always take the shortest possible route towards anything, I wouldn't be experiencing this right now.*

This doesn't happen to people who have their lives together. This doesn't happen to people with a pension pot, and distant plans for children, and do not live with a constant gripping fear that death with embrace them before they achieve anything. Nobody puts garlic mayonnaise in their herbal tea unless they are fucked-up at something. I have to stop living like I hate myself. **ZERO STARS**

SEEING THE BONES OF OUR ANCIENT ANCESTORS

I don't really know how I ended up in Mexico City in the first place – there was an 11-hour flight with my legs crammed in at an angle, half in the aisle half not, where I read a disappointing book (still *The Interestings*, fucking somehow) and then watched a disappointing *Fast & Furious* film (sort of weird they started out as street racers and now they are bombastic superspies, isn't it? Feels like the government could maybe send: literally anyone else to investigate the international crime syndicates they always seem to be driving after). I do not recall making the *decision* to go to Mexico, laying the groundwork of logistics. Have I really ever gone anywhere under my own decision in my life, or have I just done it because a girl has told me to? Anyway we're in Mexico City, even though I haven't got a job and I didn't really want to come to

FOUR STARS

Mexico City and also I forgot my wallet somehow which led to a phenomenal I mean *phenomenal* fight about that at the airport. It isn't very *hasta luego!*, apparently, to make your girlfriend buy everything you buy on holiday with her Monzo with the repeated promise that you will pay her back. Apparently that is a very fucking major issue indeed.

Before you go to Mexico City everyone who has already been to Mexico City (so: everyone you know) will tell you breathlessly about the street food, which, yes, is very good (they will not tell you what an entirely fraught experience eating the street food is – you, stood up, the most enormous man in Mexico by a good 14 inches, backpack on you because you're a tourist, narrow jennels and passageways with flatly emotionless Mexicans milling past you, men reaching past you because you are stood in front of the limes, men reaching past you because now you are stood in front of the good salsa, a paper plate growing slick and oiled in your hands, and also you've eaten five tacos but can't actually figure out how to pay, and the Duolingo app you downloaded is only on your iPad which obviously is not connected to any WiFi, so you're just saying, with a lot of hand gestures, "cinco taco chorizo? Ah ... quanto ... much?") (the tacos themselves, of course, sublime), but what they will not warn you about is that Mexico City is an endless sprawl, impossible to even see a glimpse of in the five little days you are there, so you end up bouncing around a few nice brunch spots and getting Ubers everywhere and seeing the canals and the temples and being bent down by the enduring sunshine and the heat and then when you get to your hotel every night at 7 p.m. to have a Dos Equis and 'freshen up' what you actually end up doing is watching *Seinfeld* in bed with the air conditioning blasting and murmuring into a dizzy, unsatisfying sleep. I'm sure Mexico City is a wonderful place if you can speak the language and know the people there and navigate the endless stretches of criss-crossed street and dogs sleeping on the pavement to actually see the things that *Time Out* doesn't know about, but I didn't, so I just spent 96 straight hours there looking at concrete and accidentally telling waiters *I am thank you.*

Then I went to the National Museum of Anthropology (Museo Nacional de Antropología), and stared straight down an alleyway directly into the maw of history, and had my soul altered forever. It is important to state that the Museo Nacional de Antropología is architecturally one of the most breathtaking museums I have ever been to: a huge, glistening, high-ceilinged quad that contrasts vivid against the blue sky behind it, an endless fountain greeting you as you enter and little enclaves of calm garden for you to breathe and find peace in after each overwhelming room. Unlike UK museums, which (yuk.) have people in them, the crowds at Antropología are that just-right combination of there but not there: couples walk hand-in-hand while one takes blurry unsatisfying photos of ancient artefacts on a wrong-settings iPhone; elder tourists are shown around by for-hire experts who talk them through the exhibits; at no point at all does an entire class of schoolchildren sprint suddenly into the room you're in, making that high-pitched shrieking they all make. At Antropología, they have only translated maybe one in every five descriptive plaques into English, so you get this curiously fractured and curated glimpse of the Aztecs, a sort of speed-run of four thousand years of history. Importantly, too, you never get that horrible museum urge to just fucking sit down and never use your legs ever again. There is always something goth, or interesting, lurking around the corner.

Primarily Museo Nacional de Antropología concerns Mexican history, because obviously: it tells the story of how the primitive early societies first settled and stayed in place, slowly building the early foundations of culture when mere survival wasn't the most urgent and pressing need. It tells the story of how we stopped living in caves and started building structures; how stones and sticks were sharpened into tools, which became more elaborate milling equipment for grain and herbs; how we started to tame water, and irrigate farmland. Then the next section tells you how, once humanity had built the building blocks for society, it had some fun with it: we created art, and music, and sculpture, and gods to talk about and dance to. And then you turn a corner and, fuck: we've invented war. Gorgeous societies are mysteriously abandoned or demolish themselves on the rock of a nearby rival proto-city: disease sweeps through the lands as bought from other continents due to our singular need to explore and conquer. Squabbles over how one person made up a god versus how another person made up a god got out of hand and now everyone with an interesting forehead structure is literally dead forever. Blood runs dark through the rivulets of a sacrificial altar. Every moment we stay in place for too long, Museo Nacional de Antropología warns us, every layer of complexity we add to society, the worse and worse and worse things get. We were all better off when we just spent 20 years gutting fish then died. There was never any need, for instance, to invent 'truck nuts', 'vaping' or 'Diplo at Coachella'.

I meet Lucy somewhere between 25,000 and 3,000 BC, or between Room #1 and #2, depending on how you look at it. Lucy, it should be stated, is very totally dead. She is a skeleton and not even a full skeleton: she is a collection of bones that make up roughly 40% of a— well, not a human being exactly. Something approaching a human being: an upright bipedal, but rocking a fairly small skull that suggests a fairly primal, animalistic brain. Unearthed in Ethiopia in 1974, she's thought to be 3.2 million years old, and proof that there was some long lingering interstitial stage between apes and upright humans: a whole swathe of history where we were half human and half not, where we grouped together for survival and nursed children and hunted and gathered but also had way too much body hair and couldn't say much of anything. Next to the casts of Lucy's bones was a hewn wooden bust of her holding a child, and I was suddenly and impossibly moved: she lived this little life, dying of unknown causes somewhere

FOUR STARS

between 12 and 18, walking around upright and clambering into trees and eating berries and fish and meat. She was cold and she was hot and she was sad and she was happy and she held on to babies and she carried them around. She had some of the first thoughts anyone has ever had and then they fizzed and faded into nothing. She died and she was buried and she was mourned. But she didn't know she was ever going to be anything. She lay in the ground for three million years, fossilising, until her shin poked out of the sand and she was discovered. She lived at a time when the handful of lifeforms that became all of us – all of this, every skyscraper and every plane and every moon landing and every tweet and every Diplo performance at Coachella, both the 2019 headline act and the Major Lazer appearances in 2013 and 2016 – all came from there. She had no idea what vast accelerated future was ahead of her. She had no idea at all.

NEANDERTHAL GOLBY: Ooh, *ooh*
ME: Yeah, I know. Kind of overwhelming, right?
NEANDERTHAL GOLBY: Ooh ooh, ooh *ooh*
ME: No she pre-dated you by like two and a half million years. You didn't "know that bitch".
NEANDERTHAL GOLBY: Ooh *ooh* ooh ah ooh?
ME: I don't know. I guess it's like: she lived this entire self-capsulised life, she was born and she was raised and she became this, well not a *person* exactly but an entity with a soul, she had a function and she had a use, she made others

happy and she probably made them sad too, before we even had a word for sad—

NEANDERTHAL GOLBY: Ahh, ooh

ME: Alright fine *ahh ooh* but the point is like: she lived a life. She lived an entire *life*. And then she died, and things moved on, and she just laid there, fossilising, for three million years. And I guess I'm emotional because like: she meant something back then. And she means something now. And it's kind of amazing that we are able to remember her like that. That we are able to reach back and say, "hey".

NEANDERTHAL GOLBY: Ooh

ME: I guess because I've been a bit down on myself lately. I guess because things have been hard. Well, not hard, but not easy. But then nothing is ever easy. But the hard licks sting the longest. It just feels like I've been walking around with a boulder on my chest. It just feels like even having fun has been a strenuous exertion. *Doing things I like shouldn't be hard.* And it's like: will I ever even move an inch past that. Will I ever feel good again. But I suppose, like Lucy, one day I will just be a midpoint. I live and I die and everything moves on again. One day the planet will run out of people to remember me. And I won't *matter*. But right now I'm here, and I'm flesh and I'm blood, and I'm alive, and I should be grateful for that. I'm alive I'm alive I'm alive—

NEANDERTHAL GOLBY: Ooh ahh

FOUR STARS

ME: I'm *alive*!
NEANDERTHAL GOLBY: ...
ME: ...
NEANDERTHAL GOLBY: Ooh ah ah?
ME: He's sort of a— I don't know actually. Like a DJ? But ... no, he can't just be a DJ. He's like ... famous. Most DJs are just wonky Dutch guys in masks. What's Diplo? No he can't just be a *DJ—*
NEANDERTHAL GOLBY: Ooh ah
ME: Well I can't do that because there's no 4G signal in here. It'll have to wait until we get back to the hotel.

Rest of the day I don't know: I walked through a park, dazed? I ate some Dorilocos while wearing white jeans? I got something approaching heat stroke in a pedalo? I fell asleep in a taxi? All I know was beer and dust and fear and sun and heat and sweat but not and mortality, and fear and fear and fear and that horrible holiday urge – *you need to do things! You're not doing enough things! You have to make every moment here count! This is urgent!* – and then falling asleep in the hotel with the aircon dripping down the walls. **FIVE STARS**

STARTING AN ARGUMENT ON HOLIDAY

We spent the morning on the canal boats of Xochimilco, which all the tour guides describe as 'The Floating Gardens of Xochimilco' and so you expect bounteous waterfalls, ancient lost fresh fruits glistening with beads of dew, head-spinning architecture and water that climbs up hills, but actually what quite often happens is you just bob slowly past someone's astroturfed back yard and occasionally stop off at a garden centre where you have to pay to use the toilet, and sometimes a guy floats up to your boat and has a hurried conversation in Spanish with your tour guide and then scurries along the side of the boat, legs in a kayak, to sell you a huge litre jug of michelada, which is beer with many many evil things in it, and normally I am sort of fine with being a bit scammed on holiday – what do I care, you know? With the exchange rate being what it is I've spent like £8 today – but somehow the micheladas put me in a very ghoulish and ugly mood so I got really hung up when the boat driver brought us back to the dock and told us in broken English that actually the agreed-upon fee for our cruise had doubled in the time it had taken to cruise around, and a sinister-looking guy in a large straw hat put a single flip-flopped foot on our boat to intimate that if we didn't pay it then he would make us pay it and like. Come on man it's £11 who cares, but like. For some reason I very very much decided to care.

FOUR STARS

Megan paid the £11, I paid for the next round of garden-centre toilet trips, then we found a taco place in the market that Tripadvisor said was 4.2 stars out of 5 but very, very much was not. So obviously during a small lull in conversation I decided to start a fight.

"The tables are nice in here."

"Yeah, you would say that."

"Why?"

(Because she once had sex with a guy who made tables, and I am a child.)

"Oh, for— we're on holiday."

"Yep."

"Together."

"Oh, yep."

"And that was *five years ago*."

As with every argument once I started it (and almost immediately started to lose) I tried to wind all the words back into my mouth and tried to make a sincere apology, even though every time I say the word "sorry" it clunks out of my mouth with a dull, hard metallic thud which always sounds unconvincing and then obviously the mood was broken entirely and was going to take hours and some quiet desperate crying and a very long silent trip in an Uber to repair ("You OK?" "Yeah", a doomed attempt at a hand-hold, all the old moves) and at some point she would turn around, flashing furious, and say, "You're just always so *mean* to me!" and I'd have to pretend to be hurt and wounded even though yes, she's right, that's just good analysis, I just don't really like it being put to me like that, so correctly.

We got back to the hotel and she really threw her tote on the bed and went to the bathroom for 45 minutes and I laid down and was sort of drunk and hungover at the same time, not knowing really which side of it the headache was coming from. Then a hug that felt like holding a clothes rack and a too-cheerful suggestion we go out for dinner and then she says "maybe we can just go for a walk?" and I pull a face about that prospect for half a millisecond and then she really quickly says "— or not" and then I go, "no no no no that's fine, let's . . . yeah, no yeah, let's go for a walk". Let's just pick a direction in a completely strange city we don't know and just walk aimlessly in silence. And then just stumble onto a good restaurant entirely by chance, which obviously never happens. But yeah let's do that. So we did that and ended up at a place that, essentially, was a student bar serving reheated pub food, and I didn't say anything because I was on a fucking knife edge as it was, but. I mean we definitely would have had a better time if we did not do that.

Some insane machinery inside of me does not allow me to ever truly enjoy holidays. I'm just never really there in the way that everyone else seems to enjoy them. Perhaps it is the dry itchy heat, or the fact that after days of agonising over what trainers to bring I still bought the wrong trainers, or the fact that you never really feel like you belong in the textural vista of the place, or the constant conversational loop that goes, "You speak English? Where you from? London?" and you go "Yes, London", and they go "Ah". Perhaps it's because I am always thinking about money too much so every second I am not having an absolute amount of fun I start mentally calculating the day-rate of my being here based on the airfare ($200) and the hotel fees ($200+80), and that's before I've even bought breakfast from a place that looked nice from outside but on the inside is chillingly cold from aircon and the food here is mid. I never seem to let fully go on holidays: I never succumb bodily to the sea, I never enjoy an exquisite sunset, I never climb to the top of the mountain and gaze upon the view, I never clink a cocktail glass against another cocktail glass and say "*salut!*". I just refresh Instagram on slow foreign 4G, read three pages of a book before worrying that my neck's getting burned, or spend 20 minutes in the dusty screeching heat of a subway station trying to scan a paper ticket that clearly isn't working before Megan fully yells, "OH JUST *FUCKING* GET ANOTHER ONE!" Holidays in theory are the escape hatch from your real life – the bills, the weather, the trials, the tribulations, the commute, the responsibilities, the social calendar, the long gloopy Wednesday afternoons where you can barely keep your eyes open – a vitamin-shot for the soul that leaves you healed, happy, balmed. But now it's 9 p.m. and I don't want to pay for the taxi home so we walk until our feet hurt and then I do actually get the taxi and it takes ages to arrive and when it does it costs like, nothing, it costs negative money. So now I've just ruined two people's day for no reason. And this is the break I am supposed to be taking from my life. **ZERO STARS**

A REALLY GOOD LOAD OF LAUNDRY

Did an incredible load of laundry, just then. A whites load. When I was a younger man, a more reckless man, I didn't separate my colours like this (I used to wash my *jeans*! In a washing machine! In winter! They would take weeks to dry, and when they finally had done they'd be so stiff they could stand upright!) (sometimes, when I am in need of a very good time to myself, I go down to the bathroom with a special plastic tub I bought exactly for the occasion and slowly and carefully hand wash a pair of jeans: they come out like silk, they come out smooth and soft like a fresh-licked kitten), and just shoved as many clothes as I could into the machine until the drum would creak, but now I am more mature, more rounded, an adult. I have a darks laundry basket and a whites laundry basket. I also have a separate Bag For Life filled with 'soiled whites' – i.e. white clothing with such deep mud or blood or curry stains that I don't want to wash them with actual, less-soiled white clothing, in case the turmeric or haemoglobin or soil seeps out into the wash-water, leaving everything a grimy off-grey – and a separate small pile for 'pales' (creams, yellows, any of those soft artisan socks I've started asking for for Christmas). I don't really have to worry about coloured clothing because I don't wear any colours, which is good, because otherwise I'd have to have five separate laundry baskets in my office. And that would be insane.

FOUR STARS

First you put some Lenor Unstoppables® in the drum: these will make a t-shirt smell nice for two, maybe even three wears, and does everything fragrance-wise a fabric softener promises to do but never does (I used to incorporate fabric conditioner into my routine, but I am not convinced it actually *does* anything, like a bay leaf in a stew, and also I half-watched two TikToks about how it's actually very bad for the fibres of your clothing, and nothing to me is as convincing on earth as a TikTok I half-watched and didn't save and can't even find now even when I search for it). Then I load in the clothing – particular attention paid to stains, obviously, because with a white t-shirt once a stain is set, it is *set*, so I hold each tee up to the light and dab at each small spot with a Vanish Power Gel Stain Stick®. If the load is getting too full I will go through and decide which t-shirts, socks, underpants and the like I actually *want* to wear this week and which can hold over to a less urgent, secondary whites load, and become too aware of the hierarchy inherent in my clothing and think that, if a t-shirt isn't worth the primary whites load, why do I even have it at all? By now 20 minutes have passed.

Then a liquid gel tab, then (in this particular instance) a scoop of Vanish Gold Oxi Action Multi Powder®, which I don't know what it does exactly – I have a distant feeling it contains 'enzymes' – but I really want to make sure that slop of lamb bhuna doesn't stick to that fairly new t-shirt I spent £65 on but when asked about it told Megan I got on sale for £20. Then I shut the drum, move the dial to '3' (our washing machine has 16 cycle options to choose from, but the only one that actually works without malfunctioning into an ever-spinning loop – restarting again and again, and once you notice the washing machine has been running eight hours without stopping it's too late, and the drum is filled with long soap-less water and takes forever to drain – is '3', so I select '3') (I have been on some Hotpoint forums to try and figure out how to change this but they don't know, either) and then I wait. The whirr of the machine. The quiet sound of a machine performing a difficult chore for you. The wafting fresh clean smell of laundry soap. I am in heaven.

The cyclical natures of chores inspires hatred. You finish the washing-up and then your girlfriend makes a bowl of yoghurt and granola and blueberries and eats four mouthfuls of it then leaves the bowl and spoon and yoghurt and oats by the sink, and the job has started again. You never get to the *bottom* of a good chore, because if you do it right – if you clean the shower enough, if you go round the sink with a microfibre towel, if you make the windows shine crystalline – it takes seconds of existence to undo that work again. Hoovering makes your house look and feel better, instantly, for some reason (there's no visible reason why hoovering should do this, but it does!) but then you walk over the carpet in slippers while eating a little stack of Pringles you have holding in your hand and *boom!*, it's all undone again. I do not take well to chores, I gnash and agonise against them, but I find something soothing about the earth-scorch cleanness of a good laundry load: your clothes are clean again, you are ready to start the week anew, you do not need to wear a t-shirt that smells like that anymore.

I take the machine off '3', and then briefly turn it off (a quirk of the electrics – the forums, again, keep starting threads about this that don't get answered) and then put it to 'B', which is the spin-cycle setting. This is an important rhythmic component of the laundry ceremony: the machine, after careful preparatory motions and applications by you, does all of the washing; it can now be left for 15 minutes to spin some of the surface-level dampness out of the clothes. The machine does technically have a tumble dryer setting but frankly I don't trust it. What I do instead is put all the fresh, clean laundry in a clear utility box, shuffle it (without touching the floor!) towards the airer, which I very carefully drape each single piece of laundry over. This feels like the most caring part: pinching out all of the wrinkles between the sleeve and the body section of a t-shirt, for instance, or pairing up some socks. Then you allow a cycle of the sun to run over the laundry and – "*allelujah!*" – the next day you have some clean dry pants to put on, instead of yesterday, when a minor miscalculation in scheduling meant you spent all day wearing swimming trunks. There is a quiet background hum of pride and satisfaction that I am aiming for, here, one I rarely get from anything else in my life – the soothing meticulousness of getting some good laundry done obliterates a good amount of guilt I have about, say, not paying my tax bill yet, even though 'pay tax bill' was the only thing I had on my to-do list today. I might set up the extra laundry dryer Megan hates me using because it takes up so much space and turns our flat into essentially a laundrette, and get a nice little load of pales going. Yeah I might do that, actually. Yeah I might definitely go and do that. Fuck tax. **FIVE STARS**

THIS COFFEE I JUST HAD WITH MY AGENT

Zoe asks me how things have been going which is her way of asking if I'm doing anything, and I'm not, so to deflect from that I try misdirection by actually answering the question and telling her how things have actually been, which is always a mistake, because then I end up just telling people about myself. "Yeah, good " I say. "Well: *good*. Would we say, 'good'? It's good-*ish*. Like: not good. But— hmm. Well, listen: I watched a kid get stabbed."

"You watched a kid get stabbed? When?"

"Couple ... couple of months? Yeah like. Umm yeah exactly nine weeks ago, to the day. I mean it's fine, it's fine. It wasn't like, *my* kid."

"No, but it's still: a kid."

"A kid, yeah."

"How old was—"

"The dead kid?"

FOUR STARS

"Oh he *died*?"

—*and you think of the flop and the thud and the arid silence and the howling noise of the other boy, the murderer boy, a murderer but still a boy, you think of the other boy running away, tearing his top off in flight, wrapping the knife – more like a machete than a 'knife', you suppose, though when you stay up late at night googling it you keep running over the term the police used when they were questioning you, which was 'zombie knife', which is goth, yes, but anyway the zombie knife is so called because it cuts on the way in and serrates on the way out, thus instantly rendering the victim dead, which obviously is the precursor towards becoming a zombie, though that seems a reach. This is why you don't name knives. Because that, to you, seems like a reach—*

"Yeah. Yeah, no, yeah. He died. 17."

I think of where I was at 17. They found a video of it, actually. I used to play it at house parties: me and my friend David, up deliriously late playing around with his dad's camcorder, me absolutely artlessly dressed – a stretched-out grey jumper with the sleeves pulled down over my thumbs, ass-crack jeans and some squashed brown trainers from the surf-brand Quicksilver (I'm laughing, actually. I'm laughing at how badly I was dressed) – and there I am, smooth faced and fat as a butterball, big light on in the front room, gurning to the camera about how "time is horny" or some fucking deranged shit like that. My idea of a fun Friday night was drinking an entire two-litre bottle of Dr. Pepper, a tuna-and-sweetcorn pizza, watching *Robot Wars* then seeing how much of the original *Metal Gear Solid* game we could get through without using a memory card (normally up to about Sniper Wolf). Not, you know. Getting stabbed to death outside a spa and bleeding out on a pile of towels.

"Towels?"

"Well everyone ran outside. Everyone ran over."

"With towels?"

"Yeah for. Like. "

"..."

"All the blood pouring out of his mouth and chest."

The annoying thing I suppose with the stabbing to death was I was having a nice day, up until then, and then the air went dry and chalky and silent and suddenly I was surrounded by police tape and flickering blue lights and the silence, it's the *silence* that gets you, like the atmosphere got stabbed and every vibe in the city got sucked into the vacuum that the puncture hole left, because I was having a nice day (1 x aftershave, 1 x good vintage t-shirt with the pocket that I like, 8 x books, 5 x paperback 3 x hardback), and like it was the final pint before I went back and— Anyway I was meant to go to a barbecue that night and I suppose I did but I don't really remember much between arriving and putting a load of Coronas in the fridge and then saying, "Hey, I saw a kid get stabbed" and then, two hours later, when a BBC News notification told me that yes, that kid you saw dying actually died, I think I said, *I'm probably going to leave, lads. Because of the stabbing thing, yeah.* Which was

FOUR STARS

annoying because Yiannis had made this really nice salad and was getting going on some halloumi, but. I mean you can't always eat, can you.

    I told my friend Marcel about seeing the stabbing thing which I think was a mistake because Marcel grew up on an estate in south-west London and has seen a number of stabbings and actually, I think, participated in more than one of them himself – to Marcel, getting stabbed is just a bizarre fact of life along the same lines as, 'Sometimes your washing machine won't actually wash the clothes and you'll have to spin them again' – and I suppose I told him because I was expecting deep and reassuring wisdom about stabbing, that this was the cosmic order of things, that for every one life sacrificed ten lives are saved, but actually what he said was, "Yeah I saw my first stabbing when I was 10, innit," and I was like "OK, that's young", and he said, "Yeah." Sometimes I forget that Marcel is by far, *by far*, the most threatening person I know, because he also reads high literature and speaks like he's an ancient court prince off-handedly dictating a poem, but then he'll do something bizarre and mad like unscrew a light switch and pull a wad of cocaine out of the hole, and I remember all over again. "Then 13, 13 again, then 14." I don't think I'm legally allowed to say what he did at 15 but a Hollywood director has bought the rights to it. "It just happens, innit." Next time I'm having a dark night of the soul I'm like, *OK, don't tell Marcel.*

    "So do you have any ideas for a second book?"

    "Auhhh! Zoe!"

"Yeah. You went off for a minute, there."

"No"

"Well I can't keep e-mailing them, they're expecting a manuscri—" **ZERO STARS**

HAVING AN IDEA

I've been trying to have an idea all day. The conditions, annoyingly, must be right for me to have an idea. It is like getting a rocket to take off from Cape Canaveral: explosive and impressive when it happens, and dozens of nerds gather to watch it, but ultimately atmospherically quite hard to pull off. For instance I need to have slept well, and had some breakfast. Two coffees always helps (two coffees also necessitate two glasses of water: I once watched a TikTok dentist say you need to rinse your mouth out with water after every cup of coffee you have otherwise the coffee stains your teeth irreparably, and I have been doing that diligently since. His content, sadly, has devolved into doing a lot of shoulder-heavy dances and trying to respond to viral soundtracks in the meantime. Stick to the classics! Tell me good tricks with floss!). I need to have good wordless ambient music in the background, and ideally a good smell (an incense or a candle), and it helps if my desk is tidy and also the room behind me is tidy. It helps if I am dressed in clothes. It is close to impossible to have an idea in pyjamas. It is very possible to have an idea naked, in the shower more specifically, but it is hard to write those ideas down. The outfit needs to be a good one: yesterday I couldn't have an idea because I'd started putting my outfit together with a rough theme of colour-blocking (navy jumper over navy cords, blue dappled socks), but then I went deranged and added an ecru-coloured hat with cream suede shoes, and getting that as wrong as I did distracted me all day long. It helps if no one is mad at me. It helps if I am getting a quiet burble of regular contact from my good friends, but not enough that the patter is too succulent, too irresistible. Obviously, beyond the quiet electronic ambient, I need to have absolute silence.

It helps to have had a perfect cultural digest, recently (this, obviously, is difficult: you do not know for sure whether a book is going to be good – or, pertinently, meet you with the energy you want to be met with – as soon as you open it. You cannot trust anyone's opinions about film, or TV, because they are so very often wrong). It helps, for some reason, to have watched two very mindless YouTube videos – Mr Beast torturing some followers in exchange for performative charitable cash giveaways, for instance, or a short clip of a Twitch streamer playing a game with all their reflex swearing censored out – but not too many, because that's when the mind starts to wander. Obviously Instagram is poison but I look at it anyway. I have a theory that ideas happen best to a blank mind – this is why so much of my best work is done soon after I wake up, before the Dread has managed to fall over me like a curtain – and watching no-brain cultural chow made for morons often helps with that. But if I eat too much chow then my brain gets clouded. A lot of critics have said I should just use the meditation app I have, instead, but I bristle at the idea of paying a monthly subscription to something that just tells me to close my eyes.

The pursuit of an idea is made possible by the memory of the last time you had an idea, because that feeling is gorgeous, electric: you have pulled something pure out of the ether like a golem, you have plunged your hands into the deep purple-blue celestial and bought something crackling and ethereal out with you. The feeling of having an idea is of bending your brain into a specific shape and pose that nobody in the history of earth has ever bent their brain into and felt before, and then the idea takes on a weight, an energy, a feeling: all of the possibilities of the idea glug around it like iron filings, tendrils come off the idea, extending into the infinite. Having an idea feels like: catching a huge fish from dark water. Having an idea feels like: making lightning smash into a bottle. It feels like having brief and powerful command over the sheer force of nature. You have sat and used meat to create electricity. You have travelled through time and space without moving an inch. Your brain is a supercomputer piloted by a genius. So obviously we are always chasing that.

Hm, mm— no, nothing. Just an Instagram notification. I should— mm just typing back. Mm. See this guy always annoys me. This guy always annoys me. Why do I allow this guy to annoy me? This guy always annoys me. I'm looking at that message. No. I'm not expending energy thinking of a response. But also *making the decision not to reply* is also an extension of energy. I refuse to let this man annoy me!

The whole basis of every idea is just feeling, of course, peace. I must have peace! A little chore helps, a very small one. A little snack. But it can't be a complicated chore – if I get starting a load of laundry then I'll lose half an hour. Similarly, it cannot be a complicated snack: something cold, accessible, crunchy. A few kernels of caramel popcorn, dangled into my mouth while standing in the kitchen. A single-serve waxed cheese. Not, for instance, an entire egg sandwich. That is too much happening, too many carbohydrates, too much diffusion from the idea.

I have taken a shower and it's done nothing. I have gone for a run and it has done nothing. I have watched three YouTube videos, two episodes of TV, read half a chapter (well ... eh, 12 pages) of one book. I have checked my e-mail and sent two e-mails and checked my e-mail again. I have checked my e-mail again one more time. This— this fucking guy! On Instagram! Leave me alone! I have tried whistling a little tune. What is this? Little news notification. Oh a girl— a girl who is a cheerleader got married. And she did a little cheerleading routine at her own wedding. OK. This is how dedicated I am to not having an idea, that I am watching this. I hate this, and yet I am still watching this. This is insane, this is ludicrous.

Some ideas I've had that didn't work out: it is crazy that we get mad at YouTubers for 'not having a job' and instead goofing around and, for instance, throwing a basketball off a dam onto a trampoline, because that is exactly what human beings *should* be doing, this is exactly what we were put on earth to do – to explore the outer reaches of the human condition of curiosity! – and we should not get mad at YouTubers for doing stupid goof-off stuff, we should get mad at everyone who wastes their life by doing a job that 'involves photocopying'; There Is Simply Nothing Better Than Lying To A Stranger; what if I sent my e-mails in 'medieval mode' for a month or two? Saying "mayhap", and things like that? Do you think anyone would notice? Do you think anyone would even *say* anything?; A no-miss TV pitch is just 'what if there was a cop?' and even on your worst days, even when you stand in the bathroom and screw your eyes up and face into the mirror, even you could write one of those (the cop could be called 'Aidy McPlant' and he's 45 and smooth-faced and sees things other cops don't notice. Has a limp, maybe? Has a limp once from getting shot? I'm getting chills just thinking about how much money I might make over this); I could never be a parent because I don't like yelling enough, plus I'm literally never in my life going to take a teacher seriously; yesterday I saw a guy carrying two chairs from a lift to a waiting Uber and as he was grasping at each chair by the chair-leg I was overcome by an unquenchable compulsion to simply shout at him, "CHAIR NONCE!" — the question is, *why?*, and further, *what does that say about humanity?*; online Americans are right: it *is* weird how utterly obsessed British people are with Heinz baked beans. None of these are sellable, quite a lot of these are insane. It is worth sitting through these and knowing you came up with them.

The point of course is: having an idea is possibly my only job, and I've had none. And now I am stressed about not having an idea which makes me unable to have an idea (I must have peace! Peace must be felt!). This is a self-fulfilling problem, a problem gobbling at its own tail. The guy who suffers most when I don't have an idea is me. The guy who refuses to have an idea is also me. The guy who stresses about not having an idea (taking self-inflicted psychic damage) is me. Ninety per cent of the problems I have in my life are caused by myself. The other 10% are just demands for taxes from the government.

Alright, fine, not happening today. Not happening today. Tomorrow I'll sleep well, have a good breakfast, wake up before the Dread. Tomorrow I'll have an idea. For now: Day #36 of not writing anything of worth or value. I give up. I'm going to go see who's online on the PlayStation. **ZERO STARS**

WINNING TEN GAMES IN A ROW AT *FIFA 21*

Game 9 I knew something special was happening. I have read about Michael Jordan, extensively. I have watched *The Last Dance* twice. It's a problem, actually, my obsession with Jordan: today I saw a photo of Young Jordan on Instagram, back in his Tar Heels days, and felt myself compelled once again to go to his Wikipedia page, to read up on his college stats. My fixation with Michael Jordan makes no sense at all because I don't really understand the mechanics of basketball that underlie what made him so good on the scorecard: I don't really know what a steal is, or a rebound, and it took me a couple of full months to figure out the difference between a lay-up and a three-pointer. All I know is: every time I lock eyes with a photograph of Michael Jordan I become re-obsessed with him, again, because he was the purest athlete to ever live and plus he was a winning *machine*. This is how I feel about myself when I am nine games into a ten-game run of wins on the videogame *FIFA 21*.

I was not always a *FIFA* man. No one was. The first football game I owned was *Sega Worldwide Soccer 98*, a game I mastered so completely that I once won a game of it 32–0. This was in my 'insanity era', which straddles the ages of 11 until about 17, and winning 32–0 at *Sega Worldwide Soccer* was one overwhelming facet of that. It is not normal to win a game 32–0. It is not normal to change all of the names of all the players in the in-game editor to reflect your real-life favourite players, to change 'John Hartson' to 'Christian Vieri' without changing either John Hartson's blocky, pink, pixelated visage or John Hartson's decidedly un-Vieri-like underlying statistics. At least 26 of the goals were a kick-off routine I had mastered where Christian Vieri – piloting John Hartson's body like a monster – would pass short to Stan Lazaridis, who I had renamed 'David Beckham', and this horrible, chimeric wide midfielder would lob the keeper from the halfway line again and again and again. At some point, you have to ask: *are you receiving any joy from winning this game, 32–0?* But sometimes life is not about enjoyment. Sometimes it is about pushing the very boundaries of existence until they bleed. *Sega Worldwide Soccer 98* taught me that.

In university, I slipped into it again. I find there are eras of my life when playing a football game for me is like relapsing onto hard drugs, that I find my way wandering into fragrant basements the way Victorian opioid addicts might, only instead of raw heroin I'm just asking whether we can play as international teams so I can be Brazil with Neymar. In the second year of university I made one of the great mistakes of my lifetime, which was buying a second-hand copy of *Pro Evolution Soccer 4* from an unbadged games shop for less than six pounds, and from there my grades began almost instantly to deteriorate: I became obsessed with an in-game version of Fernando Torres (running stats plus dribbling stats plus finishing stats meant he was one of the most underrated but overpowered players in the game – various friends' boyfriends, who were dragged over to our house to face me at the game I couldn't be beaten at, found this out to their horror. It didn't matter if you had Arsenal with Henry or Barcelona with Ronaldinho; *I would beat you*). I neglected to call my family for a number of weeks. I started eating cereal for most meals because it was quick to prepare and easy to balance on the soft pouch of your stomach in a hoodie while you flicked through the *Pro Evolution Soccer 4* menu screen. The girl I was having sex with at the time was on a poetry scholarship and ran completely out of things to write verses about because every evening was spent watching me stare dully at a blocky sprite version of an Atlético Madrid youth striker. I cannot know for sure because I didn't look in a mirror for about an eight-month period but I'm fairly sure I went 'physically grey'. Eventually, for my own health and that of those around me, I had to do away with the *Pro Evolution Soccer 4* disc. Ritualistically, one midnight, I walked out to a bridge overlooking the Menai Strait and frisbee'd the game into the Irish Sea. In the distance, a shock of thunder. Grey clouds loomed low above me. The rain rinsed hard then died down. The earth grumbled. On a distant hill, sylph-like demons danced their merry jig. A curse was lifted.

For a number of years, I managed to keep the old urges at bay, and these coincided with the rise of *FIFA* to overtake *Pro Evo* and then eventually eat the heart out of the chest of it. For about three hard years, as next-generation consoles took shape and the players on the screen actually started to look like something other than thumbs in kits, *FIFA* and *Pro Evo* were locked in a titanic squabble: you were either a *FIFA* boy (obvious, slightly flash, you had a gym membership and your car smelled nice) or a *Pro Evo* kid (an extra sheen of technicality, the connoisseur, doomed to one day join CAMRA and never really ever figure out how jeans should fit), two unspoken tribes clenched in battle. I was *Pro Evo* because it felt more hip and also the default controls suited the way I'd taught myself to play more easily, and then I got a complimentary copy of *FIFA 10* with an Xbox 360 and there was no going back, ever again. I lived with two housemates who fundamentally did not understand football and every time they came home to find me lulled on the sofa, my body pooled beneath me as if I'd melted, they'd ask me the following question, in the meanest tone anyone has ever said anything in: "What are you *doing*?" It took me years to realise that this was coming from a place of love. There was nothing normal about trying to get the Marouane Chamakh Arsenal side to the Champions League final by throwing it up against the computer controlled AI, like a ship bouncing hard against the shore, again and again and again.

Now it is 2022 and I am climbing out of the well of *FIFA* with my fingernails again. I never see it happen, I just blink and come to and suddenly I am looking at a wall-like menu with Kylian Mbappé cheering huge above it. I last recall playing *FIFA* in— what, 2014? 2015? When was that break-up again— 2016? But it's here again, that menu music, those quick little motions you have to make from the pause menu to change your controller layout from 'DEFAULT' to 'ALTERNATIVE'. You cannot complete a game of *FIFA* – it is a never-ending set of intangibles; you can win individual matches, or even lead a team to individual cups, but the game never runs out, you cannot 'complete' it – but that year I came as close as anyone's ever got to completing it, deliriously unbeatable with an insane inverted Chelsea team that had a 99 pace Alex Kiwomya up front instead of a slower but more devastating Diego Costa. But then I close my eyes and remember every game of *FIFA* I've ever played: cross-legged in front of the PS2 in that bedroom that eventually burned down; an all-day pass-the-greasy-controller launch day tournament that five of us had all set up to herald the new release; evenings in high flats in front of glowing TVs with the lights all off, one more game before I go and get my bus, one more game, one more game. *FIFA* used to be a social game – buying it at the supermarket at midnight then walking home with a bagful of Doritos was an autumnal ceremony the same way lighting a bonfire was! – but then it went online, and I only get matched against anonymous 12-year-olds who all know how to do nutmegs, and it doesn't work the same way anymore.

Is this how actual footballers feel as they age — once so powerful, once on top of the world, but now a certain slowness to their body that doesn't match their minds, and suddenly a game that used to come so easily to them seems alien and fully changed as youngsters run rings around them? I am 35 now: if I were a professional footballer I would be thinking about getting my coaching badges, accepting a contract for a shorter time on a lower wage, agreeing to rare cameos off the bench and firm-but-fair professionalism warnings to the youngsters coming through, instead of starting in midfield like I did every game I ever played all my life. I don't really know when this slipped away from me, but when *FIFA* introduced that new double-tap scoring system in 2018 I knew my time was short. I was still using the same pass-and-dash controls I learned in *Pro Evo*, 16 years and four consoles ago. James Milner has never had to learn what a TikTok dance is. Similarly, I am never, ever going to get my head around gyro controls.

It's been hours since I've talked. Days, maybe? When was— it might have been days. But now it's blue and purple and deep evening, and *FIFA 21* flickers glorious in front of me, and I am nine games deep into an online session that has seen me unbeaten. It's been years since this happened, but the old magic is creeping back into my fingers: with this '21 Leicester side (which I would argue is better than the '16 title-winning side in every way but for how they are being coached), every old trick I ever learned is clicking into place. The deep-down-the-wing through-pass always finds the right-wingback in Ricardo Pereira. Jamie Vardy, still a clean-finishing livewire down the middle, is impossible to mark, just loitering on the shoulder of the last defender, always ready to bolt. James Maddison is everything I hate about modern football on an interpersonal level but played in the hole he's a revelation: the ball sticks to his feet, he always finds space and pulls defenders into it, you just touch the triangle button and he slides in the perfect pass ... 1–0, 2–0, a couple of wild 4–0 scores, and then the most satisfying of all: a 4–5 reverse we win after going down three at half-time. The tenth game is another three points and some online promotion in a league system I don't fully understand. It is 1 a.m. and the sun still somehow lights the sky. It's time for bed but I am wired awake. I close my eyes and think of Youri Tielemans – playing the unfamiliar deep-but-roving role in that formation I spent so long hacking together that the TV tried to go into standby mode – making a perfectly weighted through-ball to Kelechi Iheanacho for the thousandth time today, the millionth time today. The inside of my eyelids are bright and painted with orange. Sleep, when it comes, is uneasy. **FIVE STARS**

SEEING A FRANKLY IRRESISTIBLE OFFER ON MÜLLER CORNERS WHILE YOU WERE ON THE WAY TO WHAT IS TECHNICALLY A PARTY

I think I slightly 'stopped getting invited to things' for a while there because I kept saying no to any and all social engagements, and even when and if I did turn up I would have what Michael calls 'an energy' ("It was like you were hungry. But not in a good way.") so eventually even the most stubborn and cheerful of my acquaintances have stopped telling me they, for instance, are turning 30, or going on a group holiday, or renting an entire nightclub out for a non-milestone birthday (?), or that there was an Arsenal ticket going

FOUR STARS

(I do not like going to Arsenal games, anyway. You have to stand with Arsenal fans). Socially I have made myself a leper. Anyway Jamie for some reason text me at like 9 p.m. on a Friday and said like "we've got a few people over" and it's "a cool vibe actually" and that I should "come through" and the main thing I was doing was trying to figure out if the washing machine was on a long cycle I had put it on or whether the washing machine was on a malfunctioningly long long cycle (the recurring agony of my life) so I said: "Sure, OK, sure."

I love leaving the house at 9 p.m. (I also love getting dressed very, very quickly – unthinkingly, even! Just pulling some shoes and whatever's to hand on! – because the outfit has its own bizarre élan. This is unsynthesisable, if you try and make it slowly and carefully in the cold light of day, the same way Matisse and Picasso never cracked how to draw with the unfettered anti-focus of children. It is, in a very pure sense, the only way to get dressed). Every night should start at 9 p.m., because there is just something to the timbre of everything: xenon streetlamps blurry against the crisp jet black of the sky, that first cold clear breath you take when you leave the house, the bizarre circadian rhythm unnaturalness of it, that little crackle of excitement you get. Is it naughty, leaving the house this late? Is this some primal response to the old curfews of yore that have yet to fully shake themselves out of my body? Or is it just the thrill of knowing I could realistically go to bed in one hour's time, but instead I'm in a brightly lit corner shop buying a blue bag worth of Tyskie? It is impossible to know what makes magic magical. But the point is this: any idiot can slump into the pub straight after work then a quick dinner then a cab and then the next thing and then a party. Sure. It takes a finer mind to leave the house at 9 p.m.

The flat was opposite that good supermarket in Whitechapel so I ended up there to pick up a box of beers, which was fine but bizarre: a very curious crowd affects the Whitechapel Sainsbury's at 9 p.m. on a Saturday night, as much savvy heads-of-families doing the Big Shop in what is technically quiet hours as it is students in oversized leather jackets they were wearing very bravely and having really loud between-aisle conversations laughing loudly, as it is tired shift workers buying an inexplicably big thing of crisps, as it is those weird blokes who play five-a-side on a Friday (on a Friday!) carting a rucksack full of balls around for Lucozade and a Meal Deal, as it is a butcher still somehow cleaning out the long-empty display case, as it is me. The lights are starkly bright and unforgiving. I somehow spend seven minutes in the olives and jars aisle. And then I see Müller Crunch Corners on an irresistible multi-buy deal (10 for £3). How can I resist that? It's the best yoghurt! *The* best. I can eat six, maybe seven in a row. It is the best yoghurt and yoghurt-style treat. I buy twenty. I buy a big box of beers for the normal people and a small box of ciders for the goths (if you bring cider to a party, you will instantly win over every cider drinker there – they greet you like a god – but the hit-rate of those

FOUR STARS

people being goths is 100%), but fundamentally I buy 20 pots of yoghurt.

I also buy cigarettes, for some reason. I have smoked about 14 cigarettes in my entire life, so I don't know where the compulsion comes from, but sometimes my mind just goes, *you are an adult and the only man in charge of you, you can do literally whatever you want*, and then I end up doing something strange like that. I find a bench opposite the party and smoke a single one. The flat pulses orange and full of shadows. That is where life is. That is where I am going to. This is what it is to live. This is what it is to live in one of the greatest cities on earth! This is why I'm here! How many impromptu Friday night invites to parties will I have before I die? The number will only dwindle! I! Am! A! Live!

Here's how that went:

"Hey man."

"Hey."

"Been ages. Come in—"

"Yeah hey thank you: I bought beer."

"Great great great. You know Tom? Dan? Brinny?"

"Yep, yep. All the names."

"Tato, Elima, John."

"Yeah I know all them."

"Sorry have we—?"

"We've met."

"Have you met?"

"..."

"I don't think we've—"

"Sorry, no. It's— I just say I've met people. Always. It's just easier."

"How is it easier?"

"Well now it isn't easier but normally it's easier."

"So you two *haven't* met?"

"I don't think so."

"No we haven't. No. I just said that we'd— is there space in the fridge for things?"

"Yep. Beers, I think there's some ... what are they called? Like 'hard seltzer' things?"

"Yeah, yeah. It's just I've got yoghurts. I've got quite a lot of yoghurts."

"For the party?"

"No."

"What."

"My yoghurts."

"*What?*"

"My yoghurts."

The party itself was quite good actually – I had a few beers and some really gritty cocaine and some girl in leather trousers kept unnecessarily touching her thigh against my thigh and telling me how her boyfriend didn't really "get jokes" and there was a laptop plugged into the television so everyone was taking turns DJing and I managed to get a couple of Klaxons remixes off that people didn't *like* exactly (a six-minute Soulwax remix of a Klaxons song from 2007! Ambassador, you spoil us!) but they didn't turn it off and snap the laptop shut like at other parties and I ended up slumped in a beanbag talking to a really interesting guy who was saying some cool stuff about like, the pixels in the original *Sonic the Hedgehog* game? I don't remember exactly what he was saying but it was cool. Then leather trousers girl came and just perched on the sofa next to us and kind of ruined the conversational vibe there so I decided it was time to bounce. Some mild anxiety at the end when I couldn't find Jamie to ask him if he had a Bag For Life for all the yoghurts (it turns out he was locked in the bathroom with three other people, one of whom was doing something very sinister with a cigarette that seemed to involve emptying it of all tobacco while not blinking very much) and I think I probably lost one Banana Cornflake and maybe a Strawberry Shortcake in the mix, but the Uber driver was very mellow despite how visibly I was sweating in the back seat and all in all the hangover was probably worth me leaving the house for. When I got back in Megan was in bed with her back to me and was breathing in a way that very much meant she was awake but not talking to me so I figured I'd have to wake up and have a row in the morning but until then: **FOUR STARS**

THE ENTIRE DECADES-LONG TELEVISION OUTPUT OF 'RICK STEIN'

Two inches into a bottle of white is where you feel peace, and that is where Rick Stein lives, folded into a dining chair with his hands resting softly on his belly, polite and neat like a boy. This is the beauty of Rick Stein, whose ambient sprawling televisual empire calms me like a goat soothes a horse: here Rick Stein is in France, look, wafting himself cool with a tasteless straw fedora; here is Rick Stein off the coast of Newquay, grappling with a king crab, shirt sleeves dripping with sour salt water; here is Rick Stein, dots of white flowers bouncing behind him under the soft continental breeze, saying "*à votre santé!*" and eating a cork-sized piece of cheese. It doesn't matter what year you find him in, or what continent he is drifting about in boat shoes on. Rick Stein is always doing the same thing, with the same energy, and often in the same rolled-up shirt. The theory of the multiverse dictates that there is constantly a version of Rick Stein out there, somewhere, holding up a pink prawn and marvelling at the simple beauty of it. A billion mouths form at once to whisper: "With prawns this good, it's best to keep it simple: good olive oil, good salt, and a handful of fresh parsley." This is the only recipe that the infinite Ricks really know.

Rick Stein is my favourite TV chef because, fundamentally, he is not a very 'TV' TV chef, despite him having been a TV chef for multiple decades now. The shows are all the same – Rick goes somewhere, eats fish, perhaps goes on a boat perhaps not, ambles through a farm, pats a cow firmly on the head before sampling its butter, laughs through an untranslated conversation with an ancient Spanish woman who is shouting, drives a car (he is always driving a car), swims in the sea (he always swims in the sea), then leans on a counter and whips up a sort of salad thing in mute silence, before explaining what he just did during a later scene shot later in the day. It is clear that around the year 1998 Rick Stein figured out that he could either cook, or he could talk, and he couldn't do both at once, so here's how we work it: footage of Rick Stein cooking, using only his hands and a heavy knife to do literally every job with (Rick's fingers pulling at a crab knuckle; Rick snapping a stick of celery in two with his fists; Rick plopping a cube of butter into a thin gravy with his fingertips) and then, with the dregs of a beer in front of him, sat on a log or a dock or a bench as the sun sets gauzy behind him, he tells you how much salt he used when he did that cooking earlier. Rick does not subscribe to your 'measuring systems': his proportions are more human than that, more intuitive. Yesterday I watched him use "lots of mayonnaise ". Today it was a "load" of parsley. You want to use a "fair bit" of salt, then wash the salt off so it isn't too salty. If you use too much salt it ruins the dish, but Rick will never tell you even what postcode the limit for that is in. God, it's too hot for anything like that. Figure it out on your own.

The beauty of Rick is just watching as a man grows ever-so-slightly day-drunk and pinkly sunburned in a wardrobe that can only be aesthetically described as 'the flight crew lost your dad's luggage so he had to buy all his clothes at the airport': straw fedoras, linen shirts crumpled at the front with those strange dots of middle-aged sweat, quarter-zip knits for when the evenings grow chill, absolutely never – never ever ever! – a single pair of sunglasses. A leather satchel, a haircut done over a towel in a farmhouse kitchen, an unbuttoned shirt cuff and a soft-backed notebook. Most TV travelogues are tightly, overwhelmingly inventoried – you watch as a local artisan lists off what makes their product so good in well-practised English, you gaze at some shots of a TV chef plucking their own orange from a tree, then in the same clean well-lit kitchen they do everything in they bosh something together for a family of six – but Rick seems to lurch from one location to the other based on intuition, hunger, and whether it looks like they do good arancini balls and a Peroni. He keeps turning up in professional kitchens with the chefs around him looking very genuinely surprised to see him there. He keeps leaning on gates I'm not sure you're allowed to lean against, let alone film. He breathes the clean crisp air of the coastline and tells you a story about when he read a book when he was 20. It has absolutely nothing to do with anything. It's 9 p.m. and he's eyeing up the day's third bottle of wine. Who Fucking Cares.

You would think that with an entire empire of work (27 books! 33 series! 14 restaurants!) that Rick might have some ideology or philosophy to preach, but I have looked closely and there isn't one. He likes seafood, obviously, and would like people to eat it more. He is almost constantly in another country looking at a tomato that has been grown in the sun while saying, "Why don't we have that back home?" He has a fierce and beautiful pride and love for his home county of Cornwall, which is actually a tough balance to strike: English people being in any way proud of their Englishness is somehow literally always embarrassing, except when Rick Stein rolls up his trouser legs and flops them off the promenade in Padstow and eats a big ice cream and grins. But there is no real through-line to any of this, beyond 'the top of Rick Stein's head is warm and he's eaten some good butter today'. The closest I ever see him get to an overarching credo is when jolting around on a fishing boat in late spring, gazing at a cuttlefish as it drowns dry in a lobster pot. "They make fantastic risotto with the ink, with the black ink," he says, "so when you eat them you get sort of black lips. It's a really great thing to do. A great seafood delight, to me." That's it, that's the magic: the sun is setting and the sky is pink then orange and the wind is firm and fair, and we are surrounded by salt and sweat and beer and ink, and long grass tufting merrily on a clifftop, and you eat cuttlefish risotto with the black ink on your lips because it's *a really great thing to do*. What other way to live a life is there than ambling around, doing something simply because it's great to do it?

But to over-subscribe importance to Steinism is to over-complicate it, which is against one of its primary edicts. The point of Rick Stein is he lives the mild, jolly life of an olde English king – good food and good drink and good friends and no fuss, and what could be finer, what could be finer. He sits in a pub garden with a crisp glass of white wine and worries his hands against his watch. He walks up a slightly too-steep hill and asks someone about a pepper paste their granddad invented in Romagna. He starts a remarkable number of to-camera anecdotes with, "I was just thinking the other day—" and then doesn't really finish them. A bit of cheese, bit of butter. A long drive and a snooze. In many ways, Rick's anti-TV TV – a refusal to be bombastic, or even very engaging, or really do or say anything attention-grabbing at all – is ahead-of-the-curve, futuristic ambient unentertainment, a peaceful half-hour away from a world of compulsive e-mail checking and always-on attention spans and playing with your iPad in bed. We have built towers of modern entertainment with the primary function of relaxing us – lo-fi beats, ASMR videos, re-watching *The Office* for the sixth or seventh time, ZEN Mode on *Candy Crush* – but really that can all be achieved by watching Rick Stein get slightly overwhelmed in Mexico before cooking some cod. **FIVE HUNDRED STARS**

MARY MOTHER OF GOD – CREMATE

I had tried weed twice in my life and it hadn't made me either interesting or happy so I just figured: *not for me*. I have some friends who smoked weed towards the end of our teenage years – we all have a friend like this, yes? Always wearing a hat, can become very bamboozled by a simple DVD menu, when you look at the desktop of their computer it is unlike anything you've ever seen in your life, always sending Facebook Messenger messages at four, maybe five a.m.? –

FOUR STARS

but being in the room in a squidgy soft beanbag with them never seemed to quite make sense, for me. I had beer and I had huge grotesque greasy pours of supermarket vodka topped up with an inch of Cola, and that was normally more than enough to get me out of my mind, laughing ecstatically, agonised the next morning.

I don't really know where the weed brownie came from, then, or how exactly it ended up in my mouth, but I chewed and swallowed it carefully one Sunday then, 45 minutes later, became phenomenally overwhelmed by the sound of my own mind. In there, locked in the dome, deep truths of the universe were whispered unto me: 22 Jump Street *is one of the best movies ever made, pizza crusts dipped in garlic sauce is what the gods described as ambrosia, pull a blanket up and down over your knees to feel a long-buried euphoria.* It was only many days later, after I'd text every one of my close contacts one of the most insane sentences they'd ever received and turned so inwards that, as I described it, I was "feeling the warm and distant glow of doing a good soapy load of washing up on the yuleful hog of Christmas Day", did we get the much-forwarded text from someone's sister that said: *careful before you eat those edibles, guys. turns out they're quite strong lol. maybe only have a nibble.* I had drafted an e-mail to two of my editors, deep in the funk of a high, explaining that I had very merrily damaged my brain forever and I would not be able to file to them ever again. I was stringent with dosages from then on.

Mary Mother Of God scent cones by Cremate smell like frankincense and lavender and lemongrass but something deeper, murkier, too: clean like a newly laundered tracksuit, but fragrant like every aromatic you want on a good BBQ, like some high distant zing – what is that? Grapefruit? It smells like a dry wind just rustled next to an orchard full of grapefruits – that you can't quite identify. Car air freshener, the sun lingering but not setting in the sky, jet-black windows, being surprised to discover there is someone sat behind you. The tendrils of the universe reach out and wrap me in their pink-orange glow: *it smells like buying weed from your weed dealer.*

After I self-administered the rest of the brownie – sliced into tiny atomic cubes and stored in the freezer, decanted out into my body once a week for months – I realised that I like the gluey, free-jazz, smiling-beatifically effect that marijuana had on my mind and body and soul, so I decided to find a weed dealer. By asking my friend if he could give me his weed dealer:

> why
> \> i took a load of edibles and thought i was washing up on xmas day
> \> was totally insane
> \> have u seen 22 jump street
> yes i have
> \> hits right
> hits
> ok here's his number
> \> thank u

FOUR STARS

> uh
> how does one . . . what quantities, in which, does one buy 'weed'

i normally get five grams

> you buy it by the GRAM?

yes

> can u send me like, a screenshot of ur conversations

yes

basically ur gonna have to engage in a very complicated handshake with him and then he is going to talk a lil about crypto

get £60 out in cash

The first time I met Caleb he took me on two moody laps of my block and pointed out every single delivery driver bringing takeaway to my building, explaining that they weren't actually delivery drivers, they were "undercover ops", and not to trust them. I tried to explain to him that my building was a 40-unit new build very much controlled by a management company with parquet floors that appealed to child-free cash-rich Hackney millennials who all had 20% codes for local fusion restaurants, but he still made us wait in the car – windows blacked out, engine purring – until they dissipated. It felt like a very 'me' thing to do to get arrested the first ever time I buy drugs and imprisoned for possession over a £60 bag of White Cookies wrapped inelegantly in clingfilm so, to be safe, walking home I took a very alleyway-heavy route and avoided anyone with a hot-bag on their back. I came home and smoked a joint the size of a cigar and laughed at myself for nine straight hours. **FIVE STARS**

THE McDONALD'S CHICKEN BIG MAC®, A LIMITED-EDITION BURGER EXPERIENCE

McDonald's recently announced the Chicken Big Mac, news which set every single group chat I was in simultaneously ablaze with gossip and anticipation (this, if nothing else, galvanised the idea that I was in the exact right group chats) (you wonder, you know? Are there better groups out there, having better chats. Well: no.). This was a limited edition release planned to run for a six-week period, but eventually ran instead for two separate four-week periods with a brief break in between when McDonald's unexpectedly (for them – I could have foreseen this) sold almost instantly out. The idea of the Chicken Big Mac is simple: the Big Mac, but with two battered chicken patties instead of the traditional beef – every other component part of the Big Mac remains the same. There is elegance to all the best ideas, I think, and the Chicken Big Mac drips with it: *well why don't we just do it with chicken?*, they thought. *And only do it for six weeks.* It didn't need much to formulate. The R&D lab that McDonald's runs in an underground bunker didn't have to tinker much with the recipe

FOUR STARS

(I personally believe they took the traditional McChicken patty and actually made it less salty and deliberately blander, to better make the other Big Mac components contrast and sing). But something doesn't need to be complicated to be smart. Sometimes it just needs to *be*.

THE FOLLOWING ARE SELECT EXCERPTS TRANSCRIBED AND EDITED FROM A SELF-INTERVIEW I TOOK WHILE UNDER THE INFLUENCE OF A FAIRLY POWERFUL WEED GUMMY DURING MY SECOND ENCOUNTER WITH A CHICKEN BIG MAC:

[Tape starts] *I'm about to enter into oral congress with the last Chicken Big Mac of my life. It is a limited edition burger that will cease on March 15th. I've already had one, during the initial run – it underwhelmed me a touch (it wasn't as good as the beef Big Mac, though it had all of the accoutrements) and also I am under the influence of half a weed gummy someone brought me back from LA. I have paused the TV to better get my thoughts down. I have put the dictaphone in my pocket for a hands-free sound-taking experience. OK.*

The first Chicken Big Mac I had was with my friend Adam, while slightly drunk. The best way to eat McDonald's is like this, after four to five units of alcohol, a sheen of sweat that defies whatever indoor or outdoor temperature there is, a complete abandonment of any idea of the self as ruled by manners (holding food with two hands, cheese smudged around the mouth, grunting words through the fries, exhilarated, *living*). He thought it was a masterpiece and I thought it a hollow rip-off of what came before it: for me, the Big Mac – possibly the most thought-about and intentional burger (or indeed food item!) in the world – is a perfect item. It is one of the most perfect things you can buy for less than £4. The Big Mac always tastes the same: in London, Chesterfield, Japan. The textures are the same (the lettuce is unmoved by the swaying of the seasons; the onions taste like onion but not like onion). The Big Mac is food that has been engineered in the same way they make rocket ships: every single atom of it agonised over, tested, run and re-run again. Michelin-starred chefs can think about their food, and serve it with intention, know seasonal grains and vegetables, exquisite techniques to bring out flavour and smoke and memory. But they can never compete with a Big Mac: formulated by hundreds of minds, over dozens of years, and served by thousands of hands.

[Extremely loud first bite followed by gnarly audio of chewing and swallowing] *Mm! OK. OK, OK, OK. OK!*

The point of McDonald's is not innovation. The point of McDonald's is consistency. Big Macs have tasted the same for my entire life, and in every country I have eaten one in. There is a thrill to going to McDonald's in another country, partly to see what's different – in Italy they serve beer! In Japan they offer chocolate sauce as a dip-or-drizzle for fries! – but mainly to see what's the same. The fries are the same, and the McDonald's fountain soda is the same (as in: tasting like the soda advertised, but not identical – McDonald's Coca-Cola is its own beast), the burgers are the same. The uniforms are the same, and the tiles, and the smell. McDonald's says: *Hey, you can come here and have some Chicken Selects™, and they will taste like comfort to you.* You can go into the same restaurant you had your fifth birthday in 29 years later when you've just been asked to leave a pub for spilling a tray of Jägermeister and the girl whose birthday it is started really aggressively crying. You can sit in the same chair and eat the same burger and receive the same welcome. McDonald's is not here to surprise; it is here to soothe.

A crucial part of the Big Mac experience – and it's replicated here with the Chicken Big Mac! – is that it's a double burger. It's a burger and another burger but not two burgers stacked on top of each other: the burgers are separated by a piece of bread, and that is really fucking crucial for the experience. Because you get: bread–lettuce–meat, bread–lettuce–meat, so you go soft–crunch–hard, soft–crunch–hard, soft. Wow. I cannot believe I've never noticed that before. But that is a huge part of the texture *of the Big Mac: it's not just a double burger! It's a double burger* with an extra slice!

I am a sucker for food-related consumerism that is just mild-to-medium twists on classics: I am who all the new Dairy Milk flavours are for, for instance, or when Nesquik does a new kind of cereal that is sort of Nesquik but not. Or when Coke did those horrible new Diet Coke flavours. The year everything had a salted caramel limited edition. The year everything had a chocolate orange limited edition. The white chocolate Snickers. In America, I am bamboozled in every store, most particularly CVS but I can lose an afternoon and part of an evening to a Target, because they have all kinds of remixes and untasted flavours of Snickers, Mike & Ike's, Fanta. Part of this is because I like junk food and have an insatiable sweet tooth: yes. Part of this is because I am a sucker being played like a fiddle by the big organs of consumerism: yes. But partly I just like having an entirely new experience for about the price of a Tube journey. You can have a high spike of joy for about £3 all-in. What is there not to like about that?

I think another thing that really makes the Big Mac – and it wouldn't be the Big Mac without it! – is (everyone knows Big Mac sauce; everyone knows gherkins; everyone knows lettuce, everyone knows cheese) the sesame seeds are a crucial part of the perfect bite. And that's what they're bringing here – that's what makes it different to a double chicken burger. The subtle details here: the sesame seeds on top, the extra layer of bread, the onions, even! Now: structurally, I am having more of a disintegration than I normally do with a B.B.M. (Beef Big Mac), though I am willing to attribute that to my current personal condition. Going in for another bite—

There is no more thrilling an experience than going to McDonald's as a child. It should not be that exciting

FOUR STARS

but it is: it is brain-meltingly, overwhelmingly great. You are small and the burgers are huge. There are special meals for children that come with a toy. Once adolescence hits, McDonald's becomes more pragmatic: a place to meet friends, a booth to nurse a milkshake over, a place to steal great handfuls of straws and bite the ends off and blow the paper sheaths around like bullets. In adulthood, the electric jolt of enjoyment has worn away – as with most things – unless you take a little bit of an edible and pay a frankly repulsive delivery fee to have a driver bring a brown paper bag of it to your house, and there, on the sofa, you are eight or nine or ten again, elated.

The thing with the Big Mac, is: it is so built on a foundation of pickle flavour – vinegar sharpness, the green pickle bite flavour, the texture – pickles are crucial for the Big Mac. And it's so interesting that so famously the trope, the cliche, in American movies is: "Oh, I take the pickles out of my burger" "— and I eat pickles plain!", you know? The Big Mac is built on pickles; non-pickle likers don't get the Big Mac and pick the pickles out. You can't! The pickles are crucial to what's going on here, and there's a lot going on.

I think it's easy to say: 'Big Mac sauce is a big part of the Big Mac.' Obviously it is: no other burger has it. But, you also can't take away the cheese – even though it's a relatively flavourless American slice, that cheese is doing a lot in there. Structurally, it's glue. But it belongs on the palate as well – it's doing enough to earn its place in the burger. Shout out to the cheese in

JOEL GOLBY

Big Mac. Actually: shout out to the onions, man! There's a lot of chopped white onion in the Big Mac. It's an acid profile burger! It's an acidic little burger!

I didn't really 'get into' McDonald's as an adult until I was about 24 and saw the Golden Arches glowing at me through a drunken blur on a drizzled night when the buses were barely running and I had nowhere to go, and there, bathed in that holy bright light, I housed a Big Mac, large fries, a strawberry milkshake and like six pots of BBQ sauce. The order has been refined since – I feel a sparkling drink, often a D.C. but sometimes a Sprite, helps the sheer mash of soft food go down; I like now to have a small portion of Chicken Selects® on the side to dip with – but the core of it was right: the Big Mac, the perfect burger, the fries alongside, the warm brown paper bag, the sound of my own mouth chewing, the bright lights, the fuzzy head, the sweat droplets, the straw slurp sound, the friendly call of order numbers behind me, the intense looking at the phone, the small stir of a guilty feeling, a non-admittance that I am actually here, doing this thing.

I just had a bit of the chicken patty on its own and its fine, it's flavourless. That's fine: the rest of the burger is there to prop it up. But this is what makes the B.B.M. an inch-and-a-half bigger than this: the B.B.M. is history's most consistent 10/10 burger. *That's a fact. The Big Mac can't be topped, and the Chicken Big Mac comes close, but . . . wow—*

FOUR STARS

After my first Chicken Big Mac I had delirious dreams: salt, beer, ketchup, acid, it all kept me up in a kaleidoscopic technicolour half-sleep, having frantic visions. I don't normally remember my dreams, but these all felt weirdly notable: I couldn't use a pencil sharpener after boasting to the class how good I was at and how often I sharpened my pencils; I saw Arsène Wenger in a tracksuit and jeans outside a Big Tesco but didn't react fast enough to say anything cool; I got trapped between some first-week *Apprentice* candidates trying to upsell some work shirts and I bought one for £60 then realised I'd been scammed (it was, at best, a £4 shirt) and then I made a big (crying) scene about getting a refund that was shown in full on the BBC. I woke up drenched in sweat, my mouth dry, my body aching, and I thought: *I deserve this. I have committed a sin unto myself and now I must face hell.*

I mean what a thing! What a glorious thing. Steeped in history, and lore. Every president has eaten a Big Mac. Elvis ate Big Macs. Like: every time you eat a Big Mac, you eat a Big Mac with everyone who's ever had a Big Mac. The Chicken Big Mac is a rarer beast and I feel privileged to have had not one but two, but [extremely long chewing sequence] *it's rare because it's not as good. It's rare because this burger – this perfect burger, this perfect assembly! – requires beef. It requires the flavour profile of beef. You can't just chop in another protein and call it a Big Mac. This is a pretender. This is . . . an imposter. What an era we live in. What an era we live in!* [Tape stops]

Nothing compares to a Big Mac. Even McDonald's knows this. The Chicken Big Mac will not return. It is, fundamentally, a failure in concept: you cannot improve a Big Mac, so any changes to it will only diminish the returns. You cannot rewrite history and you cannot change the future. But I experienced something with that burger, and that is what we are alive to do. I will think about it, often, and fondly. **FIVE STARS**

THE DREAM

In the dream it's either on a high rooftop or a very low rooftop but the sun is setting pink-purple blue behind us and there are birds, Mike Tyson birds, cooing grey pigeons in a walk-in coop. On the ground is lush long grass and plants that seem tropical and well-watered and amongst that is a table – brass, ornate, steampunk almost? Dare I say 'steampunk'? – loaded with grapes and cheese and delicate slivers of meat. And then something happens and I don't know what but I am in the coop with the birds and I am not in the coop with the birds and zeppelins float heavy in the sky and soft feathers touch my shoulders and thunder looms heavy and I can smell that rain is coming, I can feel the air change from heavy-hot to zip-cold and the white billboard screens on the buildings around us are now the only light. I turn around and there The Boy is, easing off the floor, holding his hand to his chest that was

FOUR STARS

once sticky and gouged hollow and now, miraculously, is healed. He looks confusedly at the towels laid all around him like blankets then tentatively tries his feet again on the uneven ground and walks slow and smooth towards me.

"Hey," he says, "what's this?"

"I dunno man, it's some sort of fever-cum-salt dream. I don't know. I have no idea."

"Where are we?"

"Again I have no idea."

"Who are you?"

"I'm the guy who watched you die."

"Ah, OK. Hey."

"Hey."

Winged bugs flurry through the air. Dark skeletons of skyscrapers stir in the smoke. There are sirens in the distance but I don't know where they're going to, what roads they are supposed to run rescue lines across. I'm wondering why, at such a clearly key point in my personal descent into mania, I decided to wear *these* trainers, a pair of dirty old Converse '70s with a hole in the toe-box and laces grey with dirt. The Boy does not deserve to have to look at these trainers during his one remaining shot at sentience. I try and hide my feet.

"Are you ... trying to hide your feet?"

"No."

"It's fine. Guys like you always wear trainers like that."

"'Guys like me?'"

"You know ... chore-jacket-and-an-IPA types."

"... well. Yeah."

JOEL GOLBY

I experience the entirety of his life in a few seconds: a trip to Ibiza with the boys, bottle service and finger-guns and models in white bikinis, the new-car-smell of a BMW, a really detailed sleeve that ends in an agonisingly intricate hand tattoo, slicking his eyebrows down in the mirror before a handshake promotion at work, whirling Instagram video of his first flat, his best friends' destination wedding, a girl smiles shyly at him in the gym, on stage in the club with a lace shirt and wraparound shades, an ill-advised period of growing his hair out, his daughter watches him scoop protein powder in an immaculate marble kitchen, a gold Rolex, a selfie on a jet ski, a year in Dubai, kissing his wife beneath the orange haze of a June sunset, his son kicks a football into the new Samsung but he laughs as it shatters on the carpet, a birthday cake topped with sparklers at a restaurant full of friends, cheering deliriously as Chelsea win the league, a hundred birthdays, a thousand Christmases. He dies in a clean well-made bed surrounded by generations of his family and as he nods into the abyss, wrinkled and grey, he knows he has lived. Why can I imagine a dead person enjoying life more than I can myself?

"You probably have to stop projecting quite so much of your stuff onto me."

"I figured."

"I'm not the reason you're like this. I was just there."

"Yeah that makes sense."

"You were already quite depressed beforehand."

"I *get it*, alright!"

FOUR STARS

— but now my hair is wet and the birds are gone and the zeppelins are ever closer and the air is cold and dark now and sometimes, you know, sometimes it feels like I'm close to feeling the right things again and then they snatch away and flutter down into nothing. Then I come to with a jolt because the door is thumping and my mouth is dry from eating a Chicken Big Mac too close to bedtime. I am, like, *gasping* for a glass of water right now. Why would I do that. Why would I do that to myself. **ZERO STARS**

REJECTION

Michael said he knew a guy at *Rammed* who said he'd read some of my stuff and they had a culture editor role coming up and would I be interested, and I tried to explain to him that I was post-salary and post-job and I was freelance now instead, I couldn't be shackled to the rock of a monthly cheque and a nine to five, and he said how many articles have you written in the past two months then and I counted it up and then went through my incomings and outgoings on Monzo and long story short I called the guy and said, "Hey." He was called – as everyone who works in media in London who is in a position to hire someone is – 'Jack'. Anyway the interview was today.

The first mistake I suppose was wearing a suit, which made me not only the only person wearing a suit in the office but possibly the only person who had ever worn a suit in this office, ever. There was a large *Rammed* neon logo behind reception and I was offered coffee-machine coffee in a *Rammed*-emblazoned mug and there were huge dark bookshelves rammed with *Rammed* and there was a folded-up ping pong table and industrial metal riveted things hanging from the ceilings. Everyone there typed in silence. TVs blared muted news. This was not a suit place. I immediately felt uncomfortable wearing a suit.

"So no to coffee?"

"Well I just know it's going to be Nespresso."

"Yeah, it's Nespresso."

"Yeah, well. You know. *Fuck* Nespresso."

"Is there a ... have Nespresso been *cancelled*? Is there a political reason for this position?"

"Cancelled, cancelled. Everyone's always obsessed with things being cancelled. No. It just tastes like shit."

"Right—"

"But it tastes like shit in a *particular* way where the office is quelled enough not to agitate against the seams and demand better coffee—"

"Right."

"A French press situation, perhaps, or an oversized drip machine that would be very easy to institute in an office of this size and keep topped up during the day."

"American-style."

"American-style, right. But instead you just get those horrible little plastic-y capsules. That space food-like un-taste from the machine-frothed milk. Entirely satisfactory, but, beneath those notes of mediocrity: disgusting."

"Right. Well we value opinionated . . . we value, ah. We like opinions, here."

"Mm."

He explained what *Rammed* was about for a bit and I sort of glazed over – 'disruption' came up a lot, but then so did 'loving legacy media' and 'big collection of magazines left over from the '90s' and 'kind of want to be a new kind of punk' but also very much in a 'not fucking up the two-year advertorial deal we have with Heineken' kind of way. The shame of course is that this suit was nice – a just-right Acne Studios blazer I picked up for a song off eBay, that had the perfect casual shoulder drape to make it smart but not *formal*, and I'd paired it with some Uniqlo trousers from a couple of seasons ago that of course they stopped fucking making because any time Uniqlo start making something good they almost immediately then pull it from the shelves and replace it with uninspiring tennis gear that says 'Roger Federer' on the sleeve – but instead of this being casual power-dressing I just felt very much like that time I walked late into an assembly at secondary school and it turned out today was Non-Uniform Day and I was the only person who didn't know that and so I had to walk past the entire assembled school in my uniform and even the headmaster was laughing at me.

"So tell me a bit about you."

"Me? I'm a . . . hmm. Male . . . person?"

"No I mean like: your career up until now."

"Jack, I'm bigger than you."

"How do you mean?"

"I'm ... bigger than you. I'm bigger than you. I shouldn't have to explain this to you. You came to me. *I am bigger than you.*"

"Right."

"Like I'm not going to explain who I am. You know who I am. Because I am—"

"— bigger than you?"

"You got it."

"Say you weren't bigger than me—"

"Hmm."

"And you had to answer that question like a normal person."

"OK."

"So tell me about your career up until now."

"No."

Society is structured to make you think there are people who are above you and below you, that people can tell you things because of how they are dressed or what their parents did or whether they got a new-reg car for passing their A-Levels or whether they got into that university you wanted to go to but ended up going to Bangor instead, that power dynamics exist and can be enforced, but they can't and there aren't. Every person you meet is just some fucking guy. Every place with a big logo is just an illusion. And I will not debase myself for some fucking editing job.

"Maybe I should tell you a little bit about the job first."

"It's editing, right?"

"Yep."

"So it's e-mails."

"The job's more— well, it's formulating ideas, and commissioning them out, and keeping track of budgets..."

"But I am a *writer*. And I know a lot of writers become editors, because this system doesn't really leave any space to be promoted into. But that's a wrong-headed way of doing it."

"Go on."

"Well you're going to have me commission writers, right? So I'm going to make up an idea, get an inferior writer to do a bad job of it, and then – as editor – I clean it up so it looks like they did a good job of it. All the writer has to do is fuck it all up. I'm the one who does the work, they're the one who gets the glory. Well, 'glory'. A byline in *Rammed*."

"Perhaps we d—"

"Here's the thing. Can I do this job? Yeah. Will I be better at it than anyone else you try and talk to? Also yes. If you want to spend the money this job frees up on making the magazine better, hire me."

"OK."

"But respectfully, don't hire me for this job. A culture editor is just an e-mail guy. Make me, I don't know, genius-in-chief. Make me an artist-in-residence for the kitchen with the coffee machine in it—"

"OK."

"Then you get all my best ideas – which is what you want from the role of a culture editor – but you also get the best writer you can possibly get on-board to write them, which is me. That's two for the price of one. Well ... we can talk about the price. One-and-a-half, maybe."

"Right. Can I ask about the column?"

"What column?"

"The column you got fired from?"

"I didn't— I didn't get fired from it. They stopped doing that column."

"I thought Ed Warburton was doing it now."

"He's doing *a* TV column. It's not *my* TV column."

"They moved it to the front of the paper."

"Exactly. Because it's a different column."

Went for a really long toilet trip afterwards, because I think you get a good read of how much an employer respects a worker by how nice the bathroom facilities are and these were passable but horrible – harsh lighting, a gurgling smell in the shared corridor between both bathrooms and an empty bottle of nice handwash that was locked in a cage with a 99p bottle of cheap handwash next to it instead, which says everything you need to know. No paper towels. One-ply toilet roll. An unbadged air dryer for the hands. This was not a place I could spend my days. I couldn't be here, every day, saying a cheerful, "Hello!" to people in the morning, telling them what I 'did' at the 'weekend', being pulled into a little room by my 'boss' to tell me that's the fifth time in ten days I've been late. Reply-all e-mail chains and warnings about leaving things too long in the fridge. *Brainstorming.* Pulling together to build a publication with no legacy and no lore, a constant plasticine wad of *branding* that gets worked and reworked and relaunched every two years to lurch after an audience that doesn't

FOUR STARS

really exist or have any sort of identity at all. Reviewing a TV show in less than 300 words! Having to schedule my own Facebook posts! Desperately trying to force the day's only news story through the prism of the 'right' way to react to it! Caring about the results of elections! No, no, no, no, no. All these people are flesh and blood and bones. They can't tell me a single fucking thing. Anyway he e-mailed almost immediately afterwards saying they were going in a different direction and to stay in touch and if I fancied it I could do my TV column for them at a drastically reduced and actually quite insulting word-rate. No. Rejection doesn't sting because it doesn't exist. I wish that moron nothing but death. **THIS STAR RATING IS BLANK**

HI TEC SQUASH SHOE IN WHITE AND DARK GREEN, SIZE 11 REGULAR FIT

I finally pulled the trigger on the Hi Tec Squash shoe, a gum-soled white-and-green leather trainer with a soft grey suede toe cap and brilliant white laces, which retail for a startlingly affordable £35. The Hi Tec Squash shoe is one of the great staple trainers because it looks good with black trousers and blue trousers (it does not need to be mentioned that the white-and-green shoe looks good with green trousers – this is a given. Everything looks good with green trousers), it costs so little that it doesn't matter if you shred the ever-loving shit out of them because they can easily be replaced, and also they sell them in the high street discount retailer Sports Direct, which is consistently one of the worst-vibes shops in the entire United Kingdom. There is an unusual windowless darkness to Sports Direct stores, the possibility of chaos: great towering displays of current-season soccer jerseys, huge bins of puntable £5 Sondico footballs, a rack of discount jogging bottoms, a child's stickily discarded Capri Sun tucked between some leggings. Sports Direct is where people go to buy equipment for a sport they're not sure they're ever going to take seriously – this is where you buy shinpads when your girlfriend's brother invites to you astroturf five-a-side and says you can't play without them, that's the rule, no honestly mate a guy on our team got fined – but it's also a weird magnet for the feral outer flaps of the Great British High Street, which every town has. There's always a guy with two haircuts yelling. Someone holds their hands up to their chest and walks with a strange trudging limp. Pre-pubescent boys with nonetheless threatening auras work around the place in packs. Someone seems to be eating from a bottomless bag of chips. In the distance, yelled into the phone, you can hear one side of a custody battle. Each Sports Direct store is somehow like this, somehow dark and similar: the size of the shop on the inside never equates to the outside of it; it is impossible to know what time it is in a Sports Direct store; without realising it, you have acquired a large mug. Culturally, though not *good*, these places are vital to the British psyche. Nowhere else can you buy a five-pack of Puma running socks while a Snapchat drug dealer, a heart-attack weekend dad and five hundred hard-faced women with prams queue far too closely behind you. You wonder in previous generations where the people with this energy would go before society invented Sports Direct to briefly house them: would they be drawn like glowing stones along the same leylines? Would they be driven by a power they couldn't sense to these same rune-engraved locations? Beneath every Sports Direct there is something dark and glowing and evil. Beneath every Sports Direct there is a thin penetrable membrane where you can reach out and touch Hell.

I went into Sports Direct and bought the shoe. While I was waiting for a shop assistant to go into a cavernous back warehouse and find a size 11, an eight-year-old boy without any visible mother or father just came and stood next to me. He had scabs on both elbows and sucked noiselessly at a long-melted ice pole.

It's a good trainer. It has a surprisingly hard tappy sole and a good stiff amount of bounce. I feel like if I hit a good sturdy wooden floor in it at just the right angle it would make this noise in a very satisfying way: *cuh—CAUK!* It does not make me think about it as an object, it does not demand to be the star of the show, it does not make me queue overnight for it: it sits beneath my trousers (blue; black) and protects my feet from injury and wind, and then I ease it off and kick it under the sofa.

I have been intrigued about the Hi Tec Squash shoe for a number of years because it has always been a foundational component in a mental game I like to play called, 'It Is The Apocalypse And You Are Locked In A Shopping Centre And For Some Reason You Need To Get A Fit Off'.

The idea behind this game is simple: whenever I am daydreaming, I normally think about how I'd do in an apocalypse event (and, at this stage, it feels like 'zombie' is the most likely), and my Plan A is always to go to a small town centre shopping centre with lockable shutters. The shopping centre has everything I'll need (an entire McDonald's! An entire Nando's with a deep-freeze!), weapons supplies (baseball bats! Flammable liquids!), huge expansive courts where you can see a zombie or something crawling at you from afar, a cinema, a bed shop, a bookshop, &c. And also, crucially, a number of clothes shops so I can spend the two years it takes for the zombie threat to recede totally finally refining my personal style.

The thing is, it's hard to actually put a good outfit together from Britain's high streets: their shops are either New Looks, River Islands, Topshops (too cheap for me to get a good fit together from; too fundamentally trend-led and young), JD Sports and Superdrys and All Saints (you have to either be 24 or have the confidence of one of those *X Factor* auditionees they only put on TV as a joke to pull them off), Urban Outfitters (*everyone* locked in a shopping centre for two years will be wearing Urban Outfitters), or GAP (trousers and hoodies *only*, no other clothes from GAP!). I can get underwear from Weekday but then I'll shred all of the actual clothes there for blankets and insulation. There are probably about three or

FOUR STARS

four things I can forage from TK Maxx but it sort of depends how closely the apocalypse fell before delivery day. Uniqlo can do a lot of my basics but you've got to really hope the end of the world falls during one of those months where they have Uniqlo U stuff in and not a load of those anime t-shirts they do. I can probably get some jeans and some good leather boots out of the dad section of John Lewis but that's about it. I will keep any prisoners I take in Primark, where the dizzying smell and atmosphere of the place will send them all mad. Due to the presence of a Boots, a Superdrug, a Holland & Barrett and a Kiehl's, I'll somehow end up walking out of this life-transforming experience looking younger and fresher than I ever did in real life. Whoever the remaining survivors have anointed as their Prime Minister or King or Emperor or whatever will marvel and shake my hand.

What was I—? Oh, right, yeah, so I went to the pub and Dan said, "Nice shoes!" and I said yeah they are my zombie apocalypse shoes and he said, "I don't know what that means" then took a really long drink of his drink and after that I wasn't really in the mood for anything so when Clee showed I made up an excuse and left, but the point is: the point is I do not need to keep caring about trainers anymore if I just wear one very simple normal trainer all the time, and that now cuts a lot of stress out of my day-to-day. Is it bad I think I'd be happier about what my feet look like while the world is on the brink of ending? On second thought I don't wish to think about the answer to that. I want to go on the Hi Tec website and see if they do any other colours or styles. **FIVE STARS**

ASKING A FRIEND FOR MONEY THAT HE TECHNICALLY OWES YOU BUT IT'S BEEN QUITE A LONG TIME NOW AND YOU FEEL AWKWARD BRINGING IT UP EVEN THOUGH IS IT YOUR MONEY AND ALSO YOUR NEED FOR THE MONEY IS NOW GREATER THAN WHEN YOU FIRST LENT IT, WHICH IN ITSELF IS EMBARRASSING, EVEN THOUGH AGAIN: IT IS YOUR MONEY

I saw Pete waiting outside the Tube station for a bus and though I thought about turning around and hiding in a shop or something there wasn't really any suitable shop there – just a kiosk that sells sweets and cigarettes and newspapers to an audience of nobody, and that's not an actual shop it's just a stand, and though I did try to hide in it for a second I rapidly realised that wasn't really working, plus I knocked a load of Fruit Pastilles over and had to pick them up off the floor and the guy was like "leave it, leave it, leave it PLEASE, just LEAVE IT!", like he was getting quite agitated at me personally despite my very clear attempts to help – and also Pete had spotted me and started taking his headphones out so I bit the inside of my mouth down really hard then smiled then walked over and said "Hi" and then "How Are You". He said he was good.

"I've been meaning to text you actually. We were all talking about you at Ed Warburton's housewarming party."

FOUR STARS

"Ed Warburton has a house?"

"Yeah he bought it with his fiancée."

"He *bought* it?"

"Yeah. Up in Green Lanes."

"How did *Ed Warburton* buy a house?"

"I don't know. With money? He's been really busy. Plus he got that book deal. It's really good to see you!"

— and all the air escapes my lungs, and the ton of metal that sits atop of my head at all times doubles in size, and the colours were sucked from the sky, and a bus in a faded shade of red whirred past me as my heart pumped hard in my neck. Of course, of course, of course. The universe is a complicated joke where I am the sole living punchline. Ed Warburton has a book deal.

"I thought you stopped hanging out with him, anyway?"

"No. Ed's a nice guy."

"I know but I thought I told you that I hated him. That he's a hack, a talentless hack. And he's my mortal enemy."

"I thought that was a joke."

"Why would I joke about that?"

"So you really wanted me to *stop hanging out with Ed Warburton*, a guy whose *stag do I went on*, because you don't like him very much since they gave him your TV column?"

"It's a different column, but yes."

"Joel, that's like. That's insane."

That helped. I told him he still owed me £500 from that time he started a vintage hat reselling business in the exact month the terms and conditions of his student overdraft changed and that I would like it back now please, and a bank transfer is fine, and even though he pulled a bit of a face about it he said "OK" and "Fine" and then we both got our banking apps out and started trying to arrange the transfer but then because it was over a certain limit we realised we couldn't do it from our phones right now he'd need to go home and use that calculator thing to set me up as a new payee but he promised to do it as soon as he got in and even though I detected a tone he did seem honest about that, at least. I asked him how the hat business was and basically he had to shutter that because it turns out not that many people like buying hats quite as compulsively as he did and he's a photographer now instead and doing really well, which part of me felt really good about on his behalf, and part of me felt this horrible cold sickening roil of jealousy, and part of me thought about that phone call from the bank I had the other week that asked me if I'd opened another account at a rival bank and started getting all my money paid into that instead because they only see money going out, they don't see any money coming in, and I had to pause a really long time before saying, "No."

Anyway I must have zoned out for a bit because Pete was like, "I think that's my bus, yeah that's my bus, yeah I really have to go but I'll send that money through later, yeah?" When I turned around the kiosk guy was picking up a packet of Fruit Pastilles that had split open and unravelled onto the wet pavement so I

FOUR STARS

ducked out of there, and to be fair to Pete the £500 did come through later on when I was lying in bed bathed insane in the blue-white light of my laptop looking up what Ed Warburton's book is about, which is a manifesto on modern masculinity that *The Times* already said is really important and he definitely got six-figures for it and honestly maybe even seven. Really bad day actually, one of my worst. **ZERO STARS**

THE LIFT UP TO SUSHI SAMBA, AND THEN BACK DOWN AGAIN

The richer you get in London, the more of it you are allowed to see: height, in this city, belongs to the middle and upper classes, and the more of it you earn the higher you are allowed to look down on the city from (this is why the highest I've lived is 'up three staircases'). There are a couple of exceptions – if I look out of my window now I can see a couple of 18-storey tower blocks – but the point of them is, from the highest window in the building, if you look down *there is nothing to look down on*. There's a car park and a bus stop that kids keep kicking the windows out of. There is 'one newsagent'. There is no point being high because there is no view. But crawl closer to the city, the dark beating heart of it, and you can scale dizzying heights to the centre of its soul, stare down and see the claws. To wit: tonight I am going to Sushi

Samba, in the Sushi Samba lift. The lift to Sushi Samba is the best bit.

The lift to Sushi Samba is an incredible lift. When you step into it, it creaks and splutters with its own weight – it is a notably heavy lift, a sensation that you shouldn't be able to ascertain from standing within it. The lift ascends slowly, headily, digital displays telling you arid facts about the restaurant you are going to, and as it rises — *pop!* — your ears feel the pressure. But the journey from the ground to Sushi Samba is not about the lift, it's about the transformation: the street, with its street sounds and that urgent feeling you just had crossing over from the Tube station because the booking was for 7.15 and it was 7.14 and apparently they are really fucking tight about the booking times, melts down into the ambience. Buildings you look up at from the ground suddenly seem small, blocky, squat. You can squint and peer but you won't see the gum on the pavements, the McDonald's box folded and run over in the road, or that guy who said something incomprehensible but in a very harsh threatening voice to you while sitting in a sleeping bag outside Tesco. All you see is the rich splendour of the city unfold in front of you, like a velvet blanket: the purr of billions and billions of pounds of infrastructure, cranes rising blinking into the sky, always building, building, building. London will never be 'finished', you realise, in the lift to Sushi Samba. You are gazing at one glorious, finite snapshot of it.

Megan pointed out we hadn't been on a date for many many months and though I wanted to explain

FOUR STARS

the very simple reason for that – it feels like a steam engine is operating inside my head! The pressure is unbearable, the pressure is immense! My skull could half-explode, my teeth just cracking in half, my jaw misaligning, hold for a heartbeat, and then full explode, like a watermelon dropped off a dam, at any second! – but I could already tell that wasn't worth articulating and would only lead to an argument about like 'having therapy' again, so I booked Sushi Samba over the phone and when they told me the deposit I had to put on my card to secure the table I swallowed hard twice and in a very weak voice agreed to it. As protest against this, against being cornered into taking my own girlfriend on a date, I did not iron my shirt. I realised in the lift up to Sushi Samba, my own gauzy semi-reflection staring back at me, that this had only punished myself. I looked like a moron, I looked like a buffoon.

"What are you having?" she says, which is a deeply uninteresting question. Look east and see the expanse of residentialia! Look down and see the gold of the city in banks! Look west and see glamour, and wealth, the ancient royal hunting grounds! Look south and see . . . well, nothing much. South's still shit.

"I never know with sushi. Just: sushi."

"Well there's meat as well."

"Alright then, meat."

"Well what meat?"

"I don't know [*the tape detects an audible low groan as we actually see the prices*] ah . . . OK."

"OK?"

"What's the . . . cheapest meat?"
"We could get something to share?"
"Mm."
"What?"
"I just don't like sharing food. It's never as fun as menus make you think."
"You think a menu is forcing me to think that?"
"HiguyscanIsetyouupwithsomedrinkstostartwith?"
"Yeah hey. Do you do beer?"
"We do beer!"
"Don't get a beer "
"Why not get a beer?"
"We're in a restaurant . . . it's a fancy meal."
"So I should order . . . 'not what I want'?"
"Well *I'm* getting a cocktail."
"Right. And are the cocktails good, here?"
"Ourbarstaffmakeaverynicecocktailyeah."
"Obviously the cocktails are nice here—"
"Alright I'll have one . . . I'll have one."
"Cocktail?"
"Yes."
"Which one?"
"It doesn't matter."

If I jumped off this building obviously I wouldn't survive the landing and they have thought about this (there are bars, there are security guys on the staircases) but the question isn't whether I would survive it (no.) but more how exactly I would explode on impact. Most falls from height are just that dull, disappointing thud, aren't they: all the organs collapse inside the body at once, and you are just left looking grey and bruised like a hard apple. But just once, just once. Just once I'd like to think if I jumped off the top of Sushi Samba my body would explode into mist at the bottom. How many pavements have I imagined my own body on—

I don't even know why I came here: this isn't how I like to eat, this isn't how I like to flex, I feel like tugging at the collar of the shirt I didn't iron and gnashing at it like skin. None of this is real, in Sushi Samba. None of this is art. It's just high up and they plate it in the kind of way that you really should bring a ringlight along to photograph it correctly. But the vibe is that of a WeWork space. I constantly feel like I'm going to get a memo about something I don't care about. 'And for a special today we have braised beef and we're also planning a purge of all the bicycles, so please let reception know if you have a bicycle, parked here, that you want to keep, because otherwise we will be destroying all the—'

"How's your corn?"

"Yeah it's good."

"You said that in a very bright voice."

"Right."

"So does that mean you're lying?"

"I mean, it's corn. It tastes nice. I like it. I answered the question."

"Right."

"OK. *OK.*"

Is this good? It doesn't feel good. But does it not feel good because I don't feel good – I haven't done for months, I haven't done for years! I feel so bad that I'm wondering if I *ever* felt good! Is 'goodness' something that I ever experienced, or were all my feelings of what were good just context-dependent, and my whole life was cruising on a 6 out of 10 level and that's what I thought good was, and now it's down to a 2 I can't even envision the giddy heights of a 6? Is that it? Or does it not feel good because it isn't good? It's hard to know what's good and what's bad from the depths of the swamp. I'm eating a £24 pork rib and it feels like ash in my mouth.

This is the kind of restaurant where they leave you for 20 minutes after you ask for the bill and then leave you for 25 minutes more when they actually put the bill on your table, which always fills me with this unbearable antsy anxious energy that I can feel radiating out of my body like heat – fucking look at me! Take my debit card! I have eaten the corn! I do not want to be here anymore! – and in that waiting period Megan took the opportunity to go to the bathroom for a really really long time. I think she is done with me but our lives are too hard to extricate to break up on a whim so she has to really, really want to before she does it. But I also think she really really wants to because, well. I haven't cried for two years but I've also extremely *seemed* like I'm about to cry, constantly, for the entire duration of that same two years. Also I think she wants a life where … I think she wants a life where sometimes she can just watch a bit of *Desperate Housewives* without me making a whole thing about it. She wants a life with someone who will sometimes say, "Shall we have some fun? Let's

FOUR STARS

have some fun. I am both capable and willing to have fun, right now", which I do not.

She's loaded the bullet in the chamber and is gathering up the nuts to pull the trigger, then. This is the realisation I come to in the Sushi Samba lift, as the misty heavens of glittering London give way back to the solid square stodge of it, that heavy lift easing back down to street level, that last thrill of glamour – walking out past a velvet rope of people queueing to have the exact same edamame/Nashi Martini/ argument about work/curated playlist/suggested tip printed on the receipt experience you just had, all squinting at you as you walk to a tinted-out car trying to figure out if you're famous or not. On the way to the cab I step on a loose pavement slab (how can a pavement slab get loose? It's a slab. It's on a foundation of sand and shale which itself is on 'the entire planet earth'. What part got loose?) and a slosh of mud-grey rainwater seeps into my shoe, a reminder that I am back on the ground, back where I belong. But in the lift to Sushi Samba I was briefly weightless. In the lift to Sushi Samba I owned this city. Oh, s— she's just text me while we're both in the same cab together. "the driver really smells :-(". Yes, I know! Stop trying to force intimacy with me on the bare bones of our remains! Shoot me in the back of the head and put me out of my misery! **FIVE STARS FOR THE LIFT, ZERO STARS FOR THE EMOTIONAL TURMOIL AND FAIR PLAY FOUR STARS FOR THE PORK RIB WHICH WAS EXCEPTIONALLY JUICY**

BEING IN LOVE WITH MY GIRLFRIEND

I couldn't fall asleep after the pork rib and the wet foot and the cab driver with the smell and the cocktail and then the beer and the bill (the bill!) and Megan was fully honk-shoo asleep with her back turned to me so I sat in an uneasy half-slumber and thought about how much I loved her, actually, and how this was actually going to be awful once she finally does it. How pathetic to be in love with someone! How weak it makes you! I always liked to think I was capable of flailing through life on my own truly independent course – shouldering people out of the way and being vulgar and horrible and impulsive and stupid and self-destructive and selfish! No gods no masters! I serve only myself! All for me, baby! *All for me*! – but instead like an idiot I've become fucking soul-bonded to another person and I'm constantly doing things to make myself better in the vain hope that it will please or impress her even one little bit. You think you're cool and you think you're fully formed and then you realise you love eating dinner with one person in particular and seeing them get out of the shower and making up little songs to sing to them on the sofa and then it's like great, great. Can't wait for this to be torn out of my life and leave a huge, raw, nerve-shredded gaping hole in my chest that takes months to heal if it ever heals at all. Very cool, very sick.

I love: I love that she mopes about the house in a huge hooded dressing gown that stinks and has coffee stains all down it, and the fact that she can never leave the house on time. I love the fact that she walks around the house when she brushes her teeth instead of just brushing her teeth in the bathroom like a normal person, so I just hear this *brrrrr!* following me around the house and then maybe she'll try and say something through the foam because somehow she's still never learned that you can't speak and brush your teeth at the same time. Or: I love the mad vampiric way she sleeps with her hands clasped, like she's moved over and is doing now, or the little muttering murmurs she makes under her breath when she's deep asleep. I love that she peers back to make sure the dog is OK every time she goes to the bar (there is no better way to spend a Saturday afternoon than having a beer with my girlfriend! It *sucks* that I won't ever get to do it again!) and that she's deeply in love with Paul Mescal but never admits she's in love with Paul Mescal. I love that she goes to gigs without me because she understands going to gigs is like being screamed at for two hours, for me, and she implicitly understands that I cannot stack the dishwasher, because of my agonies, so just quietly does it for me. I love her A5 wagyu tits and her beautiful mouth and the fact that she's always trying to do something semi-mad with her hair, and she never eats pizza crusts (she can make a pizza last all day: the perfect Sunday is both of us rolling awake, her murmuring into her dressing gown me wearing jogging bottoms like a real person, then ordering large pizzas and eating them together spread out on the sofa over the course of a day, hands lazily reaching across and interlocking, occasionally clasping occasionally not, while she rewatches *New Girl* for about the five hundredth, maybe six hundredth time, even the later seasons when it really goes off the boil). I love that she's allergic to beer but still fucking drinks beer and that she's really, weirdly good at catching and that she always beats me at pool somehow even though she isn't particularly good at pool and I take pool really seriously but I still don't really mind when she beats me. She does this really good comedy face – she raises her eyebrows cartoonishly and puckers her mouth into a snooty old society madame's rumple – and whenever she's trying a new handbag out at a shop I always knows when she feels cute with it because she holds it delicately up to her chest like a meerkat. I like to buy her tulips, and Creme Eggs, and the vegan mayonnaise she likes, and even though she doesn't really have a sweet tooth she's always really happy with a big wet tray of baklava. I love that she always tries to be friends with the neighbours even though I have a very firm anti-neighbours policy and then I always fucking end up somehow involved in some bullshit with the neighbours. I love that she always loses her glasses and always loses her phone, too, but somehow never breaks it, only loses it. I love that she always, *always* remarks on how much a pint costs – if it's a lot, or if it's surprisingly cheap, or even if it's just an average price – and that she is addicted to telling people that information. I love that she slithers in cold as hell from nights out and clonks into every single piece of furniture on the way to the bed then says, "Hello, I *love* you!" to the dog 500 times then writhes in like an S-shape next to me, freezing like an ice cube, then starts snoring ten to fifteen seconds later. That she gets really loud when she's drunk but doesn't really know it, and loves barking a horrible emo song into a karaoke microphone, and has 900 pairs of nearly identical black leather boots but still always knows which exact ones she wants to wear that night even if she can't find them. That she shows me when other boys DM her so I can just laugh and call them losers and I love how just completely safe I've always felt about our relationship until now, until me being a human block of ice has finally ruined it. I love that she listens to the worst music on earth but rarely makes me listen to it too, so there's some odd form of respect in there. That we're always bumping into her friends when we're out because so many people adore her, and that she can't be in the house without some sort of sound going on (a TV show! The radio! An app! All three!), and that she is so besotted with the dog she thinks every dog looks like our dog even though our dog is perfect and all other dogs *wish* they looked like our dog. I love that she *never* knows what colour to paint her nails. That she cooks dinner like way more than I do and it's not a big thing but it's also the nicest thing that regularly happens to me. That she's barely said anything about me going insane and buying six hundred books in a 25-month period and in fact the only action she really took was to source some very tasteful and affordable bookshelves for me to put them on from a nearby seller. I love stroking her pubes as I go to sleep and even though she hates it she very rarely says "stop doing that" unless I'm stoned and doing it very erratically, and I love that she's always stealing my hats and my coats because when she steals them that means they're cool. I love that whenever I get ready to leave the house and she says "you look nice" I walk out feeling a foot-and-a-half taller, and I love that she's weirdly handy (due to an accident I got a toothpaste cap lodged in the sink, the toothpaste cap the exact perfect diameter of the sink hole, and she got it out using a power drill, and when she held the cap aloft I just thought: *I love you I love you I love you*), and I love that she's human and she has all these things going on and she still finds time in the great swooping whirl to love me and it's like, *thank you, obviously*, but I am insane right now so I can't do it back. And I love that she's waited this long and let me have this much of her. I'm just going to hold on really tight to her ribs and kiss the big knot of ponytail at the back of her head. Tomorrow, or next Thursday, or two weeks from now, that's going to suck. But for now, for the last few gasps of it— **FIVE STARS**

THIS ACHE I'VE HAD IN MY SHOULDER FOR NINE (?) DAYS NOW AND KNOW I'M NEVER GOING TO DO ANYTHING ABOUT

I've got an ache in my shoulder now – sort of like a stitch? Sort of like a pinch? I don't know – up in the bit where the shoulder meets your neck, that gelatinous little meaty part. I don't often think about eating a human body, and where I would start on eating a human body – to be clear, only in a deeply urgent survival situation, not as a German bondage sex thing – but I do think the particular bit of shoulder I am talking about would make for a good lunch: pan-fried, lots of nice brown fond in the pan, a little baste maybe, like a cute little pork chop. I do good roast potatoes (fingerlings could be nice with this actually – just-crushed, lots of good salt and garlic and rosemary, absolutely seared in the oven) and the roast potatoes would go well with it. You kind of need a bitter green with all that. The more I think about this the more I think maybe this is a path I shouldn't be skipping down. I'm turning back before I end up on the 'perma-banned from FetLife' government watchlist I'm aimed like a missile for.

Anyway my shoulder hurts, and it's unlikeable. If I lay in bed and scroll on my phone then it hurts my phone-scrolling hand, but it's hard to know if this is a phone-scrolling injury or not – perhaps I need to reappraise how I sit in my office, maybe I need to do more deep yogic stretching. Maybe I just need to leave the house more and go for a walk. Fundamentally, the aching nag of the pain reminds me, constantly, that I'm not going to do anything about this: what am I going to do, see a doctor? "Hello, I have a small but not inconvenient pinch in my shoulder. On a pain scale I would rate it between a 2 and a 1. Can I have intrusive surgery to fix it?" Nor am I going to go to a chiropractor, or get a massage. Here's what I'm going to do: nothing, with a side order of 'wincing sometimes' and perhaps telling people about it. Occasionally I might affect a pained, deep-in-thought looking self-massage if sat alone somewhere while trying to look like an intellectual. Maybe I will find a new way of wearing backpacks, now. But this is just the reality of my life: my shoulder hurts, a little, an unexplained nagging ache, and now I am just A Person Who Has A Throbbing Twinge. It was only yesterday that I was 21. It was only the day before that that I was smooth and soft and eight years old and dumb. Now if I stand up too abruptly I go, "ah!" in a very small voice. It's just a minor little twinge in my shoulder, nowhere near the only agony I'm feeling right now, but it is a nagging little reminder that the grave is approaching faster than I'd like to think. **ONE STAR**

GETTING A PAPER CUT

I just got a paper cut in that gnarly long webbing section between the thumb and the forefinger, which I think we can all agree is the worst place to get a paper cut. I sort of knew it was coming as soon as I took the sheet of A4 out of the sheath it comes in: I heard, rather than felt, the half-textured dragging sound of paper packed too tightly, and then a sharp hot sting, and then my hand is in my mouth, no blood. It hurts in a way that is annoying: ambiently there, throbbing in a whisper, an almost-pain that has put all my other fingers on edge – like whacking a mob guy to prove a point about not ratting, then sensing anxiety in the ranks (it is actually exactly like that.) – and the cut is in that awkward position where anything more complicated than just holding my palm open above my head reopens and rejigs the slice. Days of this, then. Typing this is obviously uncomfortable in a deeply tragic way. But more than that I am embarrassed because a paper cut is such a childish, nothingy injury, like hurting yourself biting a fork, or stepping in a mess of dog shit, or falling bodily into a clutch of nettles. I used to get paper cuts all the time as a child, and then I got over it, because I wasn't an idiot anymore, and I had a healthy and casual respect for the edges of a piece of paper. This is the same reason I haven't skinned my knees for well over a decade, or why I haven't had a nosebleed during this millennium. It's doubly embarrassing because the only reason I was touching the piece of paper was to take it out of the huge sheath of paper I bought two and a half years ago when I bought a printer and have printed like seven things since (I will live fifty more years and not use up all this paper). It's triply embarrassing because the thing I was printing out was a coupon to get a free burrito. I know I'm going to get to the shop and they're going to look at this coupon like it's an alien artefact. Like they're going to go back and get a manager who also won't know what it means. Like why build the infrastructure of a free burrito coupon on your website – with the barcode, with the QR code, with the in-app activation! You made me put my e-mail address in, and then sent a confirmation e-mail, and I know I'm getting newsletters from you now forever until I die! – then not warn a single shop that this is happening, give anyone the special laser gun their till needs to read it. And I know there's going to be a queue forming all behind me while somehow three people get confused by reading the same very simple terms and conditions. I know there are going to be hurried people just in for a burrito bowl extra guac (I am going to have to pay for my own guacamole. I know this already. I have read the website. A pathetic little debit card transaction of £1.25) (I already know the manager is going to explain this fact to me with the solemnity a doctor might affect to tell me that I'm terminal). These people, these queue people. They think they're so special because they're standing in a queue. That's the rule, you idiots! Queueing is all that separates us from the animals! You're nothing! You're unspecial! You're

FOUR STARS

nothing! How dare you look at me and think: *why does that large man need a free burrito so badly?* And think: *how has his life got to this point that he can't just pay six, maybe six pounds fifty for a burrito. Why did he have to go through the humiliation of the coupon.* The cost isn't the point!, I want to say. It's the principle! I'm going to just end up yelling at a queue, aren't I. "Leave me alone!" I'm yelling. "I just got a pretty bad paper cut!" Nobody will care. I can already feel it, as I fold it up huge into my wallet: I am never going to use this coupon, because I am already pre-ashamed. This whole adventure was a bust. May as well just go to the pub already. This day is over. **ZERO STARS**

VIOLENCE

I was in the Surrey Quays Tesco late on a Saturday night (I'd taken myself to see *Mission: Impossible* on my own, but when I got there the only other people in the screening were also just men on their own, spaced out very carefully so as not to encroach on each other's personal space, which would be rich material for a Urinal Problem-style mathematical paper if the subject weren't so deeply depressing) (the film itself was a solid 4 out of 5: no one gets the blockbuster thrill of drinking a big deep Coke at the cinema and watching a stunt like Tom Cruise does) because I've been consuming a lot of Instagram content about new food releases in the UK and there was a certain new brand of American-style mustard I wanted but I went all around the jar and condiment aisles and couldn't find it. Jar and condiment aisles in large British supermarkets are soothing places to lose some calm quiet minutes of your life: all sorts of strange harissa pastes, weird new things they are doing with mayonnaise, toffee spreads, bolshy new hot sauce brands (my, personal, catnip), little tubs of breadcrumbs or crispy onions to sprinkle over a pasta. My head spins in the jar and condiment aisle, my pupils dilate, I browse in wonder. But they didn't have the fucking mustard I wanted even though @newfoodsuk said it would be out last Thursday so I gave up and went to see if they had a couple of cold beers for the extremely long train back.

Obviously the thing with supermarkets is they have the *cold* beers in a completely different section to the *beers* part of the supermarket, because the beer aisle is a load of unchilled cans or multipack boxes that you are supposed to chill at home or keep in the garage, and the actual chilled beers you want to drink now are actually at the front of the shop with the 'Dine In For £10' meal kits, meaning the only beers I had to choose from were two big bottles of Kingfisher, which I don't really like exactly but at this point who cares. I got my two big bottles and a cheap bottle opener (after years and years and years of going to supermarkets and buying beers to have on the train home, I have still somehow neglected to ever buy a keyring-sized bottle opener, meaning I own six or seven flimsy corkscrews because I always have to do this exact thing)

FOUR STARS

and headed to the front, which is where the shouting was coming from.

Shouting is a fun quirk of ours, isn't it? You can't really ever help shouting. Nobody ever intentionally shouts, really. Shouting is a sign that you've lost the wavering control you have on your emotions and you are now in a thrall to them, and to show that, you are really loud. I don't really know what the shouting was about – someone kept being called a "PUSSY!", someone else kept burbling into a walkie talkie, someone took their top off, there was lots of lunging and skittish footwork – but essentially a quite lively guy was being accused of shoplifting or something by an out-of-his-depth security guard and now both of them were yelling at each other. People just stopped to watch – swaddling big packs of toilet roll like babies, holding their car keys and a four-pint bottle of milk in the same clawed hand, holding two bottles of Kingfisher and wondering idly if they could just walk out with the Kingfisher while this was all happening, because surely that's better than paying for Kingfisher – and then the guy with his top off got a big jar of artisan white beans off a shelf (I was just round there, looking at the artichokes!) and threw it on the floor, smashing it entirely. Brine and glass and legumes spiked across the floor. For a dull grey beat I remembered the boy. A moment of silence, and then it really kicked off.

NEANDERTHAL GOLBY: Ooh agh oohb ubb ihh
ME: Yeah I know I should. Yep.

NEANDERTHAL GOLBY: Ohb ach

ME: OK but would they really notice if I—

NEANDERTHAL GOLBY: Oub

ME: How do you have more of a moral code than me? Didn't you used to have sex with your cousins?

NEANDERTHAL GOLBY: Ibb oog ach ebb oh ebb oh

ME: Yeah, yeah. Well I mean the thing is – despite my gorgeous, large physique, inherited over many many generations from you – I'm not actually very good at fighting.

NEANDERTHAL GOLBY: Oob ig

ME: I think the last significant fight I had was against Archie Langmead in Year 8. And he was about a foot shorter than me. He just wanted it more. He got me in some sort of headlock and rammed me into the door of a car belonging to one of the Spanish teachers.

NEANDERTHAL GOLBY: [*Primitive laughing sounds*]

ME: Yeah the alarm did go off, yeah. Everyone saw.

I don't even know how I ended up in that fight with Archie Langmead: I was just walking around the playground, idly wondering whatever it was I wondered at that age – "should I get into Warhammer? Are my testicles unusually small or just small in a normal way? Will my brain be able to withstand the graphical power of the PlayStation 2® without going mad?" – when I walked past a crowd of kids from my form in a

FOUR STARS

circle fighting with kids from Archie Langmead's form. I got tugged into the crowd then pushed into the colosseum, and Archie Langmead came at me, tiny like a squirrel, his little battery-sized fists held high. I think I said something along the lines of, "You alright Archie?" and then he got on me, the headlock and then the canary-yellow Seat Ibiza and then the car alarm. My glasses got all bent out of shape and I had to go to the opticians to straighten them. Of course if I saw Archie Langmead now I would simply pick him up and throw him in a canal. He is *nothing*. But back then that was the moment I realised violence wasn't for me – I didn't have the reflexes, I didn't have the urge, I didn't have the right need.

NEANDERTHAL GOLBY: Oogh ebg gha bih gah bouh?
ME: Yeah that's been about it since then. Oh no there was that Deliveroo driver who got off his moped to call my girlfriend a "cunt", but—
NEANDERTHAL GOLBY: Ogg?
ME: Yeah ahm. Hmm. I suppose my main weakness in that fight was failing to account for the fact that he was wearing a moped helmet. And those are quite hard. And so when I tried to punch his head, I punched his moped helmet.
NEANDERTHAL GOLBY: Oohg ahb igh boo bouh gouh. Obh BAH gibb ouh bo.
ME: Yeah no he hit me way harder. In . . . in the head.
NEANDERTHAL GOLBY: Ough—?

ME: And yes I fell over on my ass and cried. Are you watching me from the spirit realm, or something?

NEANDERTHAL GOLBY: Ough agh bigh boh "birri bealm"

ME: Yeah OK. I suppose the main point is I eschew violence, not from any particular moral standpoint, but just because I'm bad at it, my body doesn't make the unthinking calculations necessary for me to pull it off. But I'm going to have to go and walk over there quite closely, aren't I, and just sort of hover nearby it as if I might be good at violence, aren't I? That's the 'good citizen' thing to do.

NEANDERTHAL GOLBY: [*Really long sent of grunts I won't translate here but basically detailed this time he crushed another guy's head with a perfectly round rock – he spent more time going on about the rock, the roundness and the smoothness of it, than the actual red-raw crushing of the skull, which distantly made me wonder if he'd read* Blood Meridian *lately with his finger pressed hard to the page – and he did that because the other guy, from two caves over, 'drank from his lake'*]

ME: Right. And you think that's good, do you?

I went over and stood kind of near the incident (not too near: I had a new pair of Munchens on and I didn't want to get brine on the suede) and said a pacifying "everything alright here, mate?" and the security guard gave me a dismissive wave but the other guy was still shouting (and at some point he did say "and what is this big mong doing? Kingfisher *bitch*") but after a couple of minutes of no actual swinging fists the violence, as these things tend to do, ebbed away, and everyone walked quietly away from the incident sort of embarrassed. This is another thing with violence: it does take up a lot of energy to sustain these levels of unshackled emotion – the kind of energy that might come out of you as tears or it might come out of you as war cries, you never quite know until it bulges – and it makes you think how anyone ever sustained enough of this to get through a great big clanking field battle in olden days. Did they not get embarrassed, swinging at each other with axes in great metal suits? Did they not collectively get tired or bored, 90 seconds into battle, when the first sting of violence wore off? Anyway I paid for my Kingfisher (you don't get a peacemaker discount for hovering sort of near a security guard when it's all kicking off at Tesco Extra, so I have noted that down for next time it happens – you're on your own) and the bottle opener bent itself out of shape opening the first bottle so I just had to carry the other one home on the train until it got all warm. But I mean realistically when am I going to drink that? So that's just going to be in my fridge, forever, then. **TWO STARS**

PINTS

I have a theory that the perfect weight, of anything in the world, is a pint of beer. This is because a pint of beer does not weigh a specific amount: a pint of beer is 568ml, yes, which is more or less 568g, also yes, but that is not including the glass, which is also conducive to the overall 'perfect weight' (568g of beer in a plastic cup does not weigh the right amount, because the *vessel* does not weigh the right amount: go to a corporate-sponsored day festival and you will know this) (a pint of beer in a tankard? Heh, brother, you have gone too far. It is now too heavy. You have blasted right past perfection in your bid to look like a goth). But you cannot fill a pint glass with 568ml of water and expect the same results, either: there is something ephemeral to the beer itself, some additional heft evident in the liquid – the way it fizzes, the *swish* – that adds to the overall effect. The perfect weight on earth, therefore, is: 568ml of beer (it must be beer! Lager is best for this but arguments have been made for IPA and stout, too!) + the standard British pint glass + something else, something other: magic, tradition, history. What is it? Take another sip. I cannot tell, either. What is it? The liquid is going down but the weight still feels correct. What is going on, here? All forms of logic and sense are inverted. And now you've got a little buzz going.

It feels pertinent to remark on this. The best pints aren't just a pint, they're a stolen little moment of calmness: a simple Good Thing in an unrelenting mire of Bad Ones. Pints are rarely about the pint – in the right context, a perfect pint could be something as simple and as low as a Foster's! Though not Carlsberg. Never Carlsberg. – and are instead about the moments that led up to the pint (and the subsequent moments the pint promises: will you go home, euphorically giddy off the energy of a single stolen pint between the Tube and your house? Or will you have seven more pints and start sending some incredibly risky DMs and texts?). You watch the pour, you watch the pint snuggle and smear itself on the bar towel, you grasp it at the top with your spidered-out fingers, you remark on the perfect weight, you take a big frothy pull, and: *ahh*. That is what a pint is. That is a pint, right there.

THE GREATEST PINTS OF MY LIFE (SO FAR), NO PARTICULAR ORDER GIVEN BECAUSE I DO NOT WANT TO OVERSUBSCRIBE IMPORTANCE TO ONE PINT OVER THE OTHERS IN CASE THE PINTS – WHICH HAVE BEEN DRUNK BY ME AND PISSED OUT BY ME AND EXIST NOW AS ONLY SEWAGE ON ITS WAY TO THE SEA, REMEMBER – SOMEHOW 'GET OFFENDED';

1. On a dry-sunny July evening in 2018, I put in my greatest ever football performance on a bobbly low-angled pitch in that anonymous park behind the back of Brick Lane, and celebrated with a Litovel (top) in the nearby Star of Bethnal Green.

JOEL GOLBY

First, the football performance, which was close to perfect: for some reason that day my normally conservative, short-passing, slightly afraid defensive play was replaced by surging, roaming, un-markable running up the left wing (and then switching inside to the right whenever their defenders got too comfortable – I was everywhere! I was a monster!), scoring two and setting up six or seven. Everything was just *on* that day: my first touch was Berbatovian, I muscled through players who were bigger and heavier than me, I saw the pitch from a 360-degree angle, I was making through-passes and dinks and perfect pitch-crossing switches. I have, simply, never played like that, before or since, and it helps too that the air was so dry and dusty, and the sun setting so woozily from a high white to a low yellow to a dusky orange, and so many of my friends got to see and marvel at this astonishing performance, and I did it all in a white cotton t-shirt that smeared with the dust of other players' hands trying to catch me and seeped yellow-grey with the huge triangles of sweat my body was pumping out. After playing to exhaustion we all walked bandily back to the pub, where I ordered a single pint of Litovel topped up with a shot of lemonade, and stood in the ragtag beer garden, as some jolly faces sloped off home and more came through to replace them, watching the sun finally set purple behind me and everyone came up in turn, arm snaking three-pint unsteady around my still-damp shoulders, and told me how

FOUR STARS

fucking well I had played today, man, I've never seen anything like it—

2. On my first trip to Brighton the train was severely delayed, rendered rigid on the tracks for over an hour, before crawling along through to the coastline, and by the time we actually got there we were panting, caked with our own dry sweat, the air damp in the carriage and sand-dry at the station, and one of the first bars we passed as we dragged our roller-luggage uneasily down Queens Road was offering a two-for-one cocktail deal – my girlfriend at the time, as all girlfriends do, was enamoured with the cocktail deal – so I got her two margaritas that she pulled a face through while I drank one perfect crisp chalice of Stella, taken standing in the small street-side roped off area outside, and stared down the barrel of Queens Road as the sea sparkled blue and diamond-white beneath me. The wind was low and salty and sweet. The sun was high in the sky. And I knew the hotel room had a bath in it and as a direct result of that I was about to get some of the freakiest oral I'd ever got in my life—

3. On the day of the North London Derby – Arsenal 3, Tottenham 1 – after four pints of Guinness and a plate of actually very serviceable Pad Thai, I ambled across Putney Bridge in the direction of a used bookshop. The sun was high in the unseasonably warm blue sky; the river frittered lazily beneath me; the puttered honks and squawks of ducks and geese. I bought eight books with change from a £20 note then decamped to a nearby pub, huge and

cavernous and almost completely empty, where I sipped my way through a simple pint of Guinness while reading a Roald Dahl short story about how he was the only real hero in every single war. It was one of those glorious, endless pints, and every sip I took – little tiny fluttering sips, little mini gasps of beer, like a perfect little bird pecking at the foam! – seemed to take nothing out of the pint, and it remained chilled and settled and stout as I worked my way down through the short story and then on to the weekend crossword. In the background, at a low companionable volume, *Soccer Saturday* burbled away. I didn't speak to another human being for the next two full hours (the second pint, not as good and as endless as the first, was ordered by the barman saying, "Same again?" and me issuing a thumbs-up – together we achieved harmony). The night descended from there – I drank about five more pints, missed the last Tube and had to go back to the bar with 1% of phone battery, asking around with strangers to see if I could borrow their charger, and of course nobody had an Android charger because it was West London and they all had iPhones over there, and in the end I didn't get home until around midnight, thoroughly exhausted, bloated with pints, still carrying all these fucking books around in a repurposed Bag For Life – but for a few minutes there, somewhere between 2 p.m. and 3, I achieved it. I achieved nirvana—

FOUR STARS

4. My birthday fell on a Saturday in 2021 and after having 'quite sinister mental health' for about ten consecutive months I was delighted to start my day with a perfectly hazy over-engineered IPA – notes of cream soda, notes of mango, notes of lemongrass, notes of pepper – poured straight from the taps at my favourite brewery. My girlfriend was smiling and pretty. My dog was well-behaved and wearing a little jumper. The whole day was mine and nobody wanted me for anything. My shoulders relaxed for the first time in weeks. I did not at any point ask how much the pint cost—

5. One stolen Saturday me and the boys met up at a pub by my house at noon on the dot and racked up five of the most fiercely competitive, pendulum swinging games of pool ever committed to the bezel, Dan and I winning the series with the last ball in the last game with an outstanding cushion-bouncing near-impossible pot on the black. The pub was empty; the staff were still tinkering and tidying from the night before, restocking crisps and nuts, changing lines, fixing the projector to the wall. There was a quiet mutter of racing coverage on in the background but nothing much else. The roads outside were empty – normally clattering with trucks and buses and yelling cyclists pelting down the blue path, but for some reason it felt like everyone in the city was in a mellow, sleepy mood, and had chosen to stay more-or-less at home and quiet. I drank one pint of perfect, pure, clean Neck

Oil, then another, then one more plus a bag of Thai chilli-flavoured peanuts, and then we went somewhere – I don't really know, actually, just around, just janking about – but the taste on my lips all day was that first great pull of pint, that sweet lingering kiss of victory, the tangy spice of peanuts, the ambient joy of a Saturday well-started—

6. Michael helped me move one time, a debt I now owe him eternally, and though he did the very Michael thing of overcomplicating it – in the middle of the move we drove to and then spent several hours at an IKEA because his friend was expecting a baby and 'we had the van' so that, in his mind, logistically made sense, even though it meant at the end of the day we were doing all the moving (up two flights of stairs!) in quite angry-at-each-other silence, because it was so late and we were so tired and all the work, still, was left to do, but once we'd got all my books and jackets upstairs and I'd pinged a sheet and a duvet onto my bed we went to the second-nearest pub (the first-nearest was not giving me the correct vibe: I have an *incredibly* acute pub radar, which this did not pass, and actually I was right about this because eventually I did go to the first-nearest bar and the sister of a girl who I – through no fault of my own! – sent so mad she deleted Instagram forever was there, staring furiously at me, presumably because of the aforementioned, and that did all rather sour me on the overall atmosphere of that pub, which later, to my great relief, closed) and I bought him a

vodka-soda and myself a cheap, tall, cold, straightforwardly malty pint of Red Stripe, and I drank it outside as the new lights of my neighbourhood twinkled softly over the dark veil of the park, and Michael texted really really fast on his phone and said, "There's a party in Tottenham, do you want to go?" and I said, simply, *no*—

7. I had a particularly good pint of a foamy local ale at a pub in Hebden Bridge on the day of Queen Elizabeth's funeral, which obviously was not very ideal for her but was for me, because I'd had this long weekend booked for ages, before she died, and there was just something in the air that day – not, directly, the shroud of grief we were meant to all be feeling about it, but something weirder and actually far more enjoyable, a sort of free-day-off feeling that everyone seemed to have, people stunned to just not be at work on this particular Monday, people delighted to be around in the pub – and though I cannot remember the name of the ale exactly I had three to five more pints of it and then had this incredible conversation with a guy who told me his December tradition is to buy yule logs and eat them by slicing them in half, microwaving them for a few seconds until they are warm, then soaked in cream. "I probably go through about eight or nine logs a season," he said, and I blurred glowingly in and out of reality and thought: *yes, the Queen might be dead, but right now I am sat here with Britain's Greatest Thinker*—

8. 1 a.m., caked in dust and a day spent dancing until I sweated and then a night that was cold on top of

warm, a curious British kind of night temperature unique to this island, and it was day three of a festival and the smell of ash and fire was on the air, and the lines for the bar – glowing yellow in the night, the staff laughing and lazily mopping up spills, completely unbothered by any modicum of hospitality now, entirely in their own worlds – were empty, and I bought four plastic cups of Carlsberg and carried them up to a low hill where I sat next to one of my best friend of 20 years, shocked to silence by excess and a small amount of what we assume was MDMA that we found on the floor, and I watched a perfect DJ set while the wind lightly rustled the trees around us. We had been here when we were 19, and 29, too, and the tents were the same and the same scorched path of grass was trampled into the earth around us, and he hugged me roughly and tried to get some sort of sentence out, and then a strange boy who had lost his voice entirely shouting at the Foo Fighters the day before came and offered us both a Rennie, which we took gladly. The next day I woke up and felt like a bomb had hit me—

9. After a shifting, uncomfortable, leg-breaking long-haul flight to New York and a cab journey to the hotel and finally putting these bags down and taking these shoes off and being told no, no, you can't fall asleep now, it'll mess up your jetlag, I put on a sick Adidas x Arsenal track top and some perfectly cut jeans and went to the nearest bar we could find, which was an exceptionally movie-perfect

FOUR STARS

dive bar – sticky tables, bras and dollar bills pinned to the ceiling, strange toothless customers, loads of hand-drawn graffiti and vinyl stickers over every surface – and we had a few huge pints of Pabst or whatever made-up beer they have on draft there and made out shamelessly in the corner—

10. On an exceptionally fun group trip to a bowling alley I opted out of the rounds system to instead go to the bar upstairs and buy myself one single pint of Staropramen, which I drank alone on the balcony overlooking everyone dipping in and out of conversations with one another, whispering in ears and flirting and taunting and laughing, lopsided bowls and impossible strikes, and though it only took me away from the group for seven, maybe eight minutes, I came back and felt like my heart was soaring to be welcomed in again—

11. There is no worse place on earth than a British airport and there is no better thing to drink there than a single pint of beer, ideally if you have got there many hours early so you don't have to spent that time jittering around and trying to desperately find out where and when your gate opens, and instead stare at all these airport people doing airport things – walking around shouting into a phone while wearing a neck pillow, for instance, or five men who look like they have never met each other grimly drinking their way up to having enough energy for a stag do, or one of those bizarre people who buy luxury-brand handbags and sweatsuits at airports, wraparound shades and a diamanteéd hat,

always on FaceTime for some reason – while you slurp down first one pint of Hop House and then another. Soon you'll have to get up, and drag all this luggage around, and walk to a gate that got announced and then immediately flagged as 'Closing . . .', even though you know it isn't closing, and you and a hundred other people are going to quick-step towards it with this high-tension insanity, and then you just have to queue up for another antsy 35 minutes before eventually crab-walking inelegantly into your grey seat, and all possible relaxation and buzz has been killed and dragged out of your body and no amount of gin and tonics drunk while soaring over the ocean will get it back, but for now, but for now, but for now: you are enormous, you are a king—

12. The first pint of spring, taken when the whole office seems to realise at the same time that the sun is still out past four, and you knock off early and go to that pub down the way you always go to every Friday and still no one working there recognises you even at all, and you and a couple of hundred other nearby early-30s losers who mildly work 'in creative' buy pints and crawl along the long triangle of sunlight that creeps along the pavement, the shadows growing grey and shivering around you, and even though you weren't dressed for this and even though you've pushed all this evening's plans back you endure, picking up your rucksack and your bike and putting it down again and then picking up your rucksack and your bike and putting

FOUR STARS

them down again, moving with the triangle, more and more slender as the dusk starts to settle around you, and you're shivering now, you're freezing, and you're 30 minutes late for dinner and even if you leave now you're going to be 30 more, but someone whose round it is points to you with a single eyebrow raise that says "one more?" and you go: *Oh, absolutely, for sure—*

13. It is strange that pints come to you when you're devastated and when you're euphoric, at the quiet starts of days you don't know are about to turn legendary and at the start of the party you've been looking forward to for weeks, they mark the end of holidays and the beginning, they taste so much better after you've run all of the salt out of your body but also they don't because they are always perfect, perfect. A pint with friends: sure. A pint with strangers: you know what, why not. A pint solo: hear the angels sing. There is nothing that weighs the same and nothing that tastes the same and nothing that can measure the perfect feeling that spreads golden through your life as you sup at them. Thank you, pints, for everything. Tonight I will drink a pint in your honour. **FIVE MILLION STARS**

TRYING TO MAKE A DRUNKEN PHONE CALL TO A GIRL WHO USED TO LOVE YOU

—ah OK see I have been telling myself I really should stop checking my phone first thing in the morning – I feel like waking up and immediately beaming a rectangle of evil blue light into my eyes and brain before either of them have really started getting going yet is a bad idea but I am still addicted to it and do it every day – because I've just seen I tried to call Megan 14 times last night and connected twice and I am *wincing* now but I am remembering something where I was outside the chip shop and *yep* no she definitely picked up for one and told me *yep nope all coming back now* that this was really uncool and I was being really uncool and: *alright, it's all definitely come back now in full and vivid detail,* I tried to sing 'You Were Always On My Mind' at her and she clicked off so I phoned back and just did that to her voicemail. And I thought at the time that was *good*. Roll back over and try anew tomorrow. Stop waking up and looking at your phone. It's clearly the one and only thing that is making you insane. **ZERO STARS**

DREAD

"I'm taking you to a picnic," Michael said. "In two hours. With nice people. With normal people. You need to bring something. You need to wear some actual clothes." An attack, on my soul and my body and my afternoon. I ironed a t-shirt and took an entire handful of those quite strong CBD gummies then Googled whether that was a good idea or not. It was not. There was a bottle of Pepsi Max I got with a pizza months ago still in the fridge, so I tucked that under my arm and squirmed into my shoes. Nobody doesn't like Pepsi Max. But also nobody buys Pepsi Max unless it comes free with a pizza. The deep truth of Pepsi Max. Nobody is brave enough to confront this but me.

The dread, then. I woke up with it and as soon as Michael messaged it got worse. A dull metallic clank, a gnaw, a hum, a heavy bag of tools you can't put down. Your stomach distends down through your knees. It feels like someone – very tall and very dark and very silent – is stood too-close behind me in a queue, constantly. They are humming a low chant that makes me feel a very critical level of fear. I am constantly alert and constantly feeling like I might have to sprint 500 metres away to survive an attack. It makes it really really hard to text back Michael, "sure!" It makes it next-to-impossible to say: "sounds good!"

JOEL GOLBY

How many days has the dread been there? The dread warps time slightly, but I think it washed in softly on the Tuesday, and now it's Saturday and the water is gunmetal-cold and high, and it might not lap back out again until Wednesday, maybe Thursday. Michael looks disdainfully at the Pepsi, which has grown warm in the crook of my arm. "No Megan?" he says, and I say: "No that's not happening." And he goes "OK" then drives in silence for 25 minutes while he listens to the end of a podcast about the World Economic Forum that even if I heard the whole of I wouldn't have understood really, but fucking *hell*—

Nobody else has bought just a single bottle of Pepsi to the picnic. Everyone has cooked beautiful things and wrapped them gorgeously in foil. Michael goes to the boot of his car and gets out this exquisite heavy tray of dauphinoise potatoes and an actually unbelievably delicious edamame summer salad. A girl with bare feet and carefully plaited hair is grilling watermelon slices and tending to a chopping board of fresh mint and feta. Three lithe twinks frolic naked in the pond. There's a trestle table holding up a gallon jug of homebrew kombucha. Nobody bought a little pot of ASDA-branded coleslaw. Nobody bought a big multipack of Peperamis. There are six glistening Bruce Bogtrotteresque cakes on the side that nobody has even taken a single slice out of. Where am I?

Michael saw some guy he got arrested at a protest with so he went off so they could genuinely 'go for a walk' so I'm left here trying to make conversations while

FOUR STARS

carrying around the huge sack of sand that makes up my dread. Broadly of course they go like this:

> AUSTRALIAN GUY WHO IS 25 AND WEARING THE MOST LUDICROUS PAIR OF SHORTS I HAVE EVER SEEN IN MY LIFE: Yeah so ketamine is actually more of a hangover drug.
> THE DREAD: What do you mean
> A.G.W.I.25.A.W.T.M.L.P.O.S.I.H.E.S.I.M.L.: Well last weekend I went to a BBQ that turned into drinks that turned into bag that turned into going to someone else's house that turned into going *back* to the original house and then suddenly 11 a.m.—
> THE DREAD: Right exactly, sure
> A.G.W.I.25.A.W.T.M.L.P.O.S.I.H.E.S.I.M.L.: — and then the next day I'm supposed to go to this little day festival and it's like, starting in the middle of the afternoon
> THE DREAD: I get that. *Exactly*
> A.G.W.I.25.A.W.T.M.L.P.O.S.I.H.E.S.I.M.L.: Mm so I didn't want to do bag again so I just— *hup!* —had a little bump of ketamine and it's sort of fuzzy and takes the edge off. And also you don't want to drink so much because it'll make you throw up
> THE DREAD: Where are people pissing, around here?
> A.G.W.I.25.A.W.T.M.L.P.O.S.I.H.E.S.I.M.L.: Oh no-one is.

JOEL GOLBY

Or:

GIRL WHO RUNS A SECOND-HAND FURNITURE NEWSLETTER WHO I HAVE NO SEXUAL INTEREST IN AT ALL BUT WHO TALKS TO ME IN THE PATRONISING AND DIMINISHING WAY OF PEOPLE WHO ARE PRE-EMPTIVELY REJECTING ME FROM TRYING TO FLIRT WITH THEM EVEN THOUGH I'M FUCKING NOT: Sorry: you *injured your hand scrolling Instagram*?
THE DREAD: Yeah.
G.W.R.A.S-H.F.N.: How?
THE DREAD: Well it's like— you know how you hold your phone balanced on your little finger?
G.W.R.A.S-H.F.N.: No I use a PopSocket.
THE DREAD: Oh. Well it puts a lot of strain on your finger, your fingers, the bones of the hand, the ligaments, the *wrist*, &c. &c. My mum had carpel-tunnel syndrome, actually. They had to cut her wrists open and relieve the pressure. Her forearms puffed up tight like a pork roast
G.W.R.A.S-H.F.N.: Yeah I use a PopSocket.
THE DREAD: You said.
G.W.R.A.S-H.F.N.: You should get a PopSocket.
THE DREAD: [*Breathing for a really long time out through my nostrils*] Yeah I just don't think I'm going to do that.

FOUR STARS

Or:

GUY I VAGUELY REMEMBER HAVING ONE OF THOSE CLOSE ETHEREAL NIGHT-OUT FRIENDSHIPS WITH – "YOU'RE FUCKING SICK, MATE! WE SHOULD HANG OUT! YOU'RE A FUCKING LEGEND!" – AND THEN YOU WAKE UP IN THE MORNING WITH THE INSTAGRAM FOLLOWING NOTIFICATION FROM HIS PRIVATE 126-FOLLOWER ACCOUNT AND A MESSAGE ABOUT HOW WE SHOULD REALLY DO THAT BEER SOME TIME AND YOU KNOW YOU'RE JUST NEVER GOING TO DO THAT YOU WERE JUST BEING SILLY I MEAN REALISTICALLY YOU HAVE ENOUGH FRIENDS AND YOU DON'T EVEN DO YOUR BEST TO HANG OUT WITH THEM, LIKE WHEN WAS THE LAST TIME YOU TEXTED BACK FRED, FOR INSTANCE, AND FRED'S A NICE GUY. POSSIBLY THIS GUY'S NAME IS 'NICK'? IS IT 'NICK'? FUCKING HELL. I HAVE TO STOP DOING THIS:

'NICK'?: Pepsi Max. Great drink.

THE DREAD: Yeah you don't see it around much anymore, do you? You only really get it with pizzas. You noticed that?

'NICK'?: [*Laughing way too much for that joke*] "Only get it with pizzas"! Mate you're hilarious

THE DREAD: Yeah. Do you know if Michael is around here still, or—?
'NICK'?: We've got to get a pint in.
THE DREAD: For sure for sure for sure. Just uh ... the next month is bad. The next two months are bad.

Everyone sat down cross-legged and picked at the food (I had three plates, I had so much food that the paper plate I was eating off went grey and half-clear with a greasy morass of olive oil, pistachio shards, well-dressed salads, vegetarian sausage clumps) and started a fire that irritated my contact lenses and I got three or four either bug-bites or grass allergies, you know those ones that embed deep in the skin of your calves and when you scratch them it feels deliriously excellent but also is a terrible idea because now they pulse, red and aching, for days, burrowing even deeper into your leg as it goes, so I texted Michael (too afraid to get up from a cross-legged seated position in front of new friends, it's not an elegant way of getting up and I was afraid my full *hole* would fall out) saying it would be good to leave and soon enough later he came up behind me and tapped me on the shoulder and we drove home. I took the Pepsi Max with me for reasons I don't feel I need to explain.

"So that was fun," Michael said, and in a way he was right: for a normal person, for someone who could breathe without lifting six or seven metal plates up in their head before exhaling, that actually would have been a nice time.

FOUR STARS

"Yeah."

"You OK?"

I stared out of the window of the car as the city glimmered towards us. Red lights zipped past in a blur. The moon was big and high and yellow and lit up the fields and green woods around us, and I saw for miles, just blues and purples and browns, some small metal farmhouses lit cosily up in the distance but then, on the other side, a stadium, a skyscraper, a big ferris wheel they made for the millennium. I imagined opening the Saab door and just rolling and rolling and rolling along the road until every atom of my body had flown away from my core, no pain just oblivion.

"Yeah."

"You sure? It took you a really, really long time to respond to that question."

I felt like crying. I always feel like crying. But also you can't cry in front of Michael, can you? He'll tell people, he'll keep bringing it up. The next 40 years of my life he'll look at me, askew, as if at any given moment I'll burst out crying again. You can't do that. You can't show a man like that weakness. That would be insane.

"Do you ever feel dread?"

"Um: no, not really."

"How do you never feel dread?"

"I don't think there's an easy answer to that one."

"Is there a complicated answer?"

"There is."

"What is it?"

He drove for a while. The quiet tick of an indicator. The warm blast of the heating system. We blurred past a McDonald's but I felt no urge to go there. When he started talking he dropped as low as a whisper.

"I think when you feel dread, when you personally feel dread, you try and do everything you normally do just with dread on top of it. You think this is a functional system and it isn't. You drink the same and you eat the same and you do that strange aching smile at people you are trying to interact with—"

"'Aching'?"

"— whereas what you need to do is change the things that lead to the dread. You need to drink more water or something, but definitely less beer. You need to stop staying out so late and waking up so late, too. You wallow, a lot. You do drugs like you're 24 but you're really, really not 24. And then you're surprised when you feel dread. You have refused to grow up your entire life and now you get long grim moods where it feels like a rock is pressing your chest, and all you do is walk stiffly through it until it recedes, a little, then you hope that it's gone away."

"Hmm."

"*Hmm.*"

"You're right, I'm just annoyed that you're right."

"When was the last time you ate a piece of fruit?"

"Like, on its own?"

"Yes."

". . ."

"Exactly."

FOUR STARS

When I got home I laid flatly in bed with my hands clamped to my side and stared at the ceiling instead of sleeping. It didn't feel good. When I was a child I was convinced I was going to be an artist and when I was a young adult failing to make it as a writer I was convinced I was going to be an artist, too. *You give that little moron a mechanical pencil and he'd do something insane with it.* But somewhere along the way I lost the touch – you have to have the impulse to doodle, to spread paper out, to find out what colours work best when you press down hard on them and which require a light touch – and then words got in the way. I keep buying stationery with the distant intention of taking up drawing again but I never did. I kept telling people "I'm really good at drawing!" and scrawling out a little face on the back of the pub quiz and never doing anything with it. But now it's 3 a.m. and the lamp's on and I've pulled an old sketchbook out from under the chest of drawers that's been growing dusty beneath in my office. A Pigma 1.0mm and a Super Pro Mecha 0.4 and a Blackwing 602 I bought in New York for some reason even though you can really easily buy them in shops here. I stayed up until morning doodling tattoos I was never going to get because I'm not a tattoo person and filled six pages before the sun came up and when I turned my phone on again in the morning nobody had messaged me, no one had called. Sunday now means Thursday soon. I can bob here long enough until it's time to swim out of it. **NEGATIVE ONE MILLION STARS**

THE *FOOTBALL MANAGER 21* BRIGHTON SAVE (YEARS 2021 to 2027)

Here are my boys: Tiago Fernandes, Pedro Alemán, Vic Avdusinovic, Naim Benkouider, Luis Zecua. I am actually spoiled at the right-back slot: Tariq Lamptey is my Day #1 world-class all-star, but behind him is Scottish wonderkid Max Matthews – a dazzling attacking threat with an engine that runs all day – and, out on loan to his native Reading FC, the young Phil Vernon pushing them all the way. Though I have the all-angles attacking options of Liverpool '19 in their pomp, I feel that games are won and lost in midfield, and we have the perfect three-man interlocking combination of silks and steels: Declan Rice, picked up from a relegated West Ham, could play the entire middle of the park on his own; Michaël Cuisance, a mere €1 million from Bayern Munich, is a roving box-to-box athlete who always has a moment of goal-creating élan within him; Victor Hugo de la Torre, the now-Mexico captain, plays any role in the park (he can go forward, a glittering assist machine, or he can hold the line in front of the defence while the full-backs rove forward: he has two ways of enabling the attack, and we can flip him like a switch, as Manchester City found out to their cost). Backing them up we have Fabian Moyreyra, because sometimes you just need a pure central attacking midfielder who only lives to make cute passes and fuck up free-kick routines;

the monstrous everywhereness of young António Araújo, a 19-year-old four-star rated prospect I made an uncharacteristic January transfer for, meeting his £42 million release clause by going cap-in-hand to the board (if I play Declan Rice and António at the same time in midfield, your guys are not getting the ball. They are *not getting the ball!*); and my prized jewel, the boy I hope to swaddle and nurture and turn into a great: former Trabzonspor winger-turned-midfielder, Nazim Baltaci. Arsenal wanted Wuilker Farinez but I already had two goalkeepers better than him ready to take his place, so I sold him at a cost so eye-watering I ended the year in profit. Real Madrid and Liverpool both spent the summer squabbling over Sebastiano Esposito but he knew his greatest shot at glory would be to stick it out with me (he was right: after a European Golden Shoe, he went on to win a World Cup). I want to thank Cristian Olivera and Daniel Bragança, too, who are part of our story: though Cristian didn't often make the starting line-up (or even the bench!), he always did a job whenever he was called upon to do it, an impossible-to-deal-with pure winger on the right or a dutifully effective striker through the middle; at £26 million, Daniel was some of the best money I ever spent, three solid seasons of do-the-job midfieldery that only ended when Everton came in for him (he actually helped us most when he wasn't there anymore: in his third game on Merseyside, already the captain, he scored the penalty that caused Manchester United to drop a season-defining three points). Squads are built on these men: not just the show ponies, the tricksters, the *FIFA* cover stars and the captains, but the lads who only get nine minutes on the pitch each week but make every single one of them count. You cannot have a five-star prospect in every position on the park and also 15 of them on the bench: it means you end every matchday with ten of the best footballers in the world asking you why you didn't play them. What you need are ordinary men with big hearts and bigger engines: you need balance, harmony, smiling faces and hard work, and fundamentally you need chemistry. Brighton 2026–27 had all of that. They are the result of the most perfect 800 hours of my life.

Football Manager is a game in the same way being in prison is a good opportunity to read. It's a game, yes, but it's something more all-encompassing than that, closer to an obsession: in peak *Football Manager* phases, a lot of the game is played when the laptop isn't even open, just running over variables in my mind. I can be at lunch with someone but still distantly be deciding whether the Dennis Cirkin experiment has failed (it had – he just never did anything better than Jeremie Frimpong could do it). The decision to fill the vacant right-wing spot with newgen Tiago Fernandes or real-world Barcelona youth prospect Ilias Akhomach was a long and tortuous one (I made the right decision: Akhomach struggled for game time in an overloaded Barcelona team and ended up doing a fine-enough-but-forgettable job at Valencia instead). I knew Esposito would attract glances from the best in Europe after his 55-goal season – Inter Milan came crawling back, Bayern

FOUR STARS

Munich's name was swirled in with the rumours, even (laughably!) Tottenham had a go – and I agonised over whether to let him go and start the season with a new striker. My philosophy was built over a *Moneyball* structure, but fragmented into something other, newer, better: wage-spend is better than transfer-spend, if anyone offers over value for your players then you take it, find unexpected value among underappreciated nations, train legends don't buy them. But when a star is ascending and the rest of the team has finally assembled as a sturdy enough platform to let them shine, you let them shine. Sure, I could have sold Esposito to Madrid for £200 million and let Khoklov start the season as striker (realistically, Naïm Benkouider was about to have a glow-up season akin to Henry's at Arsenal – cutting in from the wing to suddenly make a claim to be not only the best striker in the world, but possibly to ever live). And I thought about it! Extensively! But sometimes you have to take a chance when it is offered to you. I took Sebastiano to one side and said, look. Stick with me for one more season. All the pieces are here. Declan Rice is in the form of his life. Moyreyra's finally figured out how to take corners. I've got Max Matthews on long-throw training and Victor Hugo de la Torre's gained five kilos of muscle. He said, *Boss, you've convinced me.* Forty goals later and he had his hands on the league.

"Are you thinking about that football game again?" Michael said, picking at a latte.

"..."

"..."

"Sorry, I just took a really big sip of water before you asked that. No."

"You are."

"It's the January transfer window and we're first by two points. There are a lot of crucial decisions to be made."

"How's living at your sister's?"

"Like: I need a new striker, but one who knows he isn't going to play every game yet."

"Has Megan unblocked you on Instagram yet, or—?"

"— and like: realistically it would be good to try and get a new ball-playing centre-back in place in case anyone comes in for Tosin."

"I've heard Ed Warburton has been—"

"Ed Warburton is a fucking *hack*!"

Realistically I bought Bart Meijer as youthful back-up with the 2028–29 season in mind but his dribbling developed quicker than we expected so I've thrown him on to see out the tough Champions League games. Declan Rice was made England captain and he thanked me personally at his pre-World Cup Final press conference. I have started to suspect than Fabian Luzzi has all the attributes to be a great striker, just not a great striker *for me* – the same way Chelsea once had Lukaku, De Bruyne and Salah, all at the same time, just could never figure out a role for them – and I make the difficult decision that, for the sake of his career and the sake of a valuable squad spot, I could sell him for £65 million more than I bought him for (Manchester City, those pigs, are immediately interested). You can lose a weekend to *Football Manager*, if

FOUR STARS

you plan it right: you can get home early on a Friday and get four good hours in, then up on Saturday before anyone else with the laptop whirring while you gaze freezing at the sunrise over your sister's garden, thinking about how many of your items are in boxes, how uncomfortable sleeping on a fold-out bed is, how the bar you used to take all your first dates to closed because of that pool cue episode and now you're going to have to find another one. It's less a game, more a world you build for yourself – a series of enemies (Manchester United, everyone who has ever been associated with Manchester United, and somehow Sean Dyche for some reason), stories, friendships and allies, all of whom you manipulate and flatter and train and deceive, all of whom you set up that insane asymmetrical formation that nobody in the league could deal with, all with the same goal: winning the league at the end of a long grinding season, winning the league after not really texting any of your friends back for like eight consecutive days. Winning the league by— hold on when did I last have a shower. Yesterday? Yesterday. One day is fine: you can go one day without a shower. That isn't indicative of wholesale mental descent. Hold on when did it become *Monday*—

With Brighton, I played it the right way: not buying success, but pulling it up like ore out of the ground. The 2025–26 season was desperately, agonisingly close, Manchester United (*scum.*) pipping us on the last day and winning the league by one point, though truthfully we threw it away in those last three games before it, and the temptation was of course there to quit the game, reload my laptop, play the final chicane of the season over again with a wisdom I'd gained from losing. But that's not winning, is it, it's pretending, so I told the boys before the summer: *this is a league-winning squad. And with the little Mexican boys I've got coming in, and now António Araújo has learned English, we can do the lot.* I pointed at Samuel Ronchi, a 20-year-old lost Italian boy: *there's the next best goalkeeper in the league!* I pointed at Phil Jeffrey, a 19-year-old who ascended to captain at Watford and signed for us before the summer window had even opened: *this bald child will win the World Cup for England!* I pointed at Chris Kötzsch, the European Under-21 winning superfreak who would score eight goals in his debut: *they made him in a lab like Ivan Drago!* The boys roared and chanted my name. They held me on their shoulders like a king.

From there, I'll admit, I descended: I bought a new laptop in the middle of a hard-fought season, and felt too superstitious to port the save game over to the new machine, so just fought on against a ten-year-old MacBook as well as the financial might of Manchester United; I started to actually say things, out loud, to the computer, both when the boys did well ("Yes!") and when they did badly ("More running more running more *running*!"). Entire weekends lost to data. Pressing the spacebar to skip forward on the calendar again and again and again. Tweaking the training schedule, putting the arm around individuals, making sure every aspect of the squad clicked. I went and watched games where my youth players were out on loan.

FOUR STARS

I relished the A23 Derby with Crystal Palace more than watching actual football in the actual world. And then, the final day, the win: the boys roared away to a 2–0 lead, Manchester United (*scum.*)'s heads dropped, a single static image telling me I'd won a trophy. All that work led to perfection. The only true thing to do, after that, is walk away. I closed the laptop lid. Max Matthew, Edward Moens, Bart Meijer and Martin Vandervoordt all, suddenly, ceased to exist.

I have been feeling the old urge again, recently. New versions of *Football Manager* have been released but none of them have the same pull: it has to be me, my boys, the south coast, and an unplayable offensive formation. I booted up the save on the new computer (the superstition lifted when we won the league) and tinkered quietly over the course of a summer fortnight: how to improve a perfect squad? I fire a couple of three-star coaches and hire four-star ones in their place. I play a friendly against Aston Villa and blow them away. I scout and re-scout Sandy Joyner, a two-and-a-half star (with five-star potential!) DLP currently playing in the reserves at Rangers, and think what I could turn him into if he signs for me aged 17. I feel the grip again. I forgot I had made a £102 million bid for Eduardo Camavinga, now a Ballon d'Or-winning midfielder and the perfect foundational foil for Fabian Moyreyra to play in front of, and am surprised to receive the news that it is accepted. I snip the negotiations a little, promise big on wages, back-load the payoff to Rennes so the financials make sense to the board. It's dusky-dark around me and I haven't said a word out loud to anyone today. The Brighton 2027 team I built was too perfect to live (or: I would have to give my life to make them better); 2028 can never happen. I pause the negotiations and uninstall the game. I gasp the cool air outside me and feel thankful for my freedom. **FIVE STARS**

COUCH TO 5K

I got that 'bad glimpse' of myself in the mirror getting out of a shower a few weeks ago – there is an inevitable dreadful clang awaiting men of my age with diets of my consistency (pub burgers, beer and at least one pizza a week, plus over summer my white-chocolate Magnum consumption is genuinely quite manic), and the awful bell finally rang for me – so I realised I had to download the Couch to 5K running app and shuffle my body around a nearby £12 billion wildlife park in an effort to shift some kilos and hopefully make it so my heart doesn't explode like a landmine at midnight on my 50th birthday. A friend told me his mother – in her low sixties and with a medically stiff knee – had completed the same plan last summer, and every time I gasp searing air from my lungs into the spittle-flecked sky above me after a one-minute jog down a cycle path I think humblingly of that: somewhere, out there, a woman on a course of hard painkillers is outrunning me. The other day I wore £100 worth of Nike runwear to get overtaken by a man in jeans who was jogging to his car to get out of the rain. The whole experience has taken some heavy hits out of my ego, it has to be said.

My path goes somewhere like this: a brisk walk as a warm-up and some lacklustre stretching, then, when I get to one of London's rare designated green paths, I jog lightly down it on my tiptoes – my running form changes wildly from day to day, always slow, always hefty, but I think I'm more or less on the right bit of my foot – quietly getting angry at people who cycle on the wrong side of the cycle path or walk on the wrong side of the walking path. The Couch to 5K app is meant to make you run for incrementally longer and longer distances – one minute of running turns into two minutes of running turns into 20 – and to do that, pre-recorded audio cues interrupt the podcast you're listening to every 90 seconds to tell you "you're doing *really* well". The first kilometre marker always hits at the same place on my route every day – spanking my feet in an ungainly manner down a slight off-ramp next to a canal – and each day the pre-recorded audio congratulates me in the exact same way. "Well done – keep going!" it says, cheerfully, and I think: *you said that this time yesterday, you robot bitch.* I think: *you don't know how well I'm running at all.* Sometimes pedestrians walking in the opposite direction to me gaze at me approaching from an 80- or 90-metre distance – the firm huge flap of my feet on the concrete – and assume a facial expression I can only describe as 'confused fear'. Pick-up shots in modern *Godzilla* movies show less terror. After a number of weeks of this, my per-kilometre speed seems to be inexplicably getting slower.

Today I ran 5K uninterrupted, which I think basically any functioning human body should more or less be able to do at any time – if, say, an attack broke out, I would like to be able to run five kilometres away from it without getting a stitch, and for years I have not been able to do that. I ran down the off-ramp then up again towards a stadium, then looped round a newly developed business park full of empty offices, then down towards a cluster of curated wild nature swampland – a brush of flower smell, the healing green sensation of a bush heavy with dew – then over a bridge above a rushing rivulet. The water beneath me ran mud-brown with violent jags of white. The sky above me was heavy and grey. My headphones fizzled in the damp then eventually ran out. I was left with only the echoing thoughts inside my brain – 'I can hear my breathing and my breathing is too hard', 'why didn't I learn to do this when I was a teenager like everyone else seems to have', 'this is the same with driving, everyone else learned to drive back then and I still can't', 'do we think it's too late to learn to drive, now, realistically? People do say it's harder to learn past a certain age', 'I mean when was the last time I learned something, full stop?', 'I used to be able to learn things', 'driving lessons are quite expensive though, aren't they. Though how expensive, actually?', 'try and remember to Google that when you get in' ('although realistically the chance of remembering is quite slim, we both know that'), 'that was a *heavy* breath, wow', 'does anyone else breathe this hard? Doesn't seem normal', 'what *was* I doing at 17 if I wasn't learning to drive and wasn't learning to run?', 'that's it: I was learning HTML', 'God no wonder I didn't have full intercourse until I was 20', 'weird how I am still embarrassed about that figure even though I have since had intercourse many many times', 'on my death bed I will be like: *it is embarrassing it me took so long to have full sex with a woman*', 'this is dull, isn't it. It's just the same fucking thing again and again and again', 'how many times do I have to pick this leg up and put it down again', 'how heavy do you think this leg is? I reckon surprisingly heavy', 'no way of knowing for sure though, is there', 'hmm unless I get a big bin full of water, and dip my leg into it, and then weigh the water the leg displaces', 'I think that's right, isn't it?', 'though again: realistically never going to do it', 'this is like the driving lessons and the Googling again', 'I don't even own a bin. I'd have to buy a bin just to weigh my own leg', 'and then what am I going to do with a bin?', 'Freecycle it, I suppose. Meet some sort of freak', 'only freaks go on Freecycle', 'but then they'll ask me what I used the bin for and I'll go: *I needed to weigh my leg*', 'and they'll walk away thinking *I* am the freak', 'Hmm', 'I think if we just run to that lamp-post, that's enough running for today', 'lamp-post taking ages to get to', 'is that lamp-post getting *further away*?', 'I should have done this months ago, I should have done this years ago', 'how many more of these things will I have to struggle through until I can look in the bathroom mirror again', 'right there's the lamp-post', 'mm actually kind of feels alright shall we keep it moving until the bridge?', 'yeah. Yeah!', 'this feels kind of good', 'no: nope. Got cocky', 'alright we can stop and breathe really heavily in this builder's supply warehouse car park', 'it's late enough that there won't be any builders around, to see me panting', 'no wait there's one', 'getting into his car very slowly', 'Yep off you fuck mate', 'yep he definitely slowed down there to see how pink I was', 'got a glimpse of it in the reflection of his car', '— which he probably learned to drive when he was 17, by the way—', 'and that was not a normal colour of pink to be'.

Running evangelists tell me I should expect a 'runner's high' right now, a great rush of endorphins that will make me feel good and alive in my body again, springy and supple and warm and sated, but honestly my legs hurt so much I don't think I can walk all the way home from here. Is this worth an Uber? It is and it isn't. The sky cracks into hard heavy rain above me. Drops of water pelt on the pavement like pound coins. My hair is drenched and languid, my feet are soaked with mud. I sort of feel I deserve this. Hobble home and get in the bath, maybe. Now I can finally do running I can delete that stupid app. **THREE STARS**

GETTING A NUDE

I get back from an empty-feeling date (two bars, eight gin and tonics, one continuing session of that kind of ugly public make-out that only ends when they put your thumb in their mouth and bite it and then the bartenders flash all the lights at once and say "Guys, it's Tuesday", lingering outside ordering an Uber, me seeing where the destination is, me saying, "Hold on sorry what: *Hounslow*?", her saying, "Yeah, that's where I live ", me going, "No," then, "No," then: "I'll get you next time. Hounslow? No.") to a nude, swiftly followed by another one. *u should've come back*, it said, and yeah, looks like it: a full nude body stretched cattily up in front of a mirror, all available body hair just immaculately shaved which drives me brain-turning-off insane for some reason, single finger hooked to the lip, a load of fucking detritus in the background. What's there: a wire bin with a load of straighteners in it, a mattress protector that has slipped off and just been folded up on the floor, clothes, some hair bobbles, another mirror, a letter which (I'm squinting past the ass here but—) seems to be from the council, a plate, a bottle of garlic and herb sauce. These women live in sin and they live in filth. They have developed a language of nudity that allows me to look right past it.

Every time I receive a nude I think of my father. How many nudes did he see in his lifetime? Did he have to go to special pervert cinemas just to see a titty during a dry spell? I have been receiving nudes for a decade and a half now, and the thrill only increases: from the first grainy Nokia cameraphone coy mirror nudes of my first girlfriend to the hyper-real perfect focus iPhone shots that Mia Tinder, 27, just sent of herself just after she'd squirted. Every time I get one my brain whirrs and dinks at a frequency that was previously inaccessible just a generation ago. One single modern nude would demolish the brain of a Victorian lord. It demolishes my brain, now, still. Fundamentally, my nervous system is not designed to see a girl who does ClassPass push her tits together in a Calvin Klein bralette before sending me a voicenote recording of her sucking her fingers.

We live in a golden age of pornography, both professionally and amateurly produced, and I am glad to be alive during it. My father was a photographer, and I once found his one and only porn stash, siphoned away in an old carrier bag full of negatives: a much leafed-through, artistic photography glossy where everyone's genitals were smeared or dotted with acrylic paint, and a few tasteful black-and-white nudes he'd taken of somebody else's wife. That's what you had to do to see some pussy, twenty or thirty years ago: take a roll of film of someone, drive one town over to the Boots' development lab over there, stash the sheath of them in a box on the way to an attic (and I have seen '80s nudes: they are always 'high flash-exposure, one shapeless nipple flopped out of a bra, someone looking undecided in a suspender belt, big spider plant next to a sofa, maybe a dog is in the background' affairs. Compare the original *Star Wars* (1977) to the hyper-CGI

FOUR STARS

of *The Last Jedi* (2017). '80s nudes might as well have been carved in sandstone among The Valley of the Kings). Maybe, possibly, you might find a tattered porno magazine discarded by a truck driver underneath a bush. But otherwise you were stuck on your own. Now in two texts I can direct someone to go to the work bathroom, pull their shirt up and their pants down, and see a flash of WhatsApp nipple within six minutes. That should not be allowed. That should not be allowed. I am incredibly glad it is allowed.

The worst part of a nude, obviously, is you have to answer it: someone has taken the time out of their day to angle and photograph their body for you, electronically gifting you a juvenile-powerful erection from a number of miles away, and you have to say something complimentary and hot – to make it worthwhile to them – while your brain has turned to an unending loop of a cartoon wolf doing awooga noises. "Hell yeah," I typed back, then, quickly, as if breathless: "so" "fucking" "hot", and I won't detail the rest of the conversation from there but let's just say it built to a crescendo then ended dramatically and abruptly. I already know what this girl is going to be like on Saturday and quite a lot of Sunday, how she'll sound and what she'll ask for, in a way that used to take months of polite courtship – an organised wedding in a demure country mansion! A French lady shipped over for weeks! – to find out previously. But then, I suppose, there might be something lost along the way: I am at an age now where I am craving the stability and warmth of good, solid, comfortable romance, touching feet and in-jokes and re-watching *Frasier*, going to parties separately and talking about each other like we think they're the coolest person in the world. I am ageing and tiring: how many more times can I sit through a girl with no student debt and a thing for sucking toes explain Fred Again to me? What if I've unwittingly missed my chances at the capital-L Love I've craved? The phone dings. Jesus Christ. Alright, fuck. OK. One more ... we can do this for one more. I don't know. Hmm? Ah yeah. Week, I guess, or ... month. Fucking hell. I— fuck. *Fuck.* **FIVE MILLION STARS**

TAKING BAD COCAINE AT A SEMI-THREATENING IRISHMAN'S HOUSE THE DAY BEFORE A FAIRLY BIG MEETING

The details are blurry obviously – did we meet him before the cocktail bar, or after? There was a pool table involved somewhere, but it can't have been the cocktail bar, because no cocktail bar on earth has a pool table in it, (that would be a frankly psychotic vibe. Imagine trying to navigate a tricky break with an Old Fashioned. No, I feel ill), which means there must have been another pub (can I get it together enough to open my banking app and sift through the digital receipts and figure out where we were? The decision-making flowchart that dictates my emotional wellbeing suggests

FOUR STARS

'no') – but the point is at some stage between the hours of 9.45 p.m. and 11.59 p.m., at some moment between that weird three-storey pub that felt as if, if it wasn't an active brothel right now, it had been an active brothel at least in recent living memory, and in fact might be a passive brothel currently, and then the chicken place ... this guy. There was this guy. Was he Dan's friend or just a guy? I don't think either of the potential answers to this question are necessarily healthy, or good.

Anyway the set-up was ... we were at the guy's house, and— The thing with nights is, they have magic to them, and that magic – that texture in the air, that cold glimmer of possibility, the unshackled feeling that this night could go on forever, and ever – can often lead to the best moments of your entire life. Like you are at a party and you don't know who is actually hosting the party and a girl whose name you keep forgetting is smiling and stroking your leg. Or: you and the boys, t-shirts drenched grey with your own sweat, arm around each other's shoulder, beer on the floor, smiles and chants and I-love-yous. This is where the night comes into its own: this is when the night becomes the *night*. This wasn't one of those nights. This was me illuminated by the sheer xenon glow of a petrol station forecourt at night, trying to buy four cans of Heineken through a bulletproof window, then walking down silent residential streets and sneaking into a flat to just sit upright in the kitchen.

No worse vibe on a night out than 'spare man', is there. There is no reason for a man to be outside and spare. A man has to be attached to something, whether it's a girlfriend or a boyfriend or a group. There is something sinister about a man just out there, just being a man. Coming up to your table and sitting down. "Alright boys?" the man says, and we go: *alright*. "Tell you what: the birds in here are crackers." OK—

That was it, that was it! I thought he was Gus's friend and Gus thought he was mine and by the time he'd bought us both a pint it was too late, we had slipped down the slope into the uneasy maw of his friendship and were locked into an eternal round. He said, "I'm just around the corner" and "it's five minutes away" and now we're on minute 16 of walking and my phone can't get any 4G signal and I know I have that meeting in eight hours and all I can think, all I can think in my head is *this guy knows a freakish amount of information about the 3D printing of guns*. Gus – and I am jealous forever of his ability to do this – had hit that pint (9th? 10th?) in the night where his brain turns off and he just smiles beatifically through whatever horrors unveil themselves to him. He will not text me until three or maybe four o'clock. He will sleep swaddled like a gorgeous little baby.

I want to say he was showing us deep YouTube remixes of Aphex Twin songs but I cannot recite that with authority. I want to say he ... swept a pile of toys off his sofa and told us not to go in there? I don't remember the journey from the endless street up into the flat: I just remember coming to, shocked as if dipped into a trough of water, sitting in his kitchen with all the lights on, staring at an IBM laptop I think

FOUR STARS

was made in the early '00s, drinking a Heineken that tasted like ash.

Then cocaine, obviously cocaine. There is no reason to go to a guy's flat and let him struggle with YouTube over a spotty internet connection unless there is cocaine involved. This is the problem with cocaine: obviously, at its best, it is a euphoric drug that does nothing more than make you speak in 100-word-a-second sentences and stay awake long enough to drink more pints. Fantastic, sublime. But for every gorgeous golden god-like high there's a night like this, scrabbling around, following a guy with a really large neck scar around for 45 minutes, sending a complete stranger £40 over PayPal, big lights big lights big lights, asking if anyone has a note, realising you're the only person with a note, watching – hawklike – that no one steals your note. Cocaine is fine until you want it. Then it just becomes embarrassing.

Oh no he's here—

NEANDERTHAL GOLBY: Ooh ooh! Ooh
    ooh ooh
ME: Yeahyeahyeahyeahyeahyeahno, yeah. It's fine
    it's fine it's fine. After this one, after this one.
    Then Uber, three and a half hours' sleep,
    Lucozade for breakfast, yeah.
    Yeahyeahyeahyeah. No it's fine it's fine, it's fine.
NEANDERTHAL GOLBY: Ooh ooh?
ME: No it's ... like it's an important meeting but
    it's a meeting isn't it like I just have to be there
    I just have to say things I just have to turn up
    on time.

NEANDERTHAL GOLBY: Ooh

ME: Half of meetings are just people saying things because they are in a meeting and they want to justify the meeting by saying meeting things so actually the less I say meeting-wise the more meeting things they will say and the more they'll feel like they had a meeting, so they'll walk away from the meeting brightly saying, "Good meeting!" because they said a lot in the meeting, is how meetings go, so honestly actually realistically this is a play—

NEANDERTHAL GOLBY: Ooh, ooh?

ME: Err ... Robert? Hmm, no. Is it ... no it's not 'Robert'. What's his name? Begins with an 'R', doesn't it?

NEANDERTHAL GOLBY: Ooh?

ME: No it can't be 'Robin'. No one's called 'Robin'. It'll come to me. It'll come back to me. It's fine. If I need to say anything to him, I'll just say, 'dude'. You can call anyone, 'dude'.

NEANDERTHAL GOLBY: Ooh ooh ohh-ooh?

ME: I think 'dude' is genderless, actually! Actually!

NEANDERTHAL GOLBY: Ooh ooh, a ooh a ooh. Ooh a ooh ooh, ooh ah. Ooh. A ooh ooh ah ooh!

ME: Because I wanted one more, that's why, and I wanted cocaine, and yes now I am splashing my face with water and trying to stay here in the game, but this is what we're alive for, isn't it? This is why we are here. To live—

NEANDERTHAL GOLBY: Ooh ooh ah ooh ooh

FOUR STARS

ME: Maybe I should send my cousin a book, maybe I should sober up, maybe I should get in shape, maybe I should have texted her more, maybe I should text her now?, I shouldn't text her now, obviously. It's four a.— I'm not looking at the time, I'm not looking at the time. I'm going to ... sit on the toilet and compose an e-mail—

NEANDERTHAL GOLBY: Ooh ah

ME: Alright an e-mail and then in the morning I'll go over it and make sure it's OK and then send it to her and say maybe we could meet, maybe we could meet back up, I mean we're friends still, you said we'd still be friends after and it's like we haven't done any friend-things for weeks and I saw that Instagram story you did from the inside of someone else's car and it's fine I mean it's fine I mean obviously because we're friends it's just – and I think it's OK to say it, I think I have the scope and the permission – it's just seeing that it felt like someone had taken an icicle, or a sword made out of ice, a shard of ice basically, like someone had taken a shard of ice and stabbed it into my heart and then down, down into my body, settling in the basin of my belly, the cold just spreading up, the cold just spreading out—

NEANDERTHAL GOLBY: Ooh ah ooh

ME: — no it's not a bad idea.

ROBERT? ROBIN?: Another line out here for you mate!

ME: [Really fake cheerful voice] Tha-anks!

ROBERT? ROBIN?: You OK in there yeah?

ME: Yeah, yep! Yeah dude!

NEANDERTHAL GOLBY: Ooh. Ooh ooh a ohh. Ooh ah ooh ah ooh. Ah ooh ah ooh ah ooh ooh

ME: [Sobbing for five seconds into my hands then immediately stopping] I've let everyone in my life down. I've let everyone in my life down. There is no one who is a better person for having encountered me. I am . . . I am a human curse.

NEANDERTHAL GOLBY: Ooh ooh

ME: Fuck this is quite speedy coke. Fuck this is quite speedy coke. Fuck. OK actually I'm going to have a quick shit, can you—

I don't know how I got home, I don't know where I got home from, I don't know how I woke up with half a box of chicken wings in bed with me and I don't know why I didn't have a piss until 2 p.m., I don't really know how the meeting went but the e-mails seemed fine afterwards, I don't know how I found myself in Chinatown, eyes bulging purple out of my head, fundamentally exhausted, fundamentally bereft, eating a pork bun and wondering if Uber had a deluxe service where the driver will take your keys and open the door and tuck you into bed. Will food help or make it worse? Will sleep help or make it worse? Ugh I have that thing due tomorrow. It never ends it never ends it never ends. Who ends up acting like this on a *Tuesday*? **MINUS FIVE STARS**

CONNECTING TO POSEIDON, THE ANCIENT AND ALL-KNOWING GOD OF HORSES AND EARTHQUAKES AND THE SEA, BY DIPPING EXACTLY ONE TOE IN THE WATER ON THE BEACH AT MARGATE

I am wrapped in a hoodie and a squirt of aftershave (Aesop Tacit: fresh, vegetal, liquorice-y almost?) and the air from the sea is cold, hard, freezing. Megan is moving most of her stuff out this week and I needed a place to stay so I wouldn't be slumping around the house starting small-then-large squabbles then, terrifyingly, crying in the mirror, so Isaac said I could come stay with him in Margate. Margate is having its little moment and Isaac is part of that: it used to be a town-as-an-old-person's-home, tall thin maisonettes braced against the grey dreary force of the sea, and a sort of thin un-fun seaside glee – unwinnable arcades, stiff over-frozen ice cream, a bookshop that only sells trashy romance paperbacks people on cold joyless holidays have happily left behind – but now it has, for instance, a coffee shop, and a record-and-coffee shop, and a plant shop, and a record-and-plant shop. There are a lot of women here in dresses down to their ankles who were impregnated by someone's drummer in Camden 13 years ago and the trajectory of their life was forever changed as a result of it. The locals, cars still buzzing from the reedy twinkling of the arcades, the boarded-up pub near the police station, the tattoo parlour you can't see through the windows of, hate the new influx of post-London Londoners, and bare their remaining teeth at people they deem to have 'too fancy' a pair of shoes. It's the perfect place to come to if you believe you do not personally deserve to ever have fun.

Isaac is the consummate host, because he has a spare bedroom, *Hitman III*, seven or eight hand-assembled bicycles, two businesses that don't seem to involve him ever really doing anything beyond an hour or two a day of chain-smoking roll-ups and responding to invoices, and a bag of dark-web weed the size of a sofa pillow. I got here yesterday, in sweltering, aggravating heat: the kind of heat that lingers in front of you, runs rivulets of sweat down the back of even your linen trousers, makes you need to fundamentally be horizontal, trying to limbo underneath the hotness, fronds of conversation sizzling and dying on the air. At 6 p.m. he slapped his laptop closed and told me we were going swimming in the sea, and I said: "OK." And then: "but I have never done that". And then, latterly: "also I cannot swim".

Insane that I cannot swim. Swimming, like writing your name and shitting on a toilet, is a skill learned young, very young – a sort of pre-young era of young, before hard-shaped thought and emotion and memory, where you care very deeply about dinosaurs and staying up minutes past your bedtime as if you've won anything and very little else. I was not taught to swim as a child because swimming lessons cost money and my parents never had any, and that always troubled me and seemingly nobody else. At school, they would regularly show us grim strange warning VHS tapes about playing on trainlines or approaching strangers in trenchcoats and, worst for me, messing around by canals or quietly deep brown lakes. "If you fall into the canal, tread water and cry for help," the video would say, and everyone around me, who had been taught to swim (I was once taken to a swimming pool as part of a birthday party, and walked by a class of my peers learning to swim, as I – in vivid red borrowed water-wings – was guided to the piss-warm shallow end and told to bob) (everyone else spent the hour dive-bombing and holding their breath underwater and racing from one end to another, and I floated like a duck near a small group of elderly women practising slow movements to extend the life of their hips and joints) (No adult seemed to find this strange. At no point in my childhood did someone look at me and go: "Why can't this fat little butterball fucking swim?"), but the tapes would strike a vibrant fear into me: *if you fall into a canal*, the screen seemed to say, *then I guess Joel you're just going to die.*

The sea was cool against my feet, which on a sauna-hot day was astounding, but as I crept inch-by-inch to the horizon each step of it started to pinch: zinging up my knees then thighs then crotch (my penis shrank entirely into my body), then nipples then shoulders then face. I was stood up to my ears in the sea, an astounding thing: every drop of the seas and the oceans is connected in one planet-sized slosh, and my body was encased in the same liquid that strokes languidly against the shore in LA and washes clothes in green Asian rivers and disguises teenage couples rapidly fingering along the coast of Australia. My body began to bob and swell and rise towards the sky – blue then white then pink and enormous, expansive, larger than anything – and I felt a small moment of peace there: I am a tiny speck of nothing in a very large world, and my death will trouble no one and my books are all in storage and when I go back to the flat the sofa and the bed and a lot of the pans and all the plants and the trinkets and all of her clothes will be gone, but I am here now, I guess, and my penis has gone in and my senses have been sharpened but the sky is clear and clean and I am alive. Then I caught a mouthful of gritty salt water and was reminded how much sewage is in the sea, how many turds and pieces of plastic. I walked to the shore and towelled off and became slowly anxious about strangers seeing my torso again.

The perfect British summer day is when it was warm the day before – hot, even, scorching, sweltering, vile – and now it is cold, the wind and the frigidity icing down the heat, the air dry then fresh, the wind a cooling fan rather than an icy blast. It is August and the sun goes down lazily at night – just about dips into the sea around 11 p.m., then lolls up again at 5 a.m., midnight going blue instead of black – and if this kind of cold hit me on a day in September I would be miserable, freezing, I'd wear thick socks and have a headache and not be able to read. But I can hear the lazy sounds of traffic purring over long curving roads, and seagulls clicking against the breeze, and the small static rustle of sand fizzling against the sea. There's a fair in town – it is completely insane that the aesthetic language of funfairs has not changed in my entire lifetime, the same bolted-together rides with just thicker and thicker layers of paint (the dodgems here have the following three logos on them, directly next to one another: Mercedes–Benz, Monster Energy, a picture of a go kart going so fast fire is coming out. When aliens come to our scorched earth in one thousand years they will never be able to translate our hieroglyphics!) – and last night I got powerfully stoned and meandered through it, giggling at the hazy lights blurring against the fragrant dusk, chewing candyfloss with my mouth open, standing alone beneath a whirl-i-gig spinning terrifyingly above me. The sound of fairs are: screaming but in a safe way, the jangle of coins in board short pockets, dads explaining to boys in England tops with ice cream smears down the front of them that each of these games are unwinnable. I cannot ever give my spirit over to the fair: I can never escape that the cans are glued down, that the hook-a-ducks are all £1 prizes, that the games are rigged, and this has been true since I was a boy (can you imagine taking a really pragmatic eight-year-old to a fair and trying to convince them that the penny slots were 'fun, actually'? This was a task given to one of my mother's glamorous and short-lived friends, Kelly, who soon after wasting an entire day taking me around a car park funfair, changed her phone number and went away). I can never truly have fun against the shapes of the machines we built to have fun on. All I can do is stand, and gawp, and wriggle down into my hoodie, and gaze against the lights. **FIVE STARS**

AGARIC FLY – BOLAJI BADEJO

Sandalwood is obviously the earth's most perfect scent and I frankly don't believe humanity really deserves to enjoy it, because of that. We should grow it on the moon and only let people smell it when they have passed through certain loopholes and tests: acts of great selflessness, a lifetime total sum committed to charity, other things I will never do. It is gorgeous on its own – woody in that spicy, distant, arid way – but also clean and soft-edged and sandy in a way that plays so well with others (in this case: gummy, sticky myrrh and the just-watered quench of lemon myrtle). Most of my favourite aftershaves have a robust sandalwood base: musky but not macho, erring into that 'luxury unisex' zone that I like to move around in. Burn a stick of Bolaji Badejo and close your eyes: visions of the desert, poked through with trees like teeth, smouldering and orange and on fire; a square marble pool on the edge of the Mojave; white birds fluttering into the sky, disappearing to the horizon in seconds. Hard blue, red-orange, yellow then white then sky.

Bolaji Badejo was an artist and actor who played the alien in the original *Alien* movie. They found him

FOUR STARS

in a Soho pub because he was 6 ft 10 and amazing-looking, and he prowled around that set like he was born to do it: claws, clicks, taps. When the franchise took off they offered and re-offered him the role – be the alien in *Alien*! You *are* the alien in *Alien*! – but he demurred, moved back to Nigeria, quietly died in such a way that for years they said he disappeared, his awesome crawling body replaced with a team of puppeteers and hacked-together actors. We once had a generation of Creature Actors – huge over-sized freaks, mostly, big lumps drafted from European basketball leagues to be some huge wordless beast – but there were defter, smaller versions, too: Haruo Nakajima, the guy who played Godzilla in the first 12 *Godzilla* movies, went to Tokyo Zoo to watch the elephants plod through mud (you never see the soles of an elephant's foot: it is the same with the King of Monsters) and threw bread at bears to see how they would catch it. Now we have a million gigahours of computer rendering to do the same job, and yes, it's more immersive, but is there any soul? When did you last see a shark on screen and go: *I fear this*? Anyway: it burns for 25 to 30 minutes, which is perfect, actually, because someone fed Isaac's dog too much kibble at a picnic yesterday and she did a full and funky shit in the kitchen this morning and even with all the windows open the house smells quite sharp. **FOUR STARS**

BUYING A VERY SPECIFIC PEN INSERT FROM JAPAN

Isaac was out of the house most of today doing some sort of complicated job that involved a big thing of keys and an entire emptied-out boot of a Volkswagen estate and I couldn't really be involved so I stayed inside to concentrate. This went the usual way: I walked to get a coffee, fell slightly in love with the coffee girl, ate some sort of sandy shortbread for breakfast by the sea, blinked and squinted in the sun, smelled the air as it whipped salty against me. And then I went home, listened to one and a half ambient albums, stared out of the window, locked my knees in place then unlocked them again, Googled the words 'pilates ——— should I???', closed the tab, opened the tab, closed the tab, opened another tab, noiselessly ejaculated, opened another tab, checked my e-mails, checked my e-mails, checked my e-mails again. It's been 170 days since I watched that boy die. It's been about 180 since I had a good idea.

My pen needed new inserts, though, which was a welcome distraction. I should explain about my pen: it's the Ohto Horizon Needle Point (this has also been unsuccessfully rebadged as the 'Ohto Horizon 2021 Ballpoint', and, laughably, the 'Ohto GS01', but it's still the same pen), which is an objectively perfect low- to mid-price-point pen barrel. It's cool-to-the-touch aluminium with just the right about of weight to it – it balances perfectly on the fingers, and in hand when you hold it – and the nib of the pen clicks out with a satisfying lid press and clicks out again with a stunning *thunk!* when you hit the eject button. Often, people – normal people, not pen freaks, but normal ones – have remarked on what a beautiful pen it is, what perfect balance, what a satisfying *thunk!* it has. They ask me where to buy it, and how. And I say: *well it's not as simple as that.*

The point with the Ohto Horizon is it comes with a default rollerball insert, which – and I feel I don't have to explain! – is obviously disgusting. Rollerballs slither all over paper. They have a horrible cheap inky smell, and an inconsistent line: a bobble of ink here, a short period of nothing, a big blob of ink there. They press down too hard on the page and scrape down into tomorrow's page on any good notebook, and they can only write in big ungainly splurges – huge, 1.0mm thick lines, instead of a more elegant and precise 0.4mm or even 0.3mm. I do not respect anyone who uses a rollerball. I'm choosing to not even comment on how I feel about adults who use biros.

Therefore, with the Ohto, I unscrew the top and replace the default rollerball with a needlepoint instead. But for the particular tooling inside of the Ohto Horizon, you need to have a knocked insert, which is a special stumpy ink refill that only comes in a very specific shape and size, and is not listed on most of the more popular English language stationery websites. To find the correct Hi-Tec-C refill that I need, then, you often have to go to Japanese eBay, which is effective but slow (a three-week delivery time!) and also, translation-wise, a little bit hit and miss: the last batch of inserts I bought were not blue (blue ink is disgusting.) or black, but an off-black that leaned blue, and though nobody else could notice when I showed them, I could, and it drove me deranged. Japanese eBay seems out of stock, though, so I've had to find a different website that only delivers in Japan, so I've had to set up a forwarding address, with a whole new e-mail sign-up and confirmation process, and also it's to be kept in mind that (due to the short, stumpy nature of the pen insert) the Ohto absolutely steams through these little ink refills, so to make the whole dropship-and-forward parcel process cost effective I have to buy 24 refills for my pen. I don't even question how much PayPal converts that to from yen. I cannot work without this pen.

Nobody has ever talked about this, but I have two Ohto Horizons in my rotation, because— and this will probably sound a little crazy to you! – because they help me think. I used to have a teddy when I was a kid, Stripey, a little green-headed pink-faced guy with a hard plastic nose I used to worry my nail beds over when I was stressed or sleepy, and I like to do a similar thing with my Ohtos, now, to help me think. But to *help* me think they have to be ice cold – a pen warm from my own hands feels disgusting to me – so I have to have one pen to hold and worry with and think, and another that is cooling off like a pie on a window, waiting for me to pick up and flip and whirr and think over, again. This is why I need so many inserts, really, and why I desperately need them and from Japan and as soon as possible, and because I cannot find another pen that works: nothing else really activates my brain like pressing an Ohto Horizon with a Hi-Tec-C jet black ink insert in it against my finger beds. So actually it was a good use of— Christ, three and a half *hours* of my afternoon? If Isaac comes back I'm just going to tell him I fell asleep. It's less embarrassing than what I truly did. **ONE STAR**

EXACTLY THREE DRAGS ON A CIGARETTE

1. The man wakes up face down in a double bed in a spare bedroom full of disassembled bikes and complicated server equipment and an office bin that hasn't been emptied for two months and an electronic piano with dust on it and a stiff marine-green beach towel and a tiny pointer-nosed dog sniffing wiggling at his feet and he is naked and his tongue tastes dry and his head hurts and he knows without looking that it is 2 p.m. somehow and he immediately thinks: oh no.
2. The memories are blurry but when they go they go like this: yesterday started at midday. Whatever happened before then has already slipped into the white fog of memory and therefore has already become irrelevant to the point that, essentially, it didn't happen. Probably there was a shower and

probably there was some cereal and probably there was half an episode of *Iron Chef* and probably there was one of those conversations two people have – the type intersected with long pauses while the other one focuses on typing on a laptop, errrrr . . . sorry, what's that? Yeah – where they decide what they are going to do. An early lunch, maybe, seeing as it's Friday? A brunch? And the errors all start from there.

3. Perhaps it was a mistake to go to the fry-up café that Pete Doherty from The Libertines famously completed a mega breakfast challenge at in 2018, but it wasn't the first mistake. The first mistake was made several months ago when Isaac broke up with Elle and told you he had broken up with Elle – "I've broken up with Elle, bro," he texted, he texted you those words – and you said, "Does that mean I can unfollow her faux-fur bumbag Instagram account, then?", and he said: "I'm actually pretty cut up about it." And then the 'Typing . . .' notification came up for a really long time, then went away again, and then he just said: "But yeah."

4. So it has been established that unfollowing the faux-fur bumbag (and keyring) Instagram account was the first mistake that you, personally, made.

5. The second mistake was forgetting a lesson learned repeatedly in your twenties and thought that you had carried ironclad into your thirties but, as it turns out, you were wrong, because you forgot. The lesson is this: the first break-up never sticks. You know this, you know this, you know this. The first break-up

never sticks and that's why you never say anything about the person they have just broken up with because they will get back together with them – you know this! – and then suddenly they get back together again and the half of the relationship you know is holding onto their partner with a single arm slouched lovingly around their shoulder but on their face is a smile, more of a grin actually, a thin rictus grin that says I vividly remember every bad thing you said about the person I am now re-back in love with, and hold your sins against you stronger than I hold either theirs against them or me against my own, and in this particular instance what you are saying is Elle is at the Pete Doherty fry-up café with us and she knows you unfollowed her faux-fur bumbag (and keyring) Instagram account the second after her and Isaac (as it turned out unsuccessfully) broke up.

6. (The intimation here being of course that you neither like her nor her faux-fur bumbags, or even the keyrings, which are harmless enough if a bit impractically sized.)
7. A faux-fur bumbag Instagram account is an Instagram account set up for the selling and advertising of faux-fur bumbags – perhaps if you need a soft, destructible bag for foreign currency, for instance – as well as faux-fur keyrings and also faux-fur iPad and iPhone covers, although thankfully Android devices are not covered, with the fur. When Elle and Isaac were first together you followed the faux-fur bumbag Instagram account while in the pub with her – aren't we having a fun time, here, at the pub, with your

girlfriend! You will follow her on Instagram, and cement the friendship! – but in the time since then you have found the faux-fur bumbag Instagram account a difficult follow. Seeing faux-fur bumbags and keyrings had a tremendous effect on your mood, for some reason. There is something about the *faux*-ness of the fur that runs a shiver through your entire body – there is something textural about it that repulses something buried dormant in your nerves – but also you have worked embarrassingly hard to curate your Instagram feed exactly to your aesthetic liking, and now the presence of a faux-fur bumbag follow is dragging in a number of faux-fur (and faux-suede, and faux-leather, and—) content into your algorithm, and it's getting in the way of all the New York city sandwiches and lads who wear caps getting dressed in front of a Monstera. This was an issue that has since been resolved. The day you unfollowed the faux-fur bumbag account you felt as light and as free as air.

8. The moment you order your All In Breakfast with extra black pudding you know that Elle knows that you unfollowed her faux-fur bumbag Instagram account and is holding that information against you like a gun.
9. (To the list of mistakes we must add: ordering the All In Breakfast with extra black pudding.)
10. After the All In Breakfast with extra black pudding and for some reason a 500ml bottle of Rubicon lychee-flavoured soft drink and for some reason a cup of tea out of the tea urn (two incredibly, palpably rogue drink choices, one after another) it is

FOUR STARS

1.25 p.m. and you haven't written a word all week and you know you're not going to write one now and you feel the illness rumbling within you like a sin and you know that it is an ancient curse and you know what you are going to say has passed down from man to man to man to man to man through separate strains of the family since the ancient times and in many ways you are therefore at a loss to resist both the power of the word you are going to say and the action that it is going to inspire (not just in yourself but in others) but you can feel it coming through you like a lightning bolt anyway and you know Isaac is going to say "yes" and you know it is a mistake even before you've said it and you know you are a bad influence on you and you know you're a bad influence on him and you know, to your core to your bones to the atomic molecular level dust of you that you are a bad person, you know you know you know, but you still say: "Pub?"

11. So now you are in the pub.
12. A long lazy afternoon in the pub is a beautiful thing that escapes and resists description. You are at a table and the sun is up and there are pints in front of you, big beautiful pints. Then there are some more. A packet of dry-roasted nuts is inelegantly torn open. You tell one, perfect, really good joke. You are leaning on the bar and you are fairly sure – fairly fairly sure, actually! Fairly sure! – that the barmaid is flirting with you. She is bright and hopeful and in her mid-twenties and pretty enough but also has high stubby canines like a vampire.

A fog of eroticism clouds your mind. You could not fall in love with a girl who has teeth that start in the very mountains of her gumline and point out so abruptly like that, but you can definitely imagine yourself sending her a lot of texts and going back to her house a few times and using her towel after a shower. You can imagine meeting her after work and making her laugh and, using the thudding half-words of sexual instruction, among the woozy pink light of the low lamp by her bedside, making her bounce on top of you like a toy. You tell the same joke again and it doesn't hit so hard this time. An old man with a yellow-grey ponytail and a complicated wristbrace taps you on the shoulder at the urinal while you pee. "How tall are you?" he says, and you smile and say: "Oh, only six-four." He's amazed. Thud. You are fairly sure – fairly fairly sure, actually! – he is flirting with you. You cannot imagine putting your thumb in his mouth and making him beg. You cannot imagine texting him from an Uber that you are going to 'teach' 'that ass' 'a lesson'. You cannot imagine sitting in a room that smells sweet and him saying, "I've told my friends about you, do you want to meet them?" and saying "No." You go back to the bar and the barmaid is off shift and the new one does not like you at all. Nobody has collected any glasses for an hour now and they shine like trophies on the table in front of you. You are standing back-to-back with the man with the ponytail and he is telling his friend – a man so old and pink and squinted that every feature

FOUR STARS

of his face seems to have been sucked into the same huge puckered central wink, and he is nodding and going, "Yeah, yeah." Time is moving like honey now. Time is moving like whisky. Time is moving like ooze, time is moving like the ocean. The afterwork crowd is slowly starting to fill a bar that for all the afternoon has been your domain and Isaac knows every one of them. You are introduced to two girls called Ruby and three men called Ben. You are introduced to a microscopic puppy called Laika (people love calling their dog 'Laika') who causes unfettered chaos around the feet of the bar – the extendable cord of her leash zipping around dozens of sets of selvedge jeans over Red Wings – and has to leave when she does an excitable wee on the floorboards. Nobody cleans it up. You pick at some pickled onions and the last few withered slices of a charcuterie board. Every time Isaac introduces you to someone you nod and smile and try and be a part of the conversation but they have already moved on to something you both know nothing about and cannot make any of your little jokes about – yeah I saw that article they did about it, yeah well it's fucking bullshit isn't it mate, yeah I'll see you at the hustings, yeah – and so you try and make small talk with Elle. "What's your favourite tall building?" you ask her, and she says, "What?", because the bar is getting louder now – that rising rabbling excited sound of a Friday night, the last final click of a gear on a long week of working – and you say "WHAT'S YOUR FAVOURITE TALL BUILDING" and she

says, "I don't know" and looks at her phone for a really, really, really, really long time.
13. Another mistake was not noticing when it became 10 p.m.
14. Isaac took the dog home for dinner and also to put her to bed and Elle went with him saying something about "needing to change" so you are at the pub with the table and you are looking at your phone. You are the only person sat here and you've had this table all afternoon but the pub is full now – jumping, even, the floor seems alive and springy now it's so full of people, and laughing and those loud uncontrollable pub voices, "NO I DIDN'T, NO I FUCKING DIDN'T! NO HE'S TELLING IT WRONG, NO—" – and there are a group of people stood next to your table and backing their asses and legs into the chair-backs because they want the table and they are trying to assert dominance. A guy has held the back of Isaac's chair and gone "do you mind if I—?" and you had to say, "No, sorry, my mate's sitting there", and when he left he definitely muttered something under his breath. You can't get up to the bar and you can't get up to the toilet because you will lose the table. They do not understand that this has been your table for ten hours now. You earned this table. They think you are hogging the table, when the table is already yours. If they want it they will have to kill you for it.
15. The barmaid with the fangs is not in any of the tagged photos of the pub's Instagram nor is she on the hashtag for the pub on Instagram nor is she

FOUR STARS

evident in any of the pub's 362 Twitter followers. You could check their likes on Facebook but your phone is getting hot and the battery has issued so many warning notifications that you have had to put it in Dark Mode. Another guy from the group makes a move for one of the chairs but the original guy who tried to get the chair said, "Don't bother, mate, he's a fucking twat."

16. Isaac has come back to the pub with a grave expression and said there's a housewarming party round the corner with Elle and some of Elle's mates and it's going to be quite a cool vibe but to get in we're going to need to buy two actually quite nice bottles of wine and you're going to need to walk around by the sea a bit and maybe have a burger so you sober up.

17. In the retelling of the story it will be registered that kicking the chairs over and yelling "pick that up, cunt!" at the guy who tried to take it from you earlier was very much not the vibe and yes, must go down as one of the mistakes.

18. You are never more aware of how 35 years old you look than when you are watching yourself in a kebab shop mirror eating a £4 cheeseburger while bathed in fluorescent downlight. You have never been older than you are right now. You are, once again, struck by the ability for cheap fluorescent lit kebab shops to fry chips that are too hot to eat but somehow do not melt the handful of cheese that has been sprinkled on top of them. You have a theory that kebab shop grated cheese would not melt if you

sprinkled it on lava. But nobody is ever going to do that experiment. Nobody has the guts.

19. Hold on, is— is your hair thinning? Your hair can't be thinning. Can it? Would it have gone by now? Or is it just the light? You can't compare it with Isaac because Isaac has already lost his hair but is still really alpha about it. Isaac has always made holding the heavy crown of manhood look like a simple task for light hands, but when you try it feels like an anvil. Isaac can do all the manly things you can't – drive a car, roll a cigarette, talk to women without getting flustered about it – and you always envy him for it. If you lose your hair you will be nothing, you will be nothing. No more barmaids for you ever in your life if you lose your hair. You cannot be going bald. This cannot happen to you. You feel so sick you could die.

20. Isaac knows about wine so he is choosing the bottles and you are looking at the crisps and holding a bottle of Pepsi Max that is so freezing it is like ice. You came out in an overshirt over a t-shirt and now the night has swept in and the wind has come in from the sea and you are freezing. They have a new flavour of Wotsit and you ask Isaac if that is the kind of thing you could bring to a party. No. You pick up a bottle of wine and check the price (£11) and how deep the punt is at the bottom of it (pretty deep) and tell Isaac that it's a good bottle of wine based on these facts. He checks the wine app he has on his phone. This wine is so bad there are three really angry forum threads about

how bad it is, on an app that is not traditionally even used as a forum. "Didn't you used to go out with a sommelier?" Isaac asks, and yes, you did, but but you never really ever paid attention to her or her life or what she talked about or what she cared about – particularly in regards to wine, but plenty of other stuff too – and as such that's one of the primary reasons that you, no longer, go out with a sommelier.

21. One time when you were at university and 19 and the only thing you wore was hoodies and cargo trousers and the only thing you ate was chocolate-flavoured Shreddies, a guy's friend from home drove up for the weekend and insisted you all walked up Snowdon. The guy's friend from home was one of those people you are friends with as a late adolescent in that he was very personalityless and quite actively boring but at least he had a car. As you drove up towards Snowdon, a mist descended around the vehicle, and Radio 1 broke its usual programming to instead start issuing broad weather warnings across the entire UK. What you learned that day was most people start climbing British mountains very early in the morning, not at 4 p.m., and most of them take more than a hoodie and a single half-full bottle of water with which to do it. You made it 80% of the way up the mountain before you were completely surrounded by cloud. The other two wanted to press on but every year like clockwork you hear about an unprepared stag do trying to climb this mountain dressed in

ponchos and sombreros and fake moustaches and flip-flops and having to be helicoptered down, and there's a BBC article about them where the comments have to be monitored, and it gets widely mocked on panel shows and everyone laughs at them, and you didn't want to be like them and also you didn't want to die, so you said *No*. You all trudged down the mountain in absolute silence as the darkness crept in, and you were at the back, and your penis had shrivelled entirely into your body and you were fully, fully sobbing. That was the coldest you had ever been in your life, before today, when you had to walk eight streets away along the seafront to get to a housewarming party.

22. A girl who seemed to have a bindi tattooed on her forehead asks you if you want a smoke and after you have suitably warmed up – the host found you a big fleece jacket that used to belong to her dad and that she clearly had done a lot of the fresh-smelling painting around you in – you say, "yeah, sure," but just a drag. This is your new trick: you have never been a full-time smoker, never in your life finished an entire packet of cigarettes, but sometimes 12 hours since your first beer you get the need to taste one, that sensation of smoke and fire and tar, a cool evil energy, the gush of the air between your teeth, and so you huddle together on a wall outside and you take exactly three drags of her cigarette. This is the perfect amount of cigarette: just a taste. It is good and it is hot and it is smoky and the stick feels good between your fingers and you feel like an

FOUR STARS

ancient dragon or a god puffing smoke between your lips, and it is smeared with her lip gloss and you get the strange erotic impulse again – you have already shared lips with this woman, in a way, so you may as well clench your hand in the back of her hair and kiss her – but you really, really cannot get past the fact that she seems to have a bindi tattooed on her forehead and also you don't know her name. You say: "Sorry I've forgotten, what is your name?" and she says she's told you three times already she won't tell you again. But part of you suspects that yeah, she will tell you again. You're just that charming.

23. Isaac gives you a fairly hefty bump of cocaine and you immediately need to take a big cocaine shit and when it happens it is exactly what you thought, slippery and sour, and you go through most of a roll of toilet paper and there are just not the right pieces of equipment in here, not the right pieces at all. I mean who doesn't have Aesop drops, or at least a thing of Oust? Who doesn't have that? Why is everything in this bathroom covered in talc and sticky dust and why is there a really old tub of Vaseline here? Anyway you pump a load of hand soap down the toilet and flush twice even though there's knocking outside and the water's getting very foamy and you wash your hands hot in the water and breathe once, twice, then head up shoulders back and leave.

24. The guys from the pub are here and they give you some looks and some mutters but you're quite

coke-cocky now and you've already (effectively) pulled twice today so spirits are fairly high (again this may have been the cocaine and this may have been one of your famous 'mistakes') but you march up to the main one and introduce yourself and say, "Hey, ha-ha" and he says, "What?" and you say, "Listen ah I mean it's fair to say we didn't get off to the best of starts in the pub earlier" and he is still being really stiff about it and is like "No" and you're like "Yeah, uh: listen I'm really sorry I've just been on a bit of a mad one lately I've just gone through a break-up and come down here to stay with my mate—" and you look behind you but Isaac saw this happening and has gone out in the garden to smoke a roll-up with the bindi girl, "— yeah and sorry it's just sort of all hit me this week and— Yeah." and the guy goes, "Yeah OK mate" like he's trying really hard to be the cool one and so you usher the girls in who are watching this unfold with weird terrified faces and go "I sort of threw a chair at your mate earlier" and they all laugh and now everyone's laughing because that's a completely insane thing to do and you're laughing now and you're like, "I know! I'm insane!"

25. You have organised an impromptu thumb-wrestling tournament in the kitchen with all the guys you threw a chair at earlier. It's 1 a.m. and now it's OK to smoke inside. You are drinking pink wine from the bottle. Someone opens the fridge and goes, "Ah! Pepsi Max!"
26. You are a god you are a monolith you are a planet you are a star

FOUR STARS

27. You are nothing you are dirt you are the worm that writhes within it
28. Elle pops her head into the kitchen and says her guy is round the corner and he's bringing four if anyone wants them but she's only getting two and you say, "Yeah I'll have one" and she sighs really visibly and looks around and says, "Anyone else, does anyone else want one?' and you say, "I mean I'll get two if no one—" but she's already left the kitchen by then
29. I mean it's Margate coke how good can it really be?
30. You're sat cross-legged on the floor and speaking really really quickly and telling some girl that the lighting in here is wrong, all wrong, it's insane that they – an abstract concept, the 'they', a 'they' that floats outside of the realm of this house, in a dense white fog – they got this wrong and how they got it, there's too much downlight and not enough uplight, and all the bulb colours are wrong, unsympathetic white xenon bulbs and not enough warm creamy yellows. "Philips," you say, "Philips do a colour-changing bulb now that uses a tiny amount of energy and you can control really easily via an app, and like, just think how much that would transform a room like this, a mood, a vibe." You cannot have a party without a vibe and you cannot have a party beneath the sheer white glare of a xenon bulb. "There is not even a single floor lamp in here!" you say, and you are laughing because it's insane how bad they got it. "Anyway what do you do," you say, and she says: "I live here. I decorated the room." And you say, "Well obviously the lighting isn't

finished yet" and she says, "No, it is. I like it like this." And you have two options here, the easy one being: you slowly tiptoe backwards in the imprints you have made, you rescind the critical light theory, you gobble back the last half-hour of light-based conversation.

31. The other option is you double-down and somehow keep criticising the lighting in here for ten more minutes.
32. Isaac has gone briefly missing at the party and you assume this is because he's having sex with someone, probably Elle. This is because Isaac is a horny guy. You've always kind of respected this kind of primal, impulsive horniness in him and a few other of your friends: masculinity and get-it-now horniness sort of go hand-in-hand, and you respect men in their thirties who still get a nut off at a party the same way you might respect a guy who's good in a fight or who can fix a car. Your own horniness blushes as a low, constant hum, but beyond those first few can't-keep-your-hands-off-them weeks of a relationship, your horniness does lean very truly domestic, never quite tipping into the filth: you've had sex in a bathroom once and you also did it at that place in Soho where they serve you tapas through a hatch, but realistically you are more comfortable on home turf, with a good duvet and some expensive pillows and access to a big canister of lube. One time in a moment of hysteria you did masturbate at Heathrow airport but that was more for practical reasons (staring down

FOUR STARS

the barrel of an eight-hour flight that you knew would tip into an uncomfortable doze and you hadn't ejaculated for a number of days and you knew this pent-up energy would lead to a frenzied horny half-sleep so, for the same reason they milk cows every day to stop them living in agony, you robotically brought yourself to a froth) than erotic ones. You locked yourself in a large double-width disabled cubicle and closed your eyes and thought, in very simple straightforward terms, about pink nipples and big tits. Sometimes orgasms are astonishing moments of profound ecstasy, and sometimes they are a very functional way of getting your hand dirty, and this was the latter one. I think it's very hard to nut your eyes into the back of your head when bound to the beige cubicle of a Heathrow airport bathroom.

33. You see Isaac on the stairs and say, "Hey man, where were you: suckin' and fuckin'?" and he smiles then shakes his head abruptly no and then Elle appears behind him, rotating her skirt around her waist, and then she sees you – arm frozen in the air for a congratulatory high-five – then does a low grumbling sound of frustration ("Ugh!") and storms past you both really fucking clumsily to get to the kitchen.

34. You don't really know what you've done wrong but Isaac seems to know what you've done wrong and does the 'you've done something wrong' symbol – pushes towards your chest with two flat palms out towards you – and says, "Let me handle this."

JOEL GOLBY

35. You are trying to find an outlet to put your phone charger into because you're on 1% and have been in Airplane Mode for a number of hours now and you think you've found a safe plug to take out behind a bookshelf but when you hit the switch to turn the supply off (ever since a special assembly in primary school you have been very, perhaps outsizedly afraid of electricity and electrocution) it turns out you turned off the strip-socket that was supplying energy to the TV, the speakers, the laptop that was connected to YouTube that everyone was playing music through, and the one tasteful light source in the entire house, an indoor light projector you've seen advertised underneath viral tweets, and so now suddenly all the light and music and energy in the room has been turned off and everyone is looking at you, holding your phone, saying "it's on 1%".
36. It turns out it was an old laptop and the battery didn't work so it was working solely off the direct supply and for that reason the machine needed an entire defrag and a restart after the power got back on and it was so long before anyone was able to connect to the WiFi and the TV and get the speakers started again that everyone left the room and went outside, and you are just stood behind the host of the party, The Girl Who Likes Her Lamps, and you are trying to help because you "know a bit about computers" but she's saying "you don't know about this computer" and anyway it's fine because the wheezing old machine has a USB socket and you can just about wean some energy out of it via there.

FOUR STARS

37. You are now alone in the room with the laptop and the TV and the lamp and the speaker and you are tasked with finding the exact right song necessary to bring everyone back to the party hub and you load up YouTube and pick the best song on the platform – Friendly Fires' "Paris" (Aeroplane Remix), uploaded 12 years ago and still only hovering at 678,000 views – a song so good it makes you emotional even when you're not on coke (and in the intervening minutes since you unplugged the entire party you have done a second very large bump of coke) so it makes you very, very emotional now, and you close your eyes and feel like you're travelling wingless through the sky and everything is gorgeous and suns set and clouds form and trains bullet their way through the countryside, what a world we've built, what a beautiful world we've built and there's so much of it, my god my god my god what a gift it is to be alive—
38. You open your eyes and you are alone and this was not the right song to play to get the party started again. A guy with a bisexual haircut comes in and puts some gabba on instead.
39. He's actually really sound and you end up hitting him with some of your party questions (party questions are fun, pre-loaded questions you ask people at parties) (you realise you should have mentioned this before), playing all the hits – What's Your Favourite Tall Building? What Was The Name Of The Kid At Your School Who Died? What's The Nicest Thing Anyone's Ever Done For You? – but we

get onto, obviously, the subject of bisexuality and being a bisexual and he asks you, obviously, if you've ever been with a guy and you say no, because you haven't and quite simply it's not your bag, you understand men and have many uses for them but mostly they are class to have pints and watch football and go bowling with and you just can't imagine what an absolute nightmare it is to have intercourse with them, all that hair, all those smells, their rough large hands and their deep wells of emotional resistance, and Oli (he's bisexual – his name is Oli) is like "Oh then can you only have sex with someone who is doing your emotional support for you?" and you go "No, no!" but then you think about it and annoyingly, maybe, yes, maybe this fucking bisexual is right.

40. You sense Oli is losing interest in you now he knows you're not a bisexual nor even capable of being bisexual for even one hour of your life so you offer him some of your cocaine, which you've now got way too much of, and that wins him back over. He introduces you to another bisexual, an Irish guy, and you try hitting him with some of your party questions – What Hospital Were You Born In? What Was The Incident At Your School That Forced A Special Assembly? What's The Best Meal You've Ever Eaten? – but he's really not having it and you remember that for some reason asking Irish people direct questions about themselves inspires this very strange fight-or-flight response and now you have to talk him down from trying to start on you. Oli's like,

FOUR STARS

"Pete, Pete, it's just like a fun game mate, it's just like a conversation starting game" and Pete's like, "It's fucking weird it's fucking personal" and I say, "Would a big bump of coke help smooth things over?" and Pete wordlessly acquiesces and when he's snorting an (actually massive) amount of your drugs you ask him, "So what's your shower routine?" and you can tell that internally he's going absolutely ballistic again but you can't have a go at the man who's holding the coke, can you.

41. Can you, Pete?
42. No Pete, you cannot.
43. You don't really know what's happened but you've blinked and two hours have gone by and Isaac seems to have spent a lot of it in the garden pleading with Elle to calm down and like they both have that body language people have when they are arguing but trying to do it quietly and in a way where no one notices (but you always notice) – hands in pockets, or arms crossed, or discreet full-thumb cheek brushing to get rid of tears, or turning away to look at something, or staring at the sky or ceiling, and they are doing a lot of that – while you however have somehow reignited the thumb war tournament in the kitchen with the bisexuals and that guy you threw a chair at and you're eating a whole pack of fishsticks you found in the fridge and being the referee and the atmosphere is surprisingly (almost psychotically) jovial and Oli is two-for-oh and Pete is doing his best to clamp Ben the Chair Guy into a

pin and then Elle comes in and everyone stops cheering for a sec and she goes—

44. She goes—
45. "You're all fucking children," and then she turns to you, and says, "but especially you, because not only are you a child but you're an asshole."
46. And everyone is there – the bisexuals and the bindi girl and the guy you threw a chair at and everyone who watched you accidentally unplug the entire party and the two girls who used the bathroom after you did and you overheard them in the kitchen saying, "yeah, loads of soap in there for some reason like it was just foaming up for some reason, one of the I mean absolutely the weirdest things I've ever seen at a party" – and suddenly obviously the music has stopped or at least it feels like it's stopped and everyone is looking at you in your moment of debasement and you are holding a fishstick halfway up to your mouth, and yeah now it is probably time for you to leave.
47. You walk home along the black whipped wind of the sea and you openly weep at what you have become.
48. You know you are an asshole and you know you are a person with flaws and mostly that is OK and you are allowed to bounce through life relatively unhurt but sometimes, and for some reason this happens regularly to semi-often, some people take great offence at your Kramer-like ability to bonk off walls and emerge unscratched, and they need to tell you, You Alone, that you have deep and terrible rivers of

FOUR STARS

evil running from the heart of you out to the surface, and that you are a bad person and you make life worse for other people by living, which secretly yes you did suspect but it does hurt a little to hear it said out loud, and like, Oh great, now you have to have a whole existential crisis because a mid-range bumbag-maker doesn't like you that much because you unfollowed her on Instagram which (ironically) takes energy away from the internal delvings you have already been making into your psyche about who you are, what you have become, and whether or not you are healthy or good, which obviously you have been trawling the dark waters of since Megan finally left you but now instead you have to focus on this, the next four days (minimum) of your life which will be spent wondering if it was the electricity or the fishstick that did you in, and when you slip into sleep at first it is grey and fitful and then it is deep, blank, an abyss, but only some flickering memory in there, a single candle in an abandoned church—
- you come to yourself in a dream and tell yourself, "since I last saw you I've grown a moustache, gone for a pedicure, and invested in iron, the heavy workable metal, iron; iron iron iron".
- oranges, reds, yellows, but then also purples, blues, flowers as viewed from beneath, from the level of grass.
- the scariest dream you had when you were a child was when you were a microscopic little ant-person, the side of a seed, and you were

embedded in the tyres of a huge enormous truck, and that truck zoomed out to reveal that it was itself a tiny dot in the middle of the Grand Canyon, and you always woke up with your feet itching and an uncomfortable feeling around your nipples and for a few weeks later certain shapes (wooden corners, edges of beds and tables, but also oblongs, things at a slant) made you feel terribly on-edge, and at certain periods of great and overwhelming stress in your life the ant–truck–canyon dream has returned, and you wake up itching and sweating and afraid of the edge of the bed where the dog is biting at you and know that this is what sleep is going to feel like, now, until you forget.

49. Nobody can love you until you love yourself but you wonder if you've ever loved yourself and therefore, in turn, if you've ever truly actually been loved, and also for fuck sake you forgot to charge your phone overnight again.

50. Isaac slept at Elle's and says it's "chill if you stay" but I think we both know that you should pack your bags and be at the train station again within the next hour, hour-and-a-half. **NEGATIVE A MILLION STARS**

A 10K RUN THAT FINISHES AT STRATFORD WESTFIELD

I've been getting back to it, lately. Lots of dense juice for breakfast, that type of thing. A few more vitamins into the regime. You always have to eat almonds, for some reason. I have deleted every number and cleaned every surface in my room. I have purged my Instagram of all the people I only watch because their success makes me angry (Ed Warburton, catch this block!), and replaced them with the things that soothe me instead (i.e. incredibly sped-up videos of faceless American men detailing barn-find cars; a gap-toothed midwestern janitor who cheerfully cleans up crime scenes). It's all going off: I have managed to keep a basil plant going for like seven straight weeks now, for instance. Like: I finally fucking finished *The Interestings*. I am finding that I don't screw up my eyes and scream in my head quite so often anymore. Sometimes I wake up, breathe through both nostrils, and actually think: *oh, good*. It's crazy.

I have been running, a lot, and stretching, slightly less than I should but still quite a good amount, and this has seemed to be good for me, too. Naturally athletic and agile and flexible people are always talking about the fake news of a 'runner's high', which I'll admit I never felt once over about 15 months of slow chugging 5K runs, but recently I have been becoming bouncier and more springy and my breathing sounds less like a man having a panic attack mid-air between

FOUR STARS

the top of a skyscraper and the pavement, and I'm not necessarily flush with endorphins but I get the general idea. I am wearing reflective wraparound green-orange shades and little sweat-wicking gloves. I move past buggies and bikes in short-shorts and freshly laundered Nike socks. At around kilometre six, I can feel my face feeling flush and puce, and that's when everything starts to finally relax and click: one foot up then one foot down, a rhythmic little dance, an app reminding me exactly how many miles I've dragged this particular pair of trainers around east London. I can stretch my entire body out with my arms high above my head and contort myself into a series of satisfying pops and clicks. My face doesn't look like how it got for a while, with that blurry edge. I am always drinking water and pissing pure, clear urine out again. I feel like I'm taking handsomeness pills.

I used to go to Stratford Westfield in times of deep psychic panic – at its worst I got up to three or four visits a week – but now I like to finish my runs there, flush and healthy, touching all the little hand balms in L'Occitane in a way that seems to make the shop girl there very uncomfortable. I love this strange cathedral – a John Lewis that occupies three floors! – the anonymous burbling bustle, the crowds that can't help but walk into each other, the high distant squeak of a trainer sole on tile, a series of escalators that go too slow, a strange clean complete lack of smell. There are infinite possibilities of things to do that no human has ever wanted to do: buy a gourmet cookie that somehow costs £5! Buy an astringent bottle of aftershave from a man in tight trousers! Go to a batting cage-cum-bar that is literally always empty because it is cloaked in darkness, and hit baseballs at a machine! It is possible to buy a Sky TV subscription here, though nobody has ever done that. On certain days there's a shop front that just has a full Hyundai outside it, just parked there. Why. Who is buying that.

I queue up for froyo at the froyo place even though there are more people working the stand than there are in the queue, and normally I would be incredibly frustrated that it's somehow taken two people to serve one woman who just wanted M&Ms and brownie bites on a medium cup of Original – I mean how hard is it really, I mean this is not a challenging request to the froyo stand, this should be quite straightforward, come on – but actually I feel OK. I go to Boots and get a new thing of moisturiser and tuck it in my shorts pocket so it bulges out insanely. I spend almost a full human hour, completely unbothered and undisturbed by anyone around me, prowling around the sprawling TK Maxx. I try on a translucent watch and decide that maybe I'll ask for it for Christmas. I stand on a balcony and gaze down at the food court. There is a McDonald's and a Pizza Hut and one of the country's only Popeye's. There's a security guard outside the JD Sports who looks like he was trained in the Marines. I can get a massage out in the open then walk ten feet and buy a fresh sugar pretzel. This is a lawless place without rules. I love it here.

Babies like crying in Westfield: I am convinced people take their babies there just to cry. A lot of teenagers like running through crowds, laughing and wearing backpacks. Families take trips here, seemingly bringing everything they own along with them, and all they do is walk slowly around H&M occasionally picking at a shirt sleeve and saying "Mum what do you think of that?". Young couples in too-distressed jeans love having miserable day dates there. This isn't a place to flex – this is a zone where there is an almost complete absence of taste – but a lot of people have dressed to walk around this place, lazily holding hands, looking at their phones, maybe running a single finger along a Hyundai. All forms of life are here but none of them are like me at all. It feels like wandering around an alien planet. I walk home with the liquid remains of a yoghurt and a good ache in my legs, and feel like my brain has been taken out and washed smooth. My tracking watch tells me my heartbeat is low and calm. I take the first deep breath I've taken in months. **FIVE STARS**

NOTES ON DEATH AND LOVING MY DOG

I recently heard a new theory about death, a thing I am completely and near-constantly afraid of, a fear that manifests itself in the worst ways – when I have two wet hands plunged in the washing-up, for instance, or while I'm idling on a bus with too many people on it and rushing off the bus to have an attack of panic would mean moving past too many backpacks or babies in prams – so I have to scrunch up my eyes and grasp hard onto something and repeat to myself the mantra *you only die once you only die once you only die once*, which – unless you're that eerie little '90s boy who went to heaven and came back – we all do. That brings me some small peace: you only have to go through the sheer final eternal horror of death one time, and then it's done, *thock!*, you're over the hump and you are calmly and quietly dead. I can do any difficult thing once, can't I? Death is no different.

The theory goes like this: when you die, your mind shuts down and your soul enters into a sort of purgatorial abyss, darkness maybe, perhaps some distant twilight and a floating feeling, you do not know if you are minute or enormous, but pink and purple dustclouds wash around you and you feel peace. And there, in the last electric embers of what was your mind and soul, you are thrown into a recurring loop of one of the days from your life, again: not necessarily the best day of your life, and not necessarily the worst, but *a* day, from *your* life, a sort of infinite Groundhog Day version of your own life, but you can't change it and you can never become aware of it, you just live it through, again, and then again, and then again. That is the theory. Ever since I heard it I have been trying to emulate one happy moment in my life every day, so on the off-chance today is the day I have to relive into infinity then, like, I ate a Lion bar, or laughed at a video compilation of people falling over, or shaved my beard really well, or just anything small and honest and good. The flipside of course is every time I have to artificially inject joy into my life I have to grapple with the fact that that is a fundamentally depressing thing to have to do. Normal people are just *happy*. They don't worry about reliving their life in death: that actually sounds quite nice, to them.

Megan left me with the dog this weekend while she and some new guy she met at a gig go to Marseille (and I bet he won't start a fight about nothing! I bet he won't balk at buying lunch *and* dinner in the same day! I bet he won't get too wine hungover on the Saturday that he tries to cancel the one activity she's been looking forward to ever since they booked the trip together and when she says "no, we have to do it, I really want to", I bet he doesn't drag himself around behind her sighing really heavily throughout, sort of but not quite ruining the whole day for everyone!) and as a result this animal has become the sole focus of my death–happiness over the past couple of days: I keep being really intense at him in a way I don't think he really likes, just in case this is one of the days I relive over and over as my brain flickers out into the void. I keep cradling him and singing to him. I give him little cubes of his favourite cheese (feta he will eat but doesn't love; cheddar he goes bananas for; comté is what he just had now, and I think he liked it). I take him on sunny spring walks and wrap my scarf around him when we go to the pub. I kiss him on the top of the head and make sure he always feels like he is wanted and alright. And I tell him I love him, again and again and again. I stare into his stupid brown eyes until he stops looking around for morsels of food and I say it. Sometimes I lift him up by his heavy squidgy ribcage to better make him focus on me. He kicks his little legs at the air between us. He wriggles. And then he catches my eye, and stares into me, and we both briefly float out in the abyss and through the pink and purple dustclouds, and I fix his gaze and say (out loud): "I love you, Bam." That way if I ever die (inevitable.) and I ever have to relive any day, any day, maybe even this day, at least I did one good thing and I loved the boy. At least I can feel that warm little feeling, forever. Hold on, where is— he's just had diarrhoea in the kitchen. Are you joking? Fucking *comté*! **FIVE STARS**

GOOD ROCK

Sun high in sky today. Good day. Sky blue ground soft. Trees make rustle sound, but small. I am awake no one else awake. I am sleep terribly but day is good. Day is good.

    Fire hot on dark ground. There is some meat. I cook the meat. I eat the meat. Start the day with meat, good day. Everybody wake up make *ah, ahh* noises. I say *there meat*. They go *and where water?* I say fine I go fetch. Nobody else can fetch? Nobody else can go fetch? But OK I go fetch.

FOUR STARS

I like water. Clear and blue. There animals here but I no kill them. No kill them today. That a bad habit. You kill every animal you see? No. Too much meat. Bad meat. *Yeuk.* And then the animal scared of you. You can't make sneak on them. Make it harder kill meat when you need meat. Everybody know this. Everybody know this! But do they do it? *Ah, ah.*

I scoop water in my hands I make wet face. I scoop water on my hands I make wet body. I scoop ... you get it. The hair, I make wet the hair. All sorts of hair. Crazy hair. I no bring soap because I forgot – *idiot forgot, idiot forgot!* – but I get it next time. Is basically just ash and fat from meat. Is not good soap. Is nothing fancy. I no know why I bother with soap. I feel wet I feel refreshed. I fill big sack with water, lug it. The sack is made of skin. Is goth.

Today, easy day. No hunt. Very meat. Got the wet. Sun high in sky, everybody happy. No fuss. I like day like today. Maybe I eat berry. Maybe I don't eat berry! Doesn't matter. I bring water back big sack the fire bigger everybody doing things. Brushing. Make tools sharp. Cut bad bit of vegetable from good vegetable. I like vegetable, not just meat. It can be two things. We make cave nice, high on hill. No bears get in here or wolves neither. Rarely being attacked. Is soothing. We got three more days of meat, four more days of meat. Then, yes, hunt more meat. Until then I sit on good rock.

I have woman, one, two. I have son, one, two. I have daughter, but OK. My one son he seven summers old my second son he two summers old. He live probably, wow. Thank you. Good sons. Seven summers he say *I sharpen arrow* I say *yes* he say *OK*. He tall like me. He hunt, he like hunt. When I die he protect them. I will die. I was once son seven summers, but he die. I make hole put man in hole. Cover him with leaf and stick. Favourite carving of bone. Put fire on top and then dance. Everybody sad but they dance. One day I will live in hole. They dance, they say my name. Then next cave, then next cave. I am still in hole. I am sand. I am nothing.

On good rock I have long stick I point in sand I make shape. Is OK. Sun lower now. Sky look pink and orange. Smell of fire smell of sand. Wind whips. Good day today, all good things. And yet still. I eat meat, I drink water, sure. I see animals, spears sharp. Sure. I make shape on sand, mate with woman. Tomorrow just today but again. Is good but is never *good*. I no dread the hole.

I no know what Diplo is. I no know what iMessage is. I no know what 'girl with a small forearm tattoo of a croissant and thing for getting her mouth spit in' is. I no know what tap water is or why water filter better. I no know what Arsenal banter years is. I no know what is limited edition Lego. I no know what 'import custom' is or why is make vintage hardback Vonnegut cost twice as much as it cost. I no know what mortgage is. I no know what very hype Instagram sandwich is. I never have to take anyone 'Winter Wonderland'. I never go central London and get overwhelmed and have to sit down for minute in Las Iguanas. I never spent £8 in Pret but lunch still no good. Sun go up sun go down I never have to know what 'Tyra Banks has retweeted you' notification is. This all make me good in face. Not knowing all this make me big peace and happy.

Good rock is favourite rock. Is smooth and big. I like sit on rock. Rock get me. Rock get my vibe. Rock here long ago. Rock here long again. Rock never go away. Solid boy, big boy. I am flesh and I am soft. Son, maybe he strong. Maybe he die. We no know. Clear water clear water clear water. Sun sets soft and grey. Have to remember, say thank you. Have to remember, sometimes things good. A hundred fifty thousand men beyond me, all tall. All strong. Good rock still here. I tell woman, *you bury me under good rock.* She say, *you still going on about good rock?* I say yes. Is the best thing. **FIVE SUNS**

FEAR

The running alone wasn't working so I logged onto a special website and filled out a form and an incredibly ornery man in front of a shelf full of books (I looked: all boring, all medical or journal-based, not a scrap of literature amongst them) spoke to me for 30 minutes and decided with a sigh that yes, I would need to be assigned a therapist, who I speak to now for an hour every Tuesday afternoon. It turns out everyone else has already been doing this and nobody mentioned it to me and all my friends are like "yeah" and "it's good, isn't it?" and "it really helps" and I sort of feel they could have brought it up at least once in the 24-month period where it felt like my flesh was gnawing at my skin but listen it's fine now it's done. Her name is Veronica and she seems very nice and I don't want to know a single thing about her other than that.

The main thing I have learned over the process of therapy is that everyone has secretly been speaking to me in therapy-speak for ages; they've just pretended they've found that enlightenment themselves, a discovery that I have found galling. After a particular period of loneliness – for a while there it felt like my sexual urges had been concreted over and replaced by something practical but unglamorous, like a parcel collect locker or a cash-only car wash – I redownloaded some apps and matched again with a girl I once had a particularly fraught late-night Facebook Messenger unresolved affair with, and once we were four drinks in and leaning in a little bit she turned the conversation to therapy, because she herself had been in therapy for a really long time and so wanted to talk about therapy, discuss different forms of therapy, check that I had had therapy, &c. &c. "Have you had therapy?" she said, and I said yeah, a bit, and she said, "let me guess: mummy issues," and I said mm well I mean I don't know we've not spoken that long it's mainly just a list of fears and irritations so far, and she said, "What could you possibly be afraid of?" and I was like, I don't know, everything. You used to just have to bring your birth certificate out to these things so they can figure out your compatibility based on the precise to-the-minute time of your birth. Now you have to show

FOUR STARS

them the deep dark-grey wounds of your soul and an e-mail chain that proves you've spent at least 12 weeks trying to heal them.

Veronica said it was positive that I didn't go home with her despite the overt invitation to (especially as she was wearing a top that made it clear both nipples were pierced: there isn't a points-scoring system in therapy, as far as I know about, but I think I should have been awarded +5 for that) and called that "protecting my peace" because I pre-emptively knew that sending her the text message I was going to have to send her anyway in about three more weeks was going to cause me more agony than the brief sexual thrill of seeing whether they were bars or rings. After I got the night bus back she sent me a very long and technically understanding text that was nevertheless quietly quite disparaging and "wished me luck" on my "journey to be more normal". There is no feeling like knowing that six 28-year-old women you've never met are whipping your ass in the groupchat right now. I put my Instagram on private, then thought about it a bit longer, then deleted it entirely.

A lot of my panic about doing, Veronica says, is actually about my fear of being. A lot of my angst about work is really just completely self-imposed. I like talking to her – at their best my Tuesday afternoon sessions are like an emptying of the recycling bin of my various detritus-like thoughts, like that time I spent 40 minutes telling her a story about how a friend disclosed his salary and it was a number bigger than the numbers I even *fantasise* about when I think about earning more money, and he gets that every *year* with a bonus system in December as well, and how the whole thing made me spiral quite madly back about 17 years to when I was doing my A-Levels in a very half-hearted way and how that made me wonder that maybe every decision I've ever made in my life since then has been the wrong one, because I mean fucking hell how do you even *spend* three hundred and fifty thousand pounds in one year, I mean what do you even do with that, and she just nodded through it and said "mmhmm mmhmm and anything *else*?", which wasn't helpful. But also at its core I don't really care that Veronica thinks I should get away from my desk more or forgive myself every sin I've ever committed because I see her an hour a week and she knows about as much about me as I do about her. I have spent two whole entire sessions saying how London needs a two-way system for pedestrians on pavements (though of course they wouldn't adhere to it – you've been across London Bridge) (a wholesale change like this would take government-level intervention to get the landing right, and even then), for instance, which doesn't mean anything, it's just a thought I have to expunge, and then I float back to my world where annoying things happen – like the new fridge, which starts beeping alarmingly every time it is left open for more than 20 seconds, which stresses me out not only when it is beeping but also in the seconds I leave it open leading *up to* the beeping, meaning now using the fridge is a fundamentally stressful experience where I am always on edge – they bounce off me a little easier, their edges are just a little more round. But they are still there. No amount of talking about myself can fix the fact that they are there.

What annoyed me about the therapy talk girl, I typed out in a message to her then deleted then started typing out again and then stopped, is the way she approached my therapy as being some means to an end, a simple process you have to go through to become whole and fixed and real again, like completing a Driver Awareness Course. Therapy has been good but so has running and so has been making a way more concerted effort to eat fresh vegetables and so has finally finding an oat milk I like. So has sitting in the sun and doing meditation and talking to my friends over lunch instead of drinks and being on my own in a mindful way and not a self-absolving way, and buying vinyl records and listening to them intentionally or drawing again with that nice pen I got, and logging out of Twitter, and ejaculating just with the help of my imagination instead of really soulless pornography, and not treating 12 pints with friends as a substitution for therapy but also not discounting that three pints with friends, for instance, can actually be very very healing indeed. That sometimes you need to close your eyes and smell the salty wind off the sea and feel your face glow warm in the heat and curl your toes into the grassy ground and just feel *alive*. I typed all this out but then I just thought: I don't need to explain myself to a girl who'd do that to her nipples.

A lot of my fear has been about what I would become, whether I would ever become it, whether I was languishing and wasting any potential that might live latent in my body, that I was living a piecemeal life devoid of joy simply because I was too lazy and too intransigent to do anything else. Whether the life I was living was a waste of the great efforts that generations who came before me overcame to survive and produce me. And, like, yes. But gazing in the face of it every Tuesday makes it feel infinitely less heavy and easy to solve. Start there and stop texting girls with tattoos they got at parties. **FIVE STARS**

THE NATURAL HISTORY MUSEUM WITH MICHAEL

I invited Michael to the Natural History Museum because I have to make more of an effort at all of my friendships and I figured if I showed him the skeleton of Lucy he would be so filled with gratitude – so overwhelmed by peeling through 35 million years of history to stare at the most vital of our ancestors! – that he would forget all about the coat thing. Obviously I immediately regretted this because even organising a fun and assumption-inverting trip to the museum became a hostage negotiation in the texting hands of Michael:

> > do u want to go the natural history museum tomorrow? we can go on the tube together in the morning. i will buy u lunch

FOUR STARS

hmm
quite confused by this offer
i have an interview tomorrow
> wednesday morning then
could we do wednesday afternoon?
> no.
ok wednesday morning is fine
> i'll book tickets
do you need to book? I thought they were free
> they are free but you still need to book them
> 'reserve' possibly the more appropriate verb
> ok reserve
ok don't be mad at me but i had to go to the apple store
ok so maybe i'll meet you at the museum?
no
i'm cybling back now
cycling*
no wait
i'll meet you on the tube platform
> ok
where are you?????
> on the tube platform

On and on. Anyway we finally got to the museum and once again I was struck by the difference between British museums (vile, both over-lit and under-lit, filled with children, all of the descriptions are for simpletons) and international museums (glorious cathedrals in the holy worship of history and knowledge). To see a British museum – basically two gift shops adjoined by a long corridor filled with ammonites – filled-to-crawling with British people actually gives you an accurate if particularly unflattering view of this country, its culture, its vision of the self: in British schools we like to teach our children about how innovative and world-beating Britain has always been, how it led the lights in civilisation and rule and law and order and fostering and creating geniuses, that we birthed poets and painters and the finest writers to ever live. But actually go to a British museum and you see the country as it is: slack-jawed, lumpen people staring at a wall smudged with children's handprints, just trying to do something in the endless grey abyss that stretches between one episode of *Ant and Dec's Saturday Night Takeaway* and another. We helped create culture (by stealing enough of it to describe it in the English language) but we have none of it ourselves. Anyway basically I messed up because I thought this would be the quietest day of the week but actually it was the day every single primary school in the Greater London area decided to descend on the dinosaur exhibit. It sounded like: hell.

"Maybe we should get a coffee."

"A coffee?"

"Yeah. Little walking-around coffee. Is that allowed? I don't know. Is that *allowed*?"

"I don't drink coffee."

"Tea, then."

"I don't drink tea."

"Well I don't know what you want me to do, Mike."

FOUR STARS

I didn't get a coffee in the end because once I entered the cafeteria it was one of those dreadful slow-moving one-way systems where you have to grasp a tray and side-step all around the restaurant until you can finally get one fucking latte and a granola slice and there were two groups with buggies ahead of us already and I didn't want to lose the day to getting a £4 cup of museum brew — *I am trying to be a better person I am trying to be a better person. I am trying to be a calmer man I am trying to let the pace other people walk around in in public affect me less* — so we headed straight into the Blue Room where the mammals (whales) intersected with the aquamarine exhibit (also whales). It was good but had a weirdly ancient vibe to it: all of the animals, struck in place by taxidermy many years ago and diagrammed with lacquered placards, seemed to have been there since the late-'70s or early '80s, at least one or two aesthetic discourse cycles ago, anyway. There was a big feral pig called a 'SUPERHOG'. We gazed at some clay moulds of teeth. A very boring six-minute video about the Serengeti. Another buggy, another child in a fairy dress sprinting across the pantheon, the inescapable smell of rusks and fruit-snacks. Was I this misbehaved as a child? Were any of my childhood cohort? Or are these the children of those children who were raised not to raise? I don't ever recall shouting so hard I started crying in a museum when I was a kid. But then they have *Paw Patrol*, iPads, way more TV channels, &c. &c.

"I think I hate children."

"You can't say that. Not here."

"Well what can I say?"

"'I very strongly dislike children.'"

"OK: I very strongly dislike children. I don't see the point of them. They're all sticky and they have bad vibes."

"There's a lot of them."

"There's a *lot* of them. Do we need this many?"

"Well from an evolutionary perspective . . . yes."

"Once you start saying 'people shouldn't have kids', you do become a eugenicist, I suppose."

"Yeah almost immediately."

"And from there it's a very slippery slope down to measuring the dimensions of skulls—"

"So let's not."

"— so let's not."

". . ."

"*But—*"

By then we had drifted into the map room, which was actually a map-and-crystal shop, which Michael found oddly fascinating: he kept flipping through old shop-soiled maps trying to find one from near Chesterfield, where I grew up, but obviously he doesn't know where Chesterfield is – no one does, not even me – so it just descended into him yelling, "Macclesfield, is that anything?" across a library-quiet shop while I bought us both a drawing pen (Uni-Ball PIN Fine Line 0.3mm – a fairly groovy little pen, actually, though the ink is a little brown-black rather than pure-black for my liking) (It will make a good 'bag-pen', I think). Mike saw an old man was struggling to get out of a swivel chair so he helped him up (I watched him do it, and thought, gravely: "Wouldn't it be nice if I were the type of person to even think for one atomic second about helping someone else?" and got a bit sad) and then we looked briefly at a fairly sick Gogotte before ambling through the anthropology exhibit (at some point in our history, we decided cannibalism wasn't 'very cool', but not before we tried it in every possible formation first) to go see Lucy.

"OK."

"So that's Lucy."

"That's what we came here to see?"

"Yeah."

"Where's the rest of her?"

"She's three million years old, Mike. There is no 'rest of her'. We're lucky to have a bit of jaw."

"Right. So she's not real?"

"No, she's a cast."

"Where's her real skeleton?"

"Ethiopia."

"Well, we should've gone there."

"I don't think you're *getting it*—"

Anyway in the end I explained that Lucy is special because she lived this humble simple fragile little life – meaningless, even, without note – but crucially she was this step between the dark primordial nothingness of animals and everything we have today, every thought and every idea and every building and all seven billion people on earth, because she was intelligent enough to walk as well as climb and she probably had friends and she probably had emotions and she probably felt happy and sad and anxious and angry, the same way we all do, and when she laid down at night and went to sleep – among a throng of other hominins like her, a rough little society – her primitive brain exploded into visions and colours like dreams, just like ours do, and she knew nothing of this – she knew nothing of how important she'd become! – and then one day she just curled up and finally died, and don't you think that's something, don't you think that's something? Michael finally admitted that yeah, that seemed like something, but do you want any food, so we went to this semi-bizarre silver service Polish restaurant he found on Google Maps and he had some rabbit and I had some veal, and he talked about his granddad and how he didn't come from Poland and he didn't come from Germany, how he was born in the Free City of Danzig between World Wars I and II, and how that doesn't exist now, not even the house he was born in, not even the street, and how Michael had gone back there to find it and it wasn't there and that discovery, as it turned out, made for not a very captivating radio documentary. There was a load of stuff I didn't know Michael had been up to since we fell out about the coat – a boyfriend, a new job sort of, both his grandparents died, he spent a significant number of months in Athens? – and then he said some really interesting stuff about tone and media and how he's a different journalist to how I'm a journalist because he very much doesn't care what people think of him whereas I deeply, deeply, deeply, deeply deeply

deeply care about what people think of me, and then a too clean-shaven waiter with ruddy cheeks bought us a small bowl of mashed potato with dill all over it and I remembered by first holiday to Kraków, at the frankly stupid age of 23, and how that night went wrong and two extremely tough Polish bouncers ended up frog-marching my friend to a cashpoint to withdraw £400 to pay for, what none of us wanted to admit but basically had to end up admitting, were prostitutes.

There was a skull in one of the exhibits that had been carefully repaired: the yellow-white fine texture of the polished bone they uncovered was forged together with a sort of black plaster-gum, so you could see where the pronounced brow had been bashed out and the eye socket damaged and renewed, you could see the marks but not the damage. I think maybe that's what mine and Michael's friendship is now: maybe not as strong as pure bone is, sure, but there's something that can be salvaged after the deathblow. *Fuck.* I got like five other people I have to take to the Natural History Museum and apologise to. **N/A**

MYSELF

I am a good person, I think. I try. Well, hmm: no, that is a lie, actually. My thing is that I do not try at all. The urge to do things, to make myself happy by completing them, my reaching out and taking what I want: that does not live within me. So actually I am a good person *despite not trying*. If you want to think about it like I do, that's technically more impressive. I achieve this level of mid-range, semi-miserable mediocrity without any effort at all. Imagine what I could do if I tried!

My therapist thinks I am scared of becoming my father and I said why would I fear turning into my father, he's cool, and the therapist said, "Literally every story you have ever told me about the man has been harrowing," and I thought: *hmm*. I had a girlfriend once and I was at that getting-to-know-her-don't-reveal-who-you-really-are stage and she said *tell me a funny story about your family* and I said when I was a kid my dad had to kill the dog. We had this dog called Suzie who he absolutely loved. More than me, easily. More than himself, for sure. More than the whole family, the dog. But anyway she was old, just, always. I never knew this dog as a young dog (it's like how you've never known Christopher Walken to be young: you haven't, have you? Suzie was the dog version of Christopher Walken). She was always simply ancient, scabbed up, shaking, stinking. And one day I came home from school and I was like, where's the dog. And he said: *oh, she died*. I was like damn. He was like *yeah she was eating some food over there* – he pointed to her spot in the kitchen where her food used to be – *and then she just keeled over, and that was that. Very peaceful. I buried her out in the countryside, by her favourite spot*, and he got a photo out of a landscape – dense woodland with a simple slate wall running adjacent to it (my father was a photographer, which is why he had the illustrative material on hand, so this wasn't as weird as it sounds) – and pointed out a small divot of mud where he had buried her, and said: *there*. Only I was talking to my sister years later, years after he died, and we were laughing about old things and I said, "Remember Suzie?" and she was like "God, yeah." Because it turns out Suzie hadn't died peacefully on her food mat at all. That she'd collapsed in a wheezing, unfortunate mess, and dad had rightly perceived that she was on the edge of death, and that he couldn't really afford to have her put down. So he suffocated her to death with a pillow, bawling throughout, then called my sister at work, unintelligible, and frankly from that day forward something was broken inside him that never ever got fixed again. And the girlfriend was like [*Extensively making crying noises for a really long time*]. I had always sort of thought that story was kind of fun, kind of kooky. But I guess not.

Who am I? I don't know who I am. I am starting to fear that I am nothing, and that is OK. I am the son of a son of a son of son of a son and all those names get lost the further you go back into them and that is OK, too. My dad was Tony. His dad was Stanley. Who was Stanley's dad? I can't even go back 100 years down the bloodline. So I am here, now, and one day I won't be here, and whatever lives on of me now will be swept away or fossilised within a century of my death. My bones will never be polished and cleaned and looked at as fascinating: I will never be a missing link towards anything. The earth is on the way out – wheezing on the food mat – and I will die just before it burns out in a scorch. And then it will all be over. The abyss will remember us all the same.

I do not remember a time where I was like, 'happy', 'joyous', anything like that. In childhood I was mainly just scared that someone would ask me a direct question and I would have to answer it. In secondary school I recall I had a year-long phase where I spent every break and lunch on my own, sat on benches and ledges, sighing and staring into middle distance. This wasn't even an affectation, it was just where my mind wanted us to go. By the time I snapped out of it and came to, all of my friends had girlfriends and cool long hair and opinions about the Foo Fighters. I was a million miles behind.

Am I bad to people? I think I have the capability to be mean. I can definitely be annoying, and abrupt. I'm rarely angry, which I think is quite cool. I always like to think of myself as laid-back. But then I count up all the many tensions, the miseries, the sudden fears – I didn't realise how much I truly hate the sound of hoovers, or how uptight I get about the way other people use the bathroom, or how I have waged a war on The Adam & Eve in Homerton because a barman was really moronic and annoying and by extension rude to me there once two years ago (maybe he wasn't just rude, maybe he was just stupid) (I can see myself getting annoyed about it again: *stop* spiralling about the moron barman at The Adam & Eve in Homerton! He lives rent-free in your head! He doesn't even know his *own* name, let alone yours!) – and it all paints a picture. I basically make eye contact with people I am talking to about 1% of the time I am talking to them. I viciously dabble in ugly gossip. Sometimes people commit minor infractions against me in public and I think, viscerally, about their execution. A guy in a North Face jacket with a very tiny Liberty bag dashed in front of me at the Tube barrier and I thought how his head would look split in two with an axe. Black and pink and red. Why would I think that. Why would I think that is normal.

I am a bundle of loose nerve endings and I do not know why we evolved this way. I do not know why we built the cathedral of society around us in this shape. I am too dumb and too lazy to research the answers. The biggest thing holding me back is myself. Why, Lucy, did you pull this primitive urge to feel anxiety up through your little monkey brain? Why did you clamber down from the trees and walk through the forests to the lake? Why did you muster up a world in which I have to pay rent and taxes just to stand on it? I am not suicidal, but I envision a perfect death. I flutter off the city's tallest skyscraper and fall heavy to the pavement. I leap from one billion-pound logistical monstrosity onto another one. A council worker with a clipboard has to figure out what I did.

I am tall, I have good teeth, I am technically young and I am healthy. I am good value down the pub and I have made a lot of people laugh. I don't think I've ever done racism; maybe a little sexism but I think I've learned past that now. I think I can be loving in my own way and once people are attuned to that way they can enjoy me. I give good presents and fairly good advice. (A secret I'll never tell: I have phenomenal taste in greetings cards, and write nice messages in them, too). I will not grouse or moan too much when I have to help you move. I am never going to become an angel. I will never fly high up into the sun. That is alright, that is alright. You do not have to be the best person on earth. You just have to be here. **THREE STARS**

LIFE

The strange sleep has been even stranger lately: more fluttering restless half-sleep, more of my hours of rest streaked purple and psychedelic with odd-shaped vivid nightmares. What's deeply annoying about the sleeping strangely is I can never predict what shape the strangeness will take: jolting awake at 6 a.m., before any animals make noises, sitting still in the grey-black silence waiting for something to start fluttering. Or: a feverish dream, taken in a deep writhing sleep, strange green images jagging in and out of my psyche like a knife, forgotten friends, forgotten enemies, conversations I'm too afraid to have when I'm awake (I keep having a dream where I stand in the bathroom, my hairline finally receded and patchy brown-grey, and I apply a thick stinging crème that smells of sulphur, and gaze at myself and say: "It's happened.") Sometimes I wake up in the pitch-black, at 2 or 3 a.m., and toss there for an hour or so, my bladder half-filled with urine, not quite enough to get up for but not quite enough to sleep on, either, thoughts slowly growing like bubbles (in this instance I try *not* to think, because full-sized thoughts wake me up, but the size of the thought *Don't think! Don't! Think!* is large enough to rouse me, and then in turn I think, and normally my default status is to think of Horrors). Or, sometimes, it's just me, raw eyelids at 1 a.m., in bed for three hours now – the bed warm, the light soft, the phone in hand, the book dismissed; I've taken CBD, I've smoked a very small bowl – and everything in my head refuses to turn off, no sleep to be had, and the high alarm-sound scream of not-sleeping anxiety growing ever louder. Who knows what awaits me up there tonight. Maybe there'll be a whole new type of un-sleep lying in wait for me.

A few months ago I taught myself to stop looking in the mirror. I don't really know why, exactly, I did this – I mean I kept looking in the mirror and not really liking it, I suppose, and not only not liking it (wide pores, greasy hair flopped forward so I couldn't see the hairline and become gripped with dread about it, a fat jawline, the stretched and lined signs of ageing around my eyes) but also not liking *not liking it*, which became this whole spiral thing, and I just figured: maybe stop looking, at that guy. You never realise how much you look in the mirror until you try and stop looking in the mirror: there's one in the bathroom, always, and one in the hallway, too. In the building I'm in now there's one in the lifts, and to not look at myself effectively I have to pivot all the way round and stand in the corner like the end of *Blair Witch* (when strangers share the lift with me I just stare, fixedly, at my feet). Cars pass with reflective glass; shop windows beam the vague enormous shape of yourself back at you again. When you shop at supermarkets, a high-angled camera takes the most unflattering possible live footage of your head, and booms it back at you from the self-service machine so you don't steal. Every time I ever do the wrong motions on my phone it seems to turn the front-facing camera on at me as punishment. It's very, very hard not to look at yourself for a sustained period of time. My broad findings from the experiment have been: it's fine, it's been helpful, but has it been worth all the effort? When I get rare glimpses of the monster now he seems smaller, less capable of causing harm.

The Wetherspoons Large Breakfast has been preoccupying a lot of my thinking time (you try and be a good person, you try and pray at all the right altars: read good clean literature in the mornings, stretch and exercise, raise your face to the sun, eat greens and drink water, run as far as your body can possibly go, minimise beer minimise drugs, you phase out toxic people and become a less toxic person yourself, and then your brain just whispers, as if from an enemy – *why don't we go into our mind palace and think for 45 straight minutes about the Wetherspoons Large Breakfast?*). It isn't much: the Large 1313kcal offering consists of two glueily fried eggs, one rigid slice of bacon, two brown sausages, a small ramekin of magma-hot baked beans, three perfectly salty perfectly greasy hash browns, a smattering of fried mushrooms that are emitting a sinister grey slime and two barely grilled toast slices served with a pre-packaged pat of butter the same temperature and consistency of an ice cube. The cost differs from pub to pub but with an alcoholic beverage, which is a completely insane thing to offer with a breakfast, it normally shakes out around the £6.99 mark. Somehow, this is a perfect meal. It is not a perfect meal because it is a perfect meal, obviously, but it's a perfect *item*, in that its culinary ineptness is somehow consistent from Wetherspoons to Wetherspoons, and it does a very rare thing, which is: it makes British people shut up about the 'right' way of serving a fry-up. The Wetherspoons Large Breakfast has been refined to within an inch of its life, and it's hard to go more than 20 miles within the UK without being able to buy one. I stare down at a plate of meat and eggs artlessly prepared by a half-stoned 19-year-old with the government minimum amount of safety training and I find peace.

I'm in a Wetherspoons now, actually, I think. Neanderthal Golby ushers me to a sticky, varnished pine table on a soft gluey carpet in the middle of a nondescript pub, fluttering at the edges with the low murmurs of smalltalk of other patrons, and says: "Ugg bgg. Ughh buhh ghh buggy uggh." As if to say: *I know one of your greatest disappointments is that you never got to sit and have a drink with your father. Anyway I have arranged that now, using ancient neanderthal magic, smoke and flame and also I brewed a special tea.*

And I say: Oh.

DAD: Hiya, Chunky
ME: Hi mate— Dad. Tony? Mate. Ahh. What should I call you?
DAD: I mean what do you think you'd be calling me by this stage in your life?
ME: How do you mean?
DAD: You know, if you were 35, and I was . . . God, what, 77?
ME: Yeah exactly. You'd still be dead—
DAD: —still be dead, wouldn't I?
ME: Mm yeah no way you were ever making 70.
DAD: No, yeah.
ME: Just didn't have the guts. Pff— so how's. . . um.
DAD: Can't talk about that.
ME: What, the afterli—
DAD: Yep, nope. Don't even say it. Dark. Boring. Like being locked in a dripping cave, the slate pressed close against your face, but there's a flickering light there, sometimes, off to one side, and you can't turn your head to see it. All I can say: smells like an old damp puddle. I've said too much.
ME: What else?
DAD: I mean that's it, really. Not much doing.
ME: What section do you reckon you're in?
DAD: I mean purgatory is the best guess, isn't it?
ME: Yeah.
DAD: I think I'd know if I were in hell. At least they'd let me have a fag.

FOUR STARS

ME: Wording has kind of changed on that in the interstitial years since you've been dead but I'll let it slide.

DAD: How do you mean?

ME: Don't know how much of the one pint with my dad I will ever have in my life I want to spend explaining the semantics of leftist politics in the year 2023, if that's alright.

DAD: Fine by me. Can I have one then, or what?

ME: What?

DAD: A fag?

ME: Fucking— no, you can't smoke in pubs anymore.

DAD: You're joshing me!

ME: That's what you said when Diana died. That's my most vivid memory of you. I came downstairs early on a Sunday morning and tried to watch cartoons, and all the TV channels were news, instead, every single one of them. And I watched them for about 20 minutes or so trying to work out exactly what had happened (and plus also to check that at least BBC Two – at least BBC Two, come on! – definitely weren't going to put an episode of *The Mask: Animated Series* on, you know, for the kids), and then I came through to the front room where you were there, as always, because you woke up at 5 a.m. or 6 a.m. or something stupid like that—

DAD: I never could sleep.

ME: — right and you were there in that ratty old blue dressing gown and your chest hair out and

bare feet on the wood floor in the dining room which I always found bizarre – I mean I always found it bizarre that you and Mum always sat in the dining room, every morning, with that t—
DAD: — table with all the crap on it, yeah!
ME: Yeah exactly like we had comfortable chairs in the living room, why sit stiff-backed in the dining room, it made no sense to me?
DAD: Morning light, proximity to the teapot, and a little thing called 'being civilised', by the way. You can't just slump on a sofa all your life.
ME: — *fine* and you were there putting together a roll-up with your thick yellow fingers and I said: "Dad, Diana's dead" and you gripped the dining room table with all the crap on it with both hands, your watery blue eyes popped out of your head, and you just said: "You're joshing!"
DAD: "You're joshing!" I remember that.
ME: And then I was like—
DAD: You were like— you were a little ten-year-old butterball at the time, very wimpy child, very meek and silent, which was actually fine by me, I mean it meant less ambient noise, I mean you weren't much trouble, were you, you were just weird — I remember that because, yeah, you slumped in in those ratty old Stingray M&S pyjamas, do you remember them?
ME: Obviously I remember the best pyjamas of my lifetime, yeah.

FOUR STARS

DAD: — and I don't even particularly care about Diana and the Royals and what have you — has the Queen gone, yet?

ME: She has, yeah.

DAD: God. 'King Charles'. God.

ME: Yeah.

DAD: — and ahh, yeah obviously I didn't care that much but it was *news*, you know, and obviously she was so young as well so it was shocking news, horrible news, horrible what happened to her, you know, even if you don't care, and so I'm trying to force the enormity of this news into my – and yeah obviously I'll be honest here – *hungover* brain that hadn't even had a fag yet—

ME: [*Winces imperceptibly*]

DAD: What? You're not one, are you?

ME: No, no.

DAD: Well me and your mum did wonder.

ME: Don't— just. Tell the story.

DAD: Right and then yeah you're just there in fucking Stingray pyjamas going, "What does *joshing* mean? What does *joshing* mean?"

ME: Yeah it was a very confusing word to use in that situation.

DAD: I was overwhelmed by news!

ME: And then Mum came downstairs.

DAD: Yeah and you were just like: "Mum do you know what joshing means?"

ME: And then she spat at the TV.

DAD: She didn't *spit* at the TV. She made to show her contempt for the Royal family by *pretending* to spit at the TV. God you take everything so literally.

ME: I did when I was ten, obviously. I was two years out from still believing in Santa.

DAD: Three years out. You figured it out quite early.

ME: You remember that?

DAD: Obviously I remember that. You're my son.

ME: Oh.

[*A fairly long pause where Neanderthal Golby coughs and I remember that oh yeah, here's there, too*]

DAD: Who's that?

ME: Ancient ancestor of the Golby clan. We both derived from his bloodline. Thousands of thousands of years of heritage, and we all have the same weird large torso. He's sort of been haunting my every thought for a few months. We're mates.

DAD: Yeah, OK. Listen can I have a cider?

ME: Right, yeah.

NEANDERTHAL GOLBY: *Oogh baggh go*

ME: That was almost a word, there! Yeah alright. Err— Strongbow OK? Yeah one Strongbow, one Neck Oil, whatever you're having, and ... two things of Scampi Fries and some chilli nuts.

NEANDERTHAL GOLBY: ... *oogh bagh?*

ME: Yeah obviously take my card I'm the only one here with a job.

DAD: What's *Neck Oil*?

ME: I'm not— don't. I'm not doing this with you.

FOUR STARS

DAD: Alright. What, er ... what do you do, then?

ME: Oh, for a job? Yeah I'm a writer.

DAD: Hmm.

ME: 'Hmm'?

DAD: Wasn't expecting that. Always thought you'd make a go of the illustration thing. All those cartoons you used to draw, and that. Remember that photo I took of a honeysuckle stem, and you drew it with that mechanical pencil we got you for Christmas – you must have been, what, five, six years old? — and it was *perfect*—

ME: Yeah no the more I look back on that the more I realise that was absolutely insane. It was absolutely insane I was able to do that. I can only assume the spirit of an ancient demon overtook me that day. I haven't been able to draw at that level since.

DAD: No but you did your doodling—

ME: Yeah I mean yeah, yeah. I mean I always figured I'd be like an artist or a cartoonist or an illustrator, too. But ah, you ... no cool way of saying it. The training I was getting during GCSE art was sort of derailed by you dying, in the middle of it.

DAD: Ah.

ME: Yeah, sorry.

DAD: No, no. I'm the one who died. How did I, er, you know ... 'go'?

ME: Cirrhosis of the liver. You were very yellow, by the end of it. When I went to look at your body you looked like Mr. Burns.

DAD: Ha! From *The Simpsons*!
ME: Yeah.
DAD: Love *The Simpsons*.
ME: Yeah no *The Simpsons* is good, it's ... yeah, it's good
DAD: What happened to all my stuff?
ME: Your ... stuff? I don't know. I mean everyone took a trinket or two. I got the binoculars, though I think Jemma has them at the moment.
DAD: Jemma! How is she?
ME: No this is about me. And then yeah, ah— there was this weird guy called John, who turned up to your flat, when we were clearing it out?
DAD: [*Shrugs*]
ME: Like very toothless man, had an obedient greyhound with him? Was genuinely wailing? Said he found your body and he was your best friend?
DAD: Not ringing any bells.
ME: Nothing?!
DAD: Listen, I collected a lot of strange men who like, 'have a beard that somehow has dandruff in it' over the course of my lifetime. I assume you are afflicted with this too?
ME: Right, right.
NEANDERTHAL GOLBY, FROM THE BAR: *Ough bah*
DAD: So yeah there was probably a John. There were probably a few Johns. How's Nick?
ME: Fuck alone knows.

FOUR STARS

DAD: If I had to guess I would say Nick is probably . . .

ME: — probably dead, yeah.

[*Neanderthal Golby returns with a Neck Oil, a Stella, a Strongbow and two things of Scampi Fries*]

NEANDERTHAL GOLBY: *Oohgh goobh ahh*

ME: They didn't have chilli nuts.

DAD: OK.

ME: First time I had Scampi Fries was with you. It was a revelation. We were in the Crown & Anchor on Sheffield Road, and I don't remember who you were with but I was pelting around the garden playing.

DAD: Was always quite proud that you were a 'pub kid', you know. Some people can't take their kids to the pub.

ME: This feels like authorial insertion but go off.

DAD: The *whole thing* is authorial insertion.

ME: Alright, yeah, you're right. Anyway I was playing pelt-around and you ushered me over and gave me a shandy and showed me an open packet of Scampi Fries and— wow. Just wow. I remember the exact moment I first ate one. A sunny Saturday. A blue sky above me. Arms aching from the monkeybars, my forehead dusty with sweat. And: a Scampi Fry. Do you remember that?

DAD: No.

ME: Oh.

DAD: You have to be aware that not every incident from your childhood was as important to me as it was for you. You were about five, or something. The only things you'd ever had to remember were like, two Christmases, 'the alphabet', and our home phone number in case you went missing. Obviously an incident like that is deeply imprinted on you. Look at it from my point of view: *I gave my child a crisp.*

ME: Yeah actually now when you put it like that I can see why it wasn't that memorable.

DAD: I'm gonna try and bum a cig—

ME: Alright.

[*Dad goes round the rest of the pub – men with blurry, featureless faces, murmuring together in an unlanguage, and I realise suddenly that the walls are smeared gaussian too, and the whole room feels floating – gravityless – as if I am in a dream. Anyway somehow despite all that he manages to get a pouch of Drum and some Rizla off a bloke with no discernible nose, eyes or fingers*]

DAD: Wotcha! You want one?

ME: Nah I'm good, I'm good.

[*Dad goes outside to smoke, checking in the pockets of his bodywarmer for his Zippo, and Neanderthal Golby leans over to me*]

NEANDERTHAL GOLBY: *Has this helped at all?*

ME: I don't know. I don't know. I don't know anything.

NEANDERTHAL GOLBY: *You know some things. You're not all that lost, kid.*

ME: I'm not even a kid anymore.

FOUR STARS

NEANDERTHAL GOLBY: *It is OK to be afraid.*

ME: It just— if communing with my dead father in a magical dream-like setting doesn't fix me, what will?

NEANDERTHAL GOLBY: *Yeah no I get that.*

ME: You're going to go with him, aren't you?

NEANDERTHAL GOLBY: *Yeah. You can't keep using me as a crutch.*

ME: But I *like* you!

NEANDERTHAL GOLBY: *Sometimes the people you like go away. That's part of it.*

ME: . . .

NEANDERTHAL GOLBY: *Shall I get more Scampi Fries?*

ME: [*Sighing in a way that makes me feel like I am uncracking a millenium of inherited stress over the edge of a barrel*] Yeah, go on then.

DAD: So . . .

ME: Yeah, hi. So.

DAD: Are you crying?

ME: Umm. Yeah, looks like it, yeah.

DAD: Ah.

ME: Did you ever— sorry. Did you ever, you know: worry about me?

DAD: Worry about you?

ME: Yeah. You know . . . worry what I'd be without you

DAD: No, Joe.

ME: Ah. That's nice.

DAD: Nah you were always going to be fine. You were smart, you were funny, you were good at multiple things. Do you know how many people are just really useless?

ME: Yeah.

DAD: So, you know, no. Same way you knew I would never get to 70: I always just sort of figured you'd land on your feet. You had that energy.

ME: Yeah, yeah, OK. Umm, I have a dog, do you want to see him?

DAD: Yeah!

ME: Well, had. I— yeah. His name's Bam. But he doesn't live with me anymore. But he's— look he's wearing a little leather jacket.

DAD: What's this thing you're holding?

ME: It's a Google Pixel don't— don't get distracted. Look at the dog.

DAD: Yeah sick little fella, isn't he. What is he?

ME: Just sort of a ... a mutt.

DAD: Like Suzie!

ME: Yeah. Is she in the afterlife with you?

DAD: Not actively wedged between the slate, no, but ... you occasionally get a whiff. Sometimes I can smell the dog.

ME: I'm, like, losing you, I think. I can't remember what you sound like, or what you smell like, or how you talk. I have no idea what your laugh sounded like.

DAD: [*Laughs, but in the wrong way*]

ME: Yeah, see. I think that's maybe why I fixate on the Scampi Fries, or the joshing, or whatever. It's just the few slippery things I can grip on to.

FOUR STARS

DAD: What happened with the dog?
ME: He, er. She. I had him with a girl, and she went away, and he went with her.
DAD: [*DRINKING MOST OF A PINT OF CIDER IN ONE PULL, AND NOT EVEN IN A JOYFUL WAY JUST IN QUITE A FUNCTIONAL WAY, I MEAN FUCKING HELL*] Women are smarter than us. That's why they leave.
ME: Yeah.
NEANDERTHAL GOLBY: *It's time to go.*
ME: It sucks you died, Dad.
DAD: Yeah.
ME: I really just wish it all shook out another way.
DAD: I know, I know.
ME: Ah, fuck.
DAD: What?
ME: I've just thought of a really good joke. When Mum got the late-night phone call and came to my room to tell me you'd died, I should have said—
DAD: — "You're joshing!"
ME: "You're joshing!", right! That would have been a good bit.
DAD: Wouldn't have made sense to her, though.
ME: No.
DAD: She would've thought you'd gone mad. We did wonder.
ME: What, that I'd—
DAD: Really got to go, mate.
NEANDERTHAL GOLBY: *We have to leave.*

JOEL GOLBY

ME: No, no, no, hold on!
ME: Hold on
ME: Hold on.

It's been a few weeks and the clench has been feeling better. I have been pressing my hand to my forehead less, for example, and a much smaller part of myself has constantly wanted to die. I am aware that this is a receding sea, deep and cold like metal, and one day it will swill back over the beaches, but for now, the quiet winds of peace. There's just so much every day that you can *experience*, and that's what keeps you going. There are so many: surfaces to touch, flavours to taste, emotions to make other people feel. It is an experience, I suppose, to be dreadfully scared. It's a privilege to be bored! I am trying to be that, like someone who thinks like that. I've been keeping a list of things it's worth actually living for:

- Snapping a Snickers Duo in half at the pre-cut notch in the wrapper;
- Performing a really good pure whistle in a large empty room;
- Warm bread, salted butter, honey;
- The fact that every generation Hollywood elects a big-titty actress to superstardom and along the way there's always at least one indie or arthouse-leaning project where she fully gets those tits out and like, that's always good isn't it;
- It's sort of insane to think what PlayStation graphics will be like in ten years;

FOUR STARS

- It is impossible to get away from the fact that Christmas is fucking excellent;
- HBO need to start another six-season big budget TV show that will go down in the annals of history and it always feels good to be at the start of that;
- It is always excellent to go to a party and judge the person throwing the party based on the paltry and pathetic six books they seem to have in their house;
- Going to Barcelona and taking MDMA.
- One day soon I might be on a hot bright beach and the sound of the sea will hit the shore like this – *WHHOSH!* – and there won't be any phone there won't be any e-mails, I'll be exactly 200 pages into a good 400-page paperback that won a prize, and someone I love will walk back from the bar with three Peronis, two for me one for them, both as cold as ice is;
- One day soon I will finally buy the exact right coat that will make me happy;
- You often forget this, but when it's cold you can leave a bucket of ice outside and it will freeze on top in a perfect inch-thick disc and if you wake up early enough – before the morning sun has made a move to melt it, and before anyone else can get there and take this from you – you can pick up that disc and just fucking smash it on a patio, and you feel enormous, you feel bigger than God;
- Light a match and blow it out and smell the air crackling around you;
- Brush the hair from someone's face and tilt their chin up and kiss them;

- One night you will find yourself on the upper floors of a building that has a view of the city twinkling below you and you will stand with your toes touching the glass and your nose as close as it can be without steaming the view up and that expanse of people below you, all those lives all those lights on all those souls all that money, all those little intricate routines that people are whirring on, and you will realise that it's all happening, baby, it's all happening out there;
- One day you will do pottery and find out you're really, almost weirdly good at it;
- There are so many songs to hear, so many films to see, so many books to read, but also: have you ever pissed off a stranger so much they've really embarrassed themselves by shouting at you? Jolts you full with a really bizarre, enjoyable energy;
- And then, of course, the ultimate: ten lagers, with good friends, on a hot summer Saturday. Nothing is finer than that.

That's been helping.

So, in review, life is OK. Life is good, even. Life is magical, at its best (at its worst: agony). Being alive necessarily does expose you to all the horrors of the world – poverty, death, disease, war, terror, evil, *Sunday Brunch* and the entire career of Tim Lovejoy – so to be fair I do have to knock a point off for all that. But overall, I have to give it: **FOUR STARS**

WATERING THE PLANTS BENEATH A JULY SKY AT SUNSET

Jemma's in Singapore for a month with work so I'm staying at hers for a while because her cats need feeding and also all of my worldly possessions are in storage and I'm homeless in a technical capacity and I really could use somewhere to stay. I am sleeping on the sofabed because even though the main bed is available and has an extremely expensive supportive king-sized mattress on it I am fundamentally icky about beds and other people's beds. It is strange this never happens to me in hotels (think of the skin diseases, the boiled sheets, the pounds and pounds of semen!). It is strange this thought never troubles me when a girl with seven ear piercings and an app that does my Moon Rising reading invites me back to her houseshare because she's wine-horny and pretty sure she has some drugs left over from Latitude. The reality is: there is a threshold of how much I have to know a person to feel uncomfortable sleeping in or even touching their bed, and somehow it has shaken out so I am more comfortable with strangers than with friends. Probably nothing worth exploring—

It is July and the sun is searing. The sky during British summer is the main character: bright whipped-cream clouds underlit by ominous purple-greys when rain approaches; a sudden wind that whirls up dust, dry pollen, seeds; aquamarine blue like the holiday sea; a sunset, vivid orange then dark like a bruise, midnight sky tinged navy never black. The back garden strolls up a hill and is surrounded on all sides by the other yawning green spaces of south-east London: immediately around me fences, then beyond them, tall trees fluttering lightly in a wind I can't feel. A neighbour has a spectacularly tall tree – it must be, what, a hundred-plus years old? It must have survived a *war* – that has been artlessly hacked at the top into blunt stumps. Someone is building an extension, someone's kids are playing until they're squealing. A jet hangs lazy in the air. A drone of peace surrounds me.

I feel like my head has been in a vice this year. I don't know when it started but I know the pressure is unbearable. Maybe it was not just this year, actually: was I really myself last summer? Have I really been happy since— when? It feels like my head is in a vice, it feels like my head is in a vice, it feels like my head is in a vice. But sometimes I take a good deep breath just right and it feels like it's loosening. Most days now it doesn't feel like my thoughts are going to make my eyes pop out of my head like *Casino*.

The extensive note regarding cat care and how to turn the oven on and the quirk with the bathroom tap and what days the recycling goes out and what the upstairs neighbour's phone number is also states that I have to water the plants on the patio every night in the evening once the sun starts to lull, so they don't scorch. I have never significantly had to water a plant in my life: the last time I had a garden was when I was still living at home, thirteen, fourteen, seventeen years ago. I unfurl a hose and drag it out into the light, then trudge back and turn on the outside spigot. A sudden mist. I grab the end of the hose because I am constantly worried that people are filming outside their windows, and that one day something physically stupid I do will end up on *You've Been Framed* or, worse, going viral. Getting on the news because I held a powerful hose in a stupid way just feels like its etched into my lore even before I've done it.

It feels fantastic, it feels unbelievable. I am nourishing these plants with a heavy mist of water and without me they would shrivel and clam up and die. I am completely vital to the lifespan of these green things and they are completely vital to mine. They will pump out oxygen, they will clean the air. Each molecule they photosynthesise is whispered out with a little joyful yelp: *thank you, Joel! Thank you for watering me!* I work my way around the patio, zizz mist out onto the grass nearby. A blackberry bramble threatens to drop heavy fruit onto the ground below. A fuschia is on the cusp of bloom. My dad used to garden – "Honeysuckle," he'd say, whenever he saw a honeysuckle, and I don't have any further evidence he knew the name of a single other plant – and out here are some of the accoutrements gathered from the old house: an ornamental owl he had hewn out of wood, a heavy pot I remember he used to have a bonsai in. I guess there is a way to see that I am continuing his work, here: nourishing the same pots, wetting the same soil, maintaining the same cycle, feeling the same peace against the bubbling internal pot of destruction.

The hose is off, now. Mist still sits in the air. The smell of a garden after rain is untouchable – plants breathing, mouths open, gulping and singing – and here it's similar: activated dust, green leaves crinkling and stirring back into life, soil mulch happy as a seal to be wet again. The jet lingers overhead: everyone on it excited, legs cramped up, tiny can of Coke, luggage on the hold, holiday beckoning. Clouds streak Cheeto-bright across the sky. Sometimes it has been hard to be living lately. Sometimes I haven't wanted to all too much. Right now I breathe clean air and know this is a moment worth being here for. *I am glad I am alive. I am glad I got to do this. I am glad that I am here. I am glad to water the plants.*

ACKNOWLEDGEMENTS

I got so lucky with everyone around me for this book. I have to thank the people who helped actually write it, so: Joel #1, Zoe and Olivia, (Olivia especially had to be on my case to get the book written: thank you). Then I need to thank the people who offered me space to write in: Felix, Zoe, Stephen, Monica. Then the readers: Monica again, the gorgeous John Saward. Then my friends, of which I obviously have hundreds, thousands, but I want to thank most particularly the boys who have supported me the most: Gruff, 'James', Dan. A few names I want to put in here just because it's my acknowledgements section and I can do what I want: Ed Lilo, Avery Edison, Tomas Svitorka. Michael can also be thanked. I personally have a brain disease where I read acknowledgements sections for books by authors I do not know – authors who are very frequently long since dead – and for some reason look for my name, as if Vladimir Nabokov couldn't have written *Pale Fire* without my help for some reason, so if you are doing the same thing right now, I thank you. My sister needs to get thanked in every book forever, of course, so thank you, Jemma, for everything.

Then Hannah, who put up with the most: thank you, I love you, sorry for everything obviously but I couldn't have done this without your patience and support. Also Bam, who has never been acknowledged in a book before. Thank you, Bam.